CULLODEN
AND THE '45

By the Same Author
British Foreign Policy in the Age of Walpole
The British and the Grand Tour
Natural and Necessary Enemies: Anglo-French Relations in the Eighteenth Century
The English Press in the Eighteenth Century
The Collapse of the Anglo-French Alliance, 1727–31
Eighteenth-Century Europe, 1700–89
Robert Walpole and the Nature of Politics in Early Eighteenth-Century Britain
The Rise of the European Powers, 1679–1793

Edited
Britain in the Age of Walpole
The Origins of War in Early-Modern Europe
Knights Errant and True Englishmen. British Foreign Policy 1660–1800
Politics and Society in Britain from Walpole to Pitt, 1742–89

Co-edited
Essays in European History in Honour of Ragnhild Hatton
The Jacobite Challenge
The Royal Navy and the Use of Naval Power in the Eighteenth Century
Press and Politics in Hanoverian Britain

CULLODEN
AND THE '45

Jeremy Black

ALAN SUTTON PUBLISHING LTD · Stroud

ST. MARTIN'S PRESS · New York

Copyright © Jeremy Black 1990

First published in the United States of America in 1990
Paperback edition, with corrections, first published in 1993

All rights reserved. For information, write:
Scholarly and Reference Division,
St. Martin's Press Inc. · 175 Fifth Avenue · New York · NY 10010

ISBN 0-312-05197-2 (hbk)
ISBN 0-312-10326-3 (pbk)

Library of Congress Cataloging in Publication Data

Black, Jeremy.
Culloden and the '45 / Jeremy Black.
p.   cm.
Includes bibliographical references and index.
ISBN 0-312-05197-2 (hbk)
ISBN 0-312-10326-3 (pbk)
1. Culloden, Battle of, 1746. 2. Jacobite Rebellion, 1745–1746.
3. Scotland—History—18th century. I. Title
DA814.5.857 1990   90–9034
941.07'2–dc20   CIP

First published in the United Kingdom in 1990 by
Alan Sutton Publishing Limited
Phoenix Mill · Far Thrupp · Stroud · Gloucestershire

Paperback edition, with corrections, first published in 1993

Reprinted 1995

British Library Cataloguing in Publication Data

Black, Jeremy
Culloden and the '45
1. Great Britain. Jacobite Rebellion
I. Title
941.072

ISBN 0–86299–736–4 (hbk)
ISBN 0–7509–0375–9 (pbk)

Typeset in 11/12 Ehrhardt.
Typesetting and origination by
Alan Sutton Publishing Limited.
Printed and bound in Great Britain by
WBC, Bridgend, Mid Glam.

For Timothy James Black

Note on Dates

All dates are given in the old style with the exception of events occurring on the continent where the new style (eleven days in advance) was in operation.

CONTENTS

LIST OF ILLUSTRATIONS

Cover:

Detail from a contemporary print, *The Battle of Culloden, 16 April 1746* (British Library, London; photograph: The Bridgeman Art Library)

Photographs and illustrations were supplied by, or are reproduced by kind permission of the following: Cumbria County Council, Carlisle Library (37, 38, 39); Derby Museums & Art Gallery (32, 33, 34); Mrs J. Dick-Cunyngham (30, on loan to the Scottish Record Office); Duke of Atholl (25, 45); Edinburgh Central Library (5); Harris Museum & Art Gallery (43, 44); Manchester Local History Library (54); the Mansell Collection (27, 52); National Maritime Museum, Greenwich (22); National Museums of Scotland (19, 21, 24, 35, 46); National Portrait Gallery, London (6, 9, 14, 15, 17, 20); National Trust for Scotland (3, 23, 47); Scottish National Portrait Gallery (10, 11, 13, 30, 40, 56, 57); Scottish Record Office (42); Scottish United Services Museum (28, 50); Trustees of Stonyhurst College (4, 16, 18, 58). Pictures 1, 26, 48, 49, 51, and 55 are reproduced by gracious permission of HM the Queen.

PREFACE

Seven months as a schoolteacher in Strathspey in 1975 was my introduction to Culloden and the country of the '45 and I must thank Alan Sutton, who asked me to write this book, not least for bringing back many memories. Jacobite studies have offered me various experiences: the pleasant hospitality of the Royal Archives in Windsor Castle, as well as the farcical evening when Frank McLynn, Henry Summerson and myself, having taken part as expert witnesses in a television trial of Lieutenant-Colonel James Durand, who surrendered Carlisle Castle to the Jacobites in 1745, subsequently dined at the cautious expense of the BBC, and returned at 11.30 p.m. to what purported to be the best hotel in Carlisle and were unable to gain entrance. The front door was locked, the building was unlighted and both bell and telephone were unanswered. Having failed to awaken the building or push the door in, we summoned the police, who climbed in at the back and opened the door for us. Mentioning my two colleagues of that evening gives me an opportunity to say how much I value their friendship and that of other scholars on Jacobitism. Three good friends, Eveline Cruickshanks, Frank McLynn and Philip Woodfine, have made valuable comments on earlier drafts of this work, which Linda Heitmann has produced in an exemplary fashion. I have also benefited from the advice of J. Michael Hill. I would like to thank Her Majesty the Queen and Lady Lucas for permission to use material from their collections and the British Academy, Durham University, the Huntington Library and the Wolfson Foundation for supporting my research.

Those who work on Jacobitism have been accused of 'revisionist obscurantism' and nostalgia. Having published extensively on Walpole and British foreign policy, I hope I will not be charged with only seeing one side of the hill. I personally feel that study of both Jacobitism and the '45 is salutary. The former reminds the reader that many were not comprehended within the Whig consensus and that both the Revolution settlement and the Hanoverian regime were only established by force. Consideration of the '45 is a useful corrective to deterministic approaches to eighteenth-century Britain and challenges those who find it easiest to see the past in terms of patterns. One wonders whether they would like to be explained and dismissed in a similar fashion.

I finished the first draft of this work five days after the birth of my second child, but the book is dedicated to her elder brother as hopefully he will be able to read it first, or at least to find in the pictures a passing distraction from the joyous world of Duplo and sitting in the mud, a world which in many respects I wish I could regain.

J. Black
Newcastle

INTRODUCTION

The British state faced three serious civil wars in the eighteenth century. The shortest occurred in Ireland in 1798. The rising of the United Irishmen was bloodily suppressed and, other than in Ireland, tends to be overlooked in what was by any standards a tumultous decade throughout Europe. However, the impact of the rising on the government in London was serious and casualty figures were considerable. The American revolution was more successful. The British attempt to defeat the rebellious colonists failed and the Loyalists were consequently disheartened and terrorized successfully.

Neither of these movements – the terms rebellion, revolution and civil war are fraught with complications and can arouse a surprising degree of emotion today – sought to overthrow established authority in mainland Britain, though the American cause had considerable sympathy there, and their military impact on the mainland was indirect, with the exception of American privateers.

The Jacobite movement was different. The Jacobites sought not to drive British power out of a portion of the dominions of the British Crown, though that was an objective of some Scottish Jacobites, but to change the identity of the wearer of the Crown. The movement sought support, therefore, throughout Britain. There was no continuous civil war and Jacobite conspiracies varied considerably in their nature and intentions, as did episodes of military activity, but there was a common theme of loyalty to the exiled Stuarts and opposition to those who wielded power within Britain. This was a constant theme from the invasion of England by William of Orange (William III) in 1688 until the effective destruction of Jacobitism as a plausible candidate for effecting the removal of the Hanoverians through military action. This occurred in 1746, though Jacobite conspiracies and international plans involving Jacobitism occurred thereafter, and was a result of the Jacobite defeat at Culloden and its consequences. Culloden brought to an end the '45, the most serious crisis to affect the eighteenth-century British state, and that is the subject of this book.

There is a mass of fine work already in print both on Jacobitism and on the '45. The figure of Charles Edward Stuart, Bonnie Prince Charlie, has attracted attention ever since he was born in the late afternoon of 31 December 1720. The recent bicentennary of his death saw the appearance of a number of biographies, including a first-rate one by Frank McLynn. This study does not focus on Charles Edward but rather on the military aspects of the '45. These are not, and cannot be, separated from the political context, especially the international setting, for, like the United Irishmen and the rebellious Americans, the Jacobites in the 1740s looked to France for assistance. The '45 has to be seen against several different backgrounds but one of the most important, certainly in explaining the policies of the British and the French governments, was that relatively understudied conflict the War of the Austrian Succession (1740–8). However, just as the origins of Jacobitism can be pinpointed accurately in the events of late 1688, so the causes of Anglo-French hostility can be substantially traced to the events of that year.

1 A Change of Dynasty

Problems of Invasion

The last successful invasion of England occurred in 1688. It is of importance for any history of the '45 both because it set in motion the process that was to culminate at Culloden and because in its success it was so obvious a contrast to the '45. It thus opens up the question of what was necessary in order to mount a successful invasion of England, for the central fact of Jacobite plans in 1744–5, as of the '15, was that they were designed to lead to the conquest of England. Scotland was a means to an end, indeed in many respects in 1745 a second best, after the failure of the plans for the invasion of England the previous year, though equally for William III Britain as a whole was largely a means to his desired end of a successful war with France. The removal of James II was the result of a combination of domestic conspiracy and foreign invasion. The latter was crucial militarily. The military limitations of domestic risings unsupported by foreign troops had already been made abundantly clear in 1685. After the death of Charles II and the accession of his Catholic brother James, Charles' illegitimate and Protestant son James, Duke of Monmouth sailed from the United Provinces (modern Netherlands) and landed with eighty-two companions and plenty of arms at Lyme Regis. On 6 July 1685, less than a month after the landing, Monmouth, who had been proclaimed king at the market cross at Taunton on 19 June, was defeated at Sedgemoor. Monmouth's rising had been supported by action in Scotland by Archibald Campbell, 9th Earl of Argyll, who had been living in exile in the United Provinces for a number of years. Argyll sailed with about 300 men but, like Monmouth, increased his force considerably after landing. However, Argyll's operations were affected by divided counsels and the speed of the governmental response, including the appearance of two frigates, which took Argyll's ships, a blow that was much more serious in the lands around the Clyde than where military operations did not directly require naval assistance, as in the West Country. Argyll's position was weakened by the donation of his confiscated jurisdictions to rivals. The Marquis of Atholl was placed in command of the Campbell stronghold of Inverary. Argyll found it impossible to gain the support he had envisaged. His force of about 2,000 advanced to confront a royal army near Dumbarton, but his wish to fight was overruled and the troops retreated. During the retreat the cohesion of

Argyll's force was lost and its numbers fell as clansmen disappeared back to their homes. Argyll left his men, was captured on 18 June and beheaded on 30 June 1685.

These failures recall the earlier defeats of the Covenanters, Presbyterians in south-western Scotland, who had risen as recently as 1679. They had defeated an outnumbered royal force under John Graham of Claverhouse at Drumclog, but were in turn defeated at Bothwell Bridge (1679) and Airds Moss (1680). An earlier rebellion in 1666, the Pentland Rising, had also been defeated. It is easy to jump to the conclusion that only a substantial trained force could gain victory and that this could only be provided for a rebellion from abroad. William of Orange's success appears to prove this case, and the defeat of the '45 thus appears predestined. Yet the pre-Jacobite military legacy was somewhat more complex. The forces that had defeated royal authority in Scotland and northern England in 1639–40 in the First and Second Bishop's Wars, had led the successful Irish rebellion of 1641 and that had finally defeated Charles I in England were not foreign in composition or leadership, though it is true that some of the men and more of the officers, especially among the Scots, had had military experience abroad, particularly in the Thirty Years War then raging in Germany. However, the argument that a successful rebellion required an invading foreign army, that this was 'proved' by 1688 and that therefore the '15 and the '45 were bound to fail has to consider the events of the 1630s and 1640s.

Factors of time and timing were of course important. In the 1630s and 1640s amateur forces had time to develop into trained units, a process that was pursued extensively on the Parliamentarian side in England, where the creation of the New Model Army produced a force that was to play a major role in the defeat of a foreign army, the prestigious Spanish Army of Flanders at the battle of the Dunes in 1658, a conflict in which the future James II fought on the losing side. The question of timing is more complex. Did Britain essentially alter in the mid-seventeenth century so as to make the raising of amateur forces less militarily feasible? This has been argued, especially for England, thus creating a new apparent geo-politics of insurrection, in which only Ireland and Scotland remained as kingdoms that could serve as the base for such insurrections, so that any successful rebellion would have to involve the invasion of England from abroad: from Scotland, Ireland or the continent. It is, however, dangerous to write off the possibility of raising forces in England. It was simply not the case that there were no soldiers except regulars. Militia forces might perform an undistiguished role, as against Monmouth at Axminster or in Cumbria in 1715, but the militia did fulfil useful military roles against Monmouth, for example holding Bath. During the invasion scare of 1690 the City of London raised, besides its militia, 7,400 auxiliary troops. In 1745 volunteers were raised to support the government. These took two forms: local associations where companies of volunteers were raised under the supervision of the Lord Lieutenants and financed locally, and in addition fifteen regiments were raised by loyal nobles, the men enlisting for a short term for the specific purpose of confronting the '45.

In modern times the idea of irregulars standing up to regulars successfully is far from implausible, but it relates particularly to guerilla campaigns. These appear to be a long way removed from the apparently well-ordered conflicts that characterized the eighteenth century prior to the French Revolution, with their set-piece battles, geometric battle formations and cautious, often predictable, strategy and tactics. This interpretation is based on a misunderstanding of eighteenth-century conflict, and the gap between regulars and irregulars was less weighted in favour of the former than might be imagined. This observation is equally pertinent for other European conflicts of the late seventeenth and early eighteenth centuries, especially those in Hungary, but more generally in eastern Europe. Clearly the nature of the society in question was important, especially in terms of horse-ownership and experience and more generally in the existence of social groups that were accustomed to weapons and organized semi-military activity. Regular troops could offer, if well trained and motivated, disciplined fire-power and battle field manoeuvres that were generally better controlled than those provided by irregulars, but by no means all conflicts enabled them to employ these advantages. Factors of terrain, leadership, morale and surprise still counted for much. The decisive shift in Europe towards regular forces had occurred in the related fields of fortification and siegecraft. Heavy artillery trains and skilled engineers were expensive, difficult to develop and in Britain only possessed by the royal government. New-model fortifications, the widely-spread low-profile earthworks that were more resistant to cannon than the stone walls of medieval castles, were similarly expensive, difficult and time-consuming to construct, and they were rare in Britain. By western-European standards Britain was poorly fortified, helping the invader and minimizing what might otherwise have been an important consequence of military changes.

These military themes will be discussed again in this work, but they have been introduced at the outset to encourage the reader to appreciate that the actual and potential military dimension of political possibilities and changes was far from clear to contemporaries and that any attempt to present the '45 as inevitably doomed militarily is very questionable.

*   *   *

If a man was to rob a house he would never tell the people within, whose doors were shut, that he designed to rob them and take away their money or lives, but only would enter to keep him warm or to find out some fellow that had done him mischief etc.

That was the sardonic comment of Thomas Lane, a fellow of Merton College, Oxford who had accompanied Francis Taafe, 3rd Earl of Carlingford, on his embassy to Vienna, on William of Orange's letter to Leopold I, Holy Roman Emperor and ruler of the Austrian Habsburg dominions, appealing for Leopold's support, or at least forbearance, during the attack on a fellow-Catholic sovereign. Lane summarized William's letter:

Its preamble is the King of England's engagements with France contrary to the interests of the Empire and Kingdom, the body of it, that he does not design to act anything either against the king's person or government or against the Prince of Wales and the just succession . . . that he would not disturb the Catholics in England either in their persons or free exercise of their religion, but would have the Protestant religion secured so far, that their adversaries should never be in a condition to offer violence to it, and that these were the utmost of his designs he protests before God and the Emperor'

Whether Lane's career at Merton – as bursar he suddenly left without rendering his account, carrying with him a sizeable sum belonging to the college – made him especially adept at detecting fraud is unclear, but he was right to suspect William's intentions. Politically the Glorious Revolution, as it was first termed in November 1689, revealed the value of determination in a crisis. William invaded, hoping to seize the Crown, but had to dissimulate his intentions in order to leave sufficient domestic and international opinion in the state of uncertainty and wishful thinking that would permit him to obtain his goals.

James II had made himself unpopular by the extent to which his support for Catholic initiatives had appeared to challenge existing privileges and property rights. He thus undid the effective coalition between the Crown and the Anglican establishment in the Church and, crucially, in county society that had enabled Charles II to consolidate his position after seeing off the challenge posed by the Popish Plot (1678) and the Exclusion Crisis (1679–81), an attempt to take anti-Catholic feeling to the point of altering the succession by excluding James. Charles' ability combined with his skilled use of the royal powers of dissolving and proroguing parliament enabled him to defeat the exclusionists in the sphere of legitimate political activity, while they were unwilling to foment a civil war and were faced with a king who had an adequate army and, from April 1681, French subsidies.

However, having dispensed with parliament in 1681, a condition of the French subsidies that Charles was not reluctant to accept, Charles did not rule by force. His alliance with the Tories, as those who supported Crown and Church against the Whigs, essentially backers of Dissenters and supporters of Exclusion, was known, ensured that England during his last years was relatively quiescent. Monmouth rejected the advice of the Whig leader Shaftesbury to foment a rebellion during a popular tour of the north-west in 1682, while plans for a rising and for the assassination of Charles and James, the Rye House Plot, were exposed in 1683 and led to the execution of a number of Whig leaders. As Charles strove to preserve his position, fostering royal power to that end rather than in order to pursue any agenda for expanding royal authority, his policies proved acceptable to the Tories and not intolerable to most Whigs. Monmouth enjoyed little support from former Whig gentry in 1685. In his last years Charles was like an old tiger. He had lost neither the cunning that had allowed him to survive until his old age, nor the use of his claws, but he was content to doze for most of the time.

James, in contrast, was frenetic, consumed with a sense of mission and uneasily aware that his real and alleged views were anathema to the bulk of the Crown's natural supporters. The Popish Plot had been a rude reminder of the strength of anti-Catholicism and its savage consequences. James wished to have Catholics given equal civil and religious rights and to foster Catholicism in the nation. James II's objectives were fairly moderate but his brusqueness in enforcing them alarmed Anglicans. Concern about the existence of Catholic army officers led to a breach between king and Tories in the parliament of 1685. Parliament was prorogued, new-found opponents dismissed from office and James was forced to seek a new constituency of political support. This led him to present his goal of a more secure position for Catholics as part of an attempt to create a wider-ranging religious toleration that would benefit Dissenters. A minority of Whigs cooperated with James but the majority remained suspicious of his intentions and opposed to his offers and in that position, though not in their political views, they were joined by many Tories, disenchanted by the growing breach between James and the Church of England.

By 1688 James was widely unpopular in England and from the perspective of subsequent developments it is easy to present his position as irredeemable. However, all the monarchs of England since Elizabeth had been seriously unpopular, the political situation in early 1688 was far less tense than it had been during the Exclusion Crisis, let alone in 1640 or for much of the 1620s, and it is far from clear that the movement towards what has since been generally termed, in the case of the continental monarchs, 'absolutism' was impossible in England. The foundations of a political system that would be called absolutist had it occurred on the continent had already been laid in Scotland and Ireland, and William of Orange's proclamation to the Scots aroused little response.

In England most of those who disliked James's policies were unwilling to take any illegal steps against him. Protection of privileges, refusal to heed royal lobbying and remonstrances in defence of the Church of England did not amount to intrigue or insurrection. James might receive the petition of seven bishops against the distribution and reading the Declaration of Indulgence in May 1688 by exclaiming 'This is a standard of rebellion', but it was only such if he chose to treat it thus. The political culture of the period, indeed of early-modern Europe as a whole, was not a simple matter of obedience or disobedience. The deference that a hierarchical and religious society owed God's Anointed monarch was matched by traditions of good kingship and good lordship, expectations of political behaviour and, crucially, patronage that provided a context within which royal conduct was judged and obedience elicited. There was therefore, whether explicit or implicit, a contractual element to kingship. However, if the monarch infringed the bounds of what was generally, or at least widely, held to be acceptable behaviour that did not mean that rebellion was the natural response.

Contractualism referred to attitudes rather than behaviour. It was not only prudential considerations that kept people from rebelling in 1687 or 1744. There was also no clear political course for those who were disenchanted, no institutional expression of national discontent that could organize a major rebellion. In addition, the contractual element related in general not to the renunciation of loyalty to a monarch or dynasty but rather to a willingness to defy particular policies or ministers. Most early-modern European rebellions can be seen as massive demonstrations designed to secure royal support against unpopular men or measures and to persuade the monarch to change direction, not to change the identity of the monarch or the nature of the constitution. The natural resolution of such a crisis was compromise, the abandonment of

William III as Prince of Orange in 1670, by C. Netscher

unpopular steps and the eliciting of the consensus between Crown and social elite that was the hallmark of early-modern government.

Tory hostility to James II in 1688 should be regarded in this light. Had the Tories played the major role in the crisis of 1688 then it is likely that such a compromise would have been obtained, but they neither took such a role, nor was it likely that they would have done so. Not only was James securely in control of both Scotland and Ireland, unlike his father Charles I in 1641–2, but there was no tradition of concerted secret Tory political action. Some Tories did act against James in 1688. Danby was one of the seven who signed the famous invitation to William and he seized York in late November 1688. When James' younger daughter by his first, Protestant, marriage Princess (later Queen) Anne fled London she was accompanied by several Tory peers-in-arms and by Henry Compton, Bishop of London. However, the Tories in 1688, though willing to try to take advantage of William's invasion in order to persuade James to act in an acceptable fashion, would neither have acted without William nor were interested in any change of sovereign.

It was conspiracy and invasion that drove James out, not any nationwide political movement. The conspiracy was secondary to the invasion. Though it was apparent in 1688 that James' efforts to win widespread support for his policies were unsuccessful, it was also clear that his power could only be challenged from outside England. James had built up the army of 8,565 he had inherited from his brother to a force of about 40,000 by November 1688. He also controlled a large fleet. These would be rich prizes for any ruler able to gain the alliance of Britain and that became increasingly important as the uneasy peace in western Europe established in 1684 became steadily more precarious, a process that culminated in 1688 in the outbreak of the Nine Years War, also known as the War of the League of Augsburg. The rulers best placed to win this alliance were Louis XIV and William of Orange. Louis (1638–1715) had, since he acquired effective control of France in 1661 on the death of his chief minister Mazarin, gained a reputation for aggressive diplomacy and a propensity for violence that was substantially justified, though in their own fashion other rulers acted in a similar manner. Initially Louis' energies were directed against Spain. He had grown to manhood during a long Franco-Spanish war (1635–59) and his first war, the War of Devolution (1667–8) was an attack on Spain. However, Dutch opposition led Louis to the conviction that he could only acquire the Spanish Netherlands (modern Belgium and Luxemburg) if the Dutch had been crushed. His attack on them in 1672 precipitated the rise to power of William III of Orange, who as a result became stadholder (governor) of the leading province Holland. Thereafter William and Louis duelled for military success and diplomatic influence in western Europe.

Antipathy to the Dutch as Calvinists, republicans, commercial rivals and recent enemies had led to the Second Anglo-Dutch war (1665–7) and in 1672, in furtherance of his secret Treaty of Dover (1670) with Louis, Charles II attacked the Dutch again. The war (1672–4) was far from glorious for Charles, but it indicated the potential importance of British military strength, as did the possibility of military intervention against Louis in 1678 during the period of Anglo-Dutch *rapprochement* which followed the marriage of William and his first cousin, James' eldest daughter and then heir, Mary in November 1677. To weaken William Louis helped to destroy his associate Lord Treasurer Danby by having his duplicitous negotiations with France revealed in the Commons at the end of 1678. Thus, prior to 1688 there was a tradition of both Louis and William intervening in British domestic politics. Precisely because they were able and willing to intervene and because many British politicians were keen to obtain their support and money, it was important for Charles and later James to try to ensure that such intervention was either friendly or unsuccessful. Danby's fall was an object lesson in the dangers of provoking Louis, but James was careful to avoid associating himself too closely with Louis' policies. However, the ambiguous nature of his support for Louis became less acceptable to William as international relations deteriorated. Individual steps, such as the Catholicization of the English army and the attempt to recall British soldiers serving in the Dutch army, appeared threatening in the light of the danger that James would assist Louis and in turn seemed to prove this danger. In early 1688 William decided to intervene in England, but concern about his likely reception and about James' military strength led him to insist on an invitation which was sent by the 'Immortal Seven' in June, the month when the birth of a son to James' second wife, the Catholic Mary of Modena, appeared to threaten the establishment of a Catholic dynasty.

Dutch invasion preparations during the summer of 1688 were too prominent to be kept secret for long, though James remained very unwilling to accept that they were directed against him. Nevertheless, in August naval and military moves were ordered, garrisons were reinforced, and troops ordered to England from Ireland and Scotland. However, these moves took time, and Sir John Lowther of Whitehaven writing from London on 6 October stated 'that the Scotch forces are coming for England we take for granted . . . once it was said they should meet the Irish at Chester and now that they shall come for York'.[2] William's first invasion attempt in mid-October was defeated by the weather, with the loss of many supplies, including over a thousand horses, crucial to the mobility of any invasion force. This blow helps to explain why on 26 and 28 October the council of war of the English fleet, under George Legge, Lord Dartmouth, decided not to leave their anchorage at the Gunfleet, off Harwich, in order to sail to the Dutch coast and wait for William's fleet there, as James, a former Lord High Admiral with military experience in the Second and Third Anglo-Dutch Wars, suggested. The anchorage appeared to cover the likely Dutch landing sites, Harwich, Yarmouth and Bridlington Bay, while, far from it being likely that William would seek to evade the English fleet, it was more probable that, as with English plans for landings on the Dutch coast during the Third Anglo-Dutch War, the Dutch would first seek to engage and defeat it. The alternative was to run the risk that even if the English fleet could be avoided, while it remained undefeated it would be able to attack the Dutch while landing or after they had landed, with very serious consequences.

Yet that was precisely what William intended. Planning to arrive as liberator not conqueror, he wished to avoid battle, which anyway he might not win, while it was too late in the year to risk waiting to invade until after a naval victory had been obtained. As Louis, who had invaded the Rhineland in 1688, might attack the Low Countries the following year, it was unacceptable to wait. Thus, William tried what foreign supporters of the Jacobites were always to be loath to risk, an invasion of southern England in the face of an undefeated navy and a substantial army. His success is a warning against writing off Jacobite plans as bound to fail, but equally it is worth pointing out that chance played a major role in this success. Dartmouth tried to sail on 30 October believing, correctly, that William was about to sail, but the strong north-easterly wind that brought the Dutch out on 1 November made it impossible for Dartmouth to round the Gunfleet shoal on the 30th and the 1st. When he eventually sailed on 3 November, the Dutch were already passing Dover and when William landed at Brixham on 5 November the English fleet was only off Beachy Head. A council of war that day determined not to attack what appeared to be the larger Dutch fleet and thereafter the English fleet was kept from intervening by storms.[3]

Though he had evaded the royal fleet William was not in a strong position militarily. He had landed at a considerable distance from London and much of the royal army was near the city, unlike in 1745 when it was mostly in the Low Countries. The mobility of William's men, especially of the cavalry, crucial to any rapid advance, was impaired after the sea crossing and William stayed at Exeter from 9 until 21 November hoping to refresh his troops and win English support. However, Exeter did not offer William the enthusiastic reception Charles Edward Stuart was to receive in Edinburgh in 1745, while relatively few members of James' army deserted to him. On 19 November James reached his forces encamped on Salisbury Plain. His strength was nearly twice that of William and, unlike much, though not all, of the royal forces in 1745, he was not

Etching showing the flight of James II (above) and the battle of the Boyne (below) by de Hooghe

out-manoeuvred into abandoning the position nearest London. A lot of James' army had still not been brought over from Ireland. James' soldiers were mostly loyal, though many of the officers were untrustworthy.

However, 1688, unlike 1745, became a political crisis in which James, having lost his superior military position, was increasingly forced onto the defensive. A failure of nerve, to which poor health, indecision and the seriousness of the situation contributed, led James to agree at a council of war on 23 November to retreat to London, instead of advancing on William and the following day he left the army. This helped to weaken morale among his troops, while James' general military and political position was eroded by the fact that, unlike in 1745, a number of provincial uprisings took place. By 5 December Derby, Nottingham, York, Hull and Durham had been seized for William, though the extent of loyalty towards James and the role of local circumstances, especially determined leaders, is indicated by the fact that Carlisle, Chester and Newcastle resisted such attempts successfully. Negotiations between James' commissioners and William began at Hungerford on 8 December, but William refused to halt his march towards London, whence James fled towards France on the night of

10–11 December, ordering his commander in chief to cease hostilities. The French envoy Barrillon reported that many were opposed to William gaining power but he suggested that this opposition would collapse at his arrival and that no one would dare oppose his designs.[4] The situation proved far more complex but essentially Barrillon was correct. William controlled the military situation, James reached France on his second attempt and James' army disintegrated. William made clear that he wanted to be ruler, declaring on 3 February 1689 that he would be neither regent nor prince consort, and thus one of the many innovations of the Revolution Settlement was the creation of a joint monarchy, that of William and Mary. James II and his baby son had been debarred, the former on the grounds that he had deserted the kingdom, while Anne's rights to the succession were subordinated to those of William. The desertion theory is difficult to sustain as the second time James left London he was ordered out by William under Dutch escort. William's Declaration alluded to the 'imposture' of the Prince of Wales' birth and said that the 'facts' would be established. No inquiry ever took place, which led to complaints by Seymour and Reresby. Parliament did not declare the prince an 'impostor', but it debarred all Catholics from the succession. However, far from settling Britain, the events of 1688–9 were to be the first stage in the War of the British Succession, a war that was to involve both conflict in England, Ireland and Scotland and foreign intervention.

2 Civil War, Plots and Risings 1689–1723

Men may very well be excused if for the present they suffer politics and affairs of state to engross their thoughts; because the subject matter is no less than what concerns their religion, property and peace, and he that can be thoughtless or careless of the event of things when an invasion threatens, will justly be suspected of favouring in his heart a change in our constitution.

Lord Perceval, a Whig, 27 August 1715[1]

William's success in England neither ensured the compliance of Ireland and Scotland nor freed him from the necessity of having to defend his position in England against domestic conspiracy and the threat of foreign invasion. William's chances were lessened considerably by his success in obtaining what had been his essential purpose in invading England. In 1689 his new dominions joined the coalition arrayed against Louis XIV, thus ensuring that Louis, whose resources were fully stretched on a number of fronts, would provide James with military support. The years 1689–91 were not typical for Jacobitism, as the cause of the exiled Stuarts came to be known from the Latin for James, *Jacobus*, for during that period James II and his supporters controlled part of Britain, including for a while most of Ireland. This situation did not look forward to that of later Jacobite activity but back to the last period of Stuart dispossession, the misnamed English Civil Wars and the Interregnum. However, William III, like Cromwell before him, was to succeed in having the Stuarts and their supporters driven from Scotland and Ireland, thus forcing them to become reliant on the foreign support that was offered in accordance with a diplomatic and military agenda, timetable and constraints that rarely suited the Jacobites and over which they had little influence, let alone control. The campaigns against William in Ireland introduced the problem of cooperating with France, militarily and politically, and this was to be a central theme until the failure of the '45.

James' prospects were best in Ireland, but it was in Scotland that the first battle was fought. On 4 April 1689 the Scottish Convention resolved that James had not abdicated, but had forfeited the throne through his misdemeanours. A Claim of Right laying down fundamental constitutional principles and attacking episcopacy (church government by bishops) was accepted on 11 April and followed by the proclamation of William and Mary as joint monarchs. However, the same month the most active of James' Scottish supporters, John Graham of Claverhouse, Viscount Dundee, raised James' standard outside Dundee. The Presbyterians were not as numerous as they claimed to be. Only William III's backing, which arose from opposition by the Episcopalians to the transfer of the Crown, made them strong. The Episcopalians always claimed to be the majority. Viscount Dundee retired into the Highlands to obtain recruits, pursued by the royal army under General Hugh Mackay of Scourie. The two forces confronted each other at the Pass of Killiecrankie while seeking to control Blair Castle in Perthshire, which commanded a crucial north–south route through the Highlands. Dundee had only 2,000 men. As in 1745, the Highland rising had scant support from abroad or from Jacobites elsewhere, while Dundee faced the classic problem of irregular warfare: keeping his men together. Mackay's force was twice as large, but on the evening of 27 July 1689 Dundee had the advantage of height. After an inconsequential exchange of fire, the Highlanders threw down their guns and charged with their broadswords. Mackay's line collapsed at once under the charge, but at the close of the battle Dundee was killed by a musket ball. Victory led the doubtful clans to flock to James' standard and Dundee's successor, Colonel Cannon, who had brought 300 infantry from Ireland to reinforce the force, found himself in command of 5,000 men. However, swift moves by Mackay and Cannon's indecisiveness kept the Jacobites out of Perth and Aberdeen. Cannon refused to engage Mackay and instead attacked the apparently vulnerable garrison of untrained Covenanters at Dunkeld. He was, however, repulsed and retreated to Mull, while the Highlanders dispersed to their homes. Cannon was replaced by Major General Thomas Buchan, but he was surprised and defeated on 1 May 1690 by Mackay's cavalry on the Haughs of Cromdale. Reinforced by clansmen, Buchan entered Aberdeenshire but he proved unwilling to attack Aberdeen, and loss of support and Mackay's advance led to his retreat into the mountains in Lochaber where his forces dwindled.

Most of the Highland chiefs swore allegiance to William in late 1691, a process facilitated by indemnity, bribes and being allowed to obtain the permission of James VII (James II of England). The Scottish campaigns are instructive in a number of respects. War was far faster moving in Scotland than it was in the Low Countries and Rhineland, where operations centred around lengthy sieges. The importance of bold generalship and, in particular, a willingness to risk battle were also demonstrated. The cautious war of manoeuvre conducted by, among others, William III in the Spanish Netherlands was expensive, required large forces if positions were to be protected, and was a formidable drain on supplies. It was not surprising that the areas where position warfare was classically conducted, the Low Countries, the Rhineland and Lombardy, were relatively wealthy agricultural regions served by good communications. In Scotland, as in eastern Europe and Iberia, the situation was different. It was not easy for forces, both offensive and defensive, to remain in a given area for any length of time, without exhausting their supplies and a premium was therefore placed on movement. In the context of Scotland this meant an advance from the Highlands to seize wealthier lowland areas. A refusal

Soldier's Leap, Killiecrankie, where it is said that a soldier leapt 18 ft across the gorge in 1689 to escape Highland troops

to engage in battle or attack towns did not preclude troops from gaining food from lowland regions, but it reduced the political significance of their presence. The crucial factor about Killiecrankie was the failure to exploit the victory, a failure that ensured that the battle had more in common in its political consequence with the generally inconclusive engagements in the Low Countries in the 1690s than with the battles in eastern Europe. Charles XII was to show at Narva (1700), when the Swedes defeated the Russians, that a smaller attacking force, boldly led and taking advantage of local circumstances, could defeat a larger army. However, the Swedes were a disciplined force able to exploit advantages and to respond to a strategic plan. Jacobite generals did not enjoy the same degree of control in Scotland.

The decisive battles involving James II's cause were fought in Ireland. Ireland was more accessible than Scotland to French naval power and, therefore, troops and supplies, better able to support operations than the Scottish Highlands and, in early 1689, more under the sway of James' supporters. James II left France for Ireland in March 1689, continuing the process that had begun with his elder brother Charles, and that James himself had exemplified by going to Edinburgh during the Exclusion Crisis, of Stuarts visiting Scotland and Ireland only during periods of adversity. Most of the island was soon won for James, but Derry, fearing Catholic massacre, resisted a siege and was relieved by the English fleet in July 1689. The following month William's army, mostly of Danes and Dutch, landed and occupied Belfast. Naval power thus offered William military flexibility and prevented James from controlling all of Ireland. Arguably the French should have made more of an effort to deprive William of his naval weapon, but the Irish Sea was quite a distance from their principal bases and the English benefitted, as they were to do in 1744–6 when moving troops between Britain and the Low Countries, from closer proximity to their bases and from the advantage in terms of naval strength that the Dutch alliance brought.

Arriving in Ireland in June 1690, William marched on Dublin to find the outnumbered Jacobites drawn up on the southern bank of the River Boyne. As with the Spey in 1746, the line of the Boyne was not held. On 1 July William was able to outflank the Jacobite left flank, before crossing with his own left. Defeated on both flanks, the Jacobites retreated to Dublin where James II made the decision to return to France, a move that weakened his cause in Ireland. Dublin was taken easily by William, though he failed at Limerick in August. The following month John Churchill, then Earl of Marlborough, took Cork after an action lasting two days, indicating that the defence did not have all the advantages, while Kinsale fell to him in October. The following year Athlone fell to the Dutch general Ginkel, while his second-in-command Hugh Mackay carried Irishtown by assault after crossing the deep ford of the Shannon. At Aughrim on 12 July 1691 Mackay turned the Jacobite flank by leading his cavalry across a bog on which he had laid hurdles. The Jacobite force broke, their infantry suffering heavy casualties in the retreat. Limerick surrendered and by the Treaty of Limerick all the Jacobite forces in Ireland surrendered, about 11,000 Irishmen, the 'Wild Geese', going to serve James in France.

The Irish campaigns had been far from static. Bold generalship had been important and success in battle had been more important than the holding of fortified positions, Though Derry, and Athlone and Limerick had successfully resisted in 1689 and 1690 respectively, the Boyne had given William a number of Jacobite strongholds and Aughrim was followed by the fall of Galway. Both of the major engagements had been won by the attacking force and in each case tactical considerations relating to the terrain and to the ability to take advantage of developments had been crucial, while the vulnerability of armies to flanking attacks had been clearly demonstrated. There was no suggestion that the battles were foregone conclusions, though the greater priority attached to Ireland by William III rather than Louis XIV was important in terms of the resources available to the combatants.

Louis, however, hoped to assist James by an invasion of southern England. On 28 June 1690 the Anglo-Dutch fleet under Torrington with 56 ships of the line was defeated by a large French fleet under Tourville with 75 of the line off Beachy Head. Tourville, whose instructions when he left Brest were to attack Portsmouth and then blockade the Thames, was unable to exploit the victory. There was no army ready to invade and Tourville simply made a raid on Teignmouth. Rumours that the French were going to land in the Romney Marshes, in Sussex or on the Exe proved false. There were only 6,000 regular troops in southern England, but William was fortunate that there was no Jacobite activity there. The militia was raised, the horses of Catholic gentlemen seized and leading Catholics and disaffected nobles sent to the Tower. Whether these measures would have proved more effective than James II's less determined last-minute moves in 1688 had there been an invasion is unclear, but William was fortunate that the Jacobite cause was not progressing in Scotland or Ireland. It was unfortunate for the Jacobites that they were unable to exploit the longest period in the history of their movement when the French had control of the Channel. Though they were undefeated, the French were less of a threat in 1691 because of the large number of ships the English put to sea and the French decision to concentrate on privateering. The following year Louis decided to invade England in support of James but in an engagement which began off Barfleur on 19 May 1692 the Anglo-Dutch fleet under Russell defeated the outnumbered Tourville, ending the plan. Louis returned to the scheme in 1696 when, unable to defeat William in the Spanish Netherlands and promised Jacobite support in England, he concentrated troops near the coast. A small

'James III' as Prince of Wales by Gennari

inner group of officers planned the assassination of William, but neither James nor Louis was party to this and the rest of the Jacobite plot cum invasion was quite separate. However, the plans were not kept secret and the English assembled a formidable fleet of 80 men of war off Dunkirk, dissuading the French from making any move.

The following year Louis made peace at Rijswijk, recognizing William. Sir John Lowther noted 'the Jacobites are stunned'. The 'might have beens' were over for a while. Jacobite chances had not been destroyed by Williamite successes in Scotland and Ireland. Had Tourville waited for the Toulon fleet in 1692 the battle of Barfleur might have taken a different course and had William been killed during the war it is possible that policies of reinsurance on the part of politicians who continued links with the exiled James might have weakened the English response to a French invasion. However, the peace of 1697 left the Jacobites adrift, not least because it was followed by a diplomatic *rapprochement* between William and Louis as they sought to solve the vexed problem of the Spanish Succession by negotiating two partition treaties (1698, 1700). They were to be rescued from limbo by the breakdown of Anglo-French relations in 1701. Louis' decision to recognize the prince born in 1688 as King James III on his father's death that year played a role in exacerbating relations, but the two powers were already on a collision course that stemmed from Louis' acceptance of the Spanish crown for his second grandson, the Duke of Anjou.

During the war of the Spanish Succession, which lasted as far as the English were concerned from 1702 until 1713, France offered the Jacobites far less assistance than during the previous Nine Years War. The situation was clearly less propitious for French action. The previous conflict had revealed the difficulties of mounting an invasion, the English fleet was even stronger, the Jacobites were no longer in control of much of Ireland and Scotland and their claims to be able to create disorder in England had been discredited. The French did not offer assistance, and then far less than in 1692 and 1696, until after the situation had changed. The Union of England and Scotland in 1707 raised hopes of discontent in Scotland, while the failure of France to defeat her opponents suggested the need for a decisive blow against Britain, just as the defeat at Dettingen (1743) was to do. In 1704 at the battle of Blenheim the Duke of Marlborough thwarted the French plan to knock Austria out and in 1706 the French were driven out of Italy and the Spanish Netherlands as a result of defeats at Turin and Ramillies. France was forced back to the defence of her frontiers. The Union was widely unpopular in Scotland and had only been brought about by judicious bribery. It led the Jacobite nobility and gentry to draw up an urgent Memorial for presentation to Louis. They argued that the presence of 'James VIII and III' would be essential for success and promised that when he landed an army of 30,000 would be quickly formed. This force would be a national one, Highlanders and Lowlanders, Presbyterians, Episcopalians and Catholics. Money, arms and ammunition and experienced officers were requested, as was an invasion force large enough to resist the 2,000 men of the Scots army and any English troops that might be sent. One memorandum said that the son of George of Hanover was illegitimate and could not succeed under the Act of Settlement. In Paris the proposals were given an English dimension by the

Duke of Chevreuse. English support was assumed and, looking back to the Bishops' Wars against Charles I, it was argued that an invading force of Scots would be able to subsist in northern England, where there were no strong fortresses nor any troops. Newcastle and its coalfield were to be seized and London thus put under pressure. Hopefully England and Ireland would rise but, even if they failed to do so, the effect of the invasion would be to force the British to withdraw their forces from the Continent and thus undermine the anti-French coalition. James would be sent from Dunkirk with 5,000 men.

Louis decided to support the project hoping that the recall of British troops would enable France to invade the Spanish Netherlands where plans for a pro-French rebellion were being encouraged. However, secrecy was lost and on 27 February 1708 Sir George Byng anchored a squadron off Dunkirk. The French naval commander Forbin wished to call off the expedition, but James persuaded Louis to order Forbin to sail, which he did on 6 March, avoiding Byng in the mist. Forbin reached the Firth of Forth on 12 March, followed a day later by Byng. Forbin succeeded in evading the superior British force and returning to Dunkirk, but James and the troops were landed neither in the Firth of Forth nor further north. An opportunity had been lost. James and the troops could have been landed on the 12th, especially if the initial landfall had been in the Firth and not, as a result of error, 100 miles further north. Edinburgh Castle was in no state to resist a siege and the Scots army was not powerful enough to block Jacobite plans. On the 12th the Earl of Leven, Anne's commander-in-chief in Scotland, had written complaining about having 'few troops . . . It vexes

Facies Arcis EDENBURGEENÆ *The Southside of the Castle of* EDINBURGH.

Edinburgh in the eighteenth century by Sleazer

me sadly to think I must retire towards Berwick if the French land on this side the Forth'. Much of the Scottish aristocracy was prepared to rise for James. On 1 April a loyal peer David Carnegie, 4th Earl of Northesk wrote from Edinburgh of his desire to hear that the French had disembarked in Dunkirk:

> ... we have for some time been in great doubts and fears, if it end this way we have reason to be very thankful, for we were on the brink of being destroyed, we cannot doubt but the Queen who has shown so great a regard to this part of the island, will lay down such methods, as may both secure us by sea and land, for it will be very odd if they leave this project, on so slender a repulse as they got, I'm very hopeful, however, it will appear that there has not been such a disposition of rebelling in Scotland as the French have boasted of.[2]

The immediate British response had been to march ten regiments of foot from Ghent to Ostend and then transport them to first the Tyne and then Leith. Though the troops returned in turn to help Marlborough gain the third of his great victories at Oudenarde, it is clear that the Union would have been defended. Whether 1708 could have prefigured 1745 with the Jacobites gaining effective control of Scotland before invading England is unclear. The English Jacobites pledged no support in 1708, unlike in 1745 when they promised help if the French landed. In some respects James was in a stronger position in 1708. He not only had French troops with him, but the French had clearly committed themselves and were therefore likely to send more assistance if they could. Furthermore, there was more support for the Jacobite cause in Scotland in 1708 than there would be in 1745, as the list of those nobles arrested by the government in 1708 makes clear. The Union was very unpopular, Scotland had been badly battered economically over the previous fifteen years, the Stuarts were the ancient Scottish kings and James appeared a better option than the Electress Sophia of Hanover, who was the alternative, and legally recognized, heir to Anne. As in 1745, the French did not control the sea, while in 1708 the French position in the Low Countries was worse, though this was to become clearer after Oudenarde. Had there been a struggle in northern England between the troops brought back from Ostend and James it is difficult to predict the result. The Scots would have been relatively untrained, while the experience of a French expeditionary force in Ireland in 1690–1 was scarcely encouraging. On the other hand Scotland might well have united against Union to a sufficient extent to permit James to field a large army. Though the size of the British fleet would have lessened the danger of a supporting French invasion that would still have had to be faced, as in 1744–6, and it would have been impossible to recall all the troops from the Low Countries without running the risk of a separate Franco-Dutch peace. The '08 was over too fast for its possible military implications to be probed, but it is a reminder of the unpredictability of events in this period, an unpredictability that military success and dynastic chance both displayed.

In 1709 the French planned an invasion of Scotland from Brest, but the plans were abandoned: the British navy was too strong, Louis had to concentrate his resources on defending his frontier against Marlborough and France was exhausted financially, as indeed was Britain. The Jacobite option was in effect abandoned militarily, though the fall of Anne's Whig ministers in 1710 and their replacement by Tories who, for domestic political reasons of their own, sought Jacobite support suggested that James might be able to gain the throne without an invasion. Contrary developments appeared to be at work in 1710–14. On one hand James' foreign position deteriorated, as he lost French support without gaining the backing of other rulers. As early as 1706, Louis was prepared, as part of a peace settlement, to recognize Anne as queen and the Protestant Succession in the House of Hanover, as parliament had determined by the Act of Settlement of 1701. This was agreed to in the preliminary peace articles signed on 27 September 1711, while the French were informed that James, who had followed his father in accepting Louis' hospitality in the palace of St Germain outside Paris, would have to leave France in accordance with the resolution of the House of Lords of March 1709 preventing the government from entering into a treaty with any ruler sheltering James. As a result James left France for Lorraine. On the other hand the British political situation appeared to be increasingly propitious for James. There was the hope that concern about Hanoverian intentions would drive the Tory ministry to turn to him, though his refusal to accept the advice that he should conform to the Church of England lessened his appeal. Anne was a Stuart, James' half-sister, an Anglican and a woman whose foreign non-Anglican husband, Prince George of Denmark (died 1708), did not enjoy power or advance policies that challenged national interests. There had been little prospect of Jacobite action in England during her reign. However, the possible succession of a Hanoverian was a different matter. The Act of Settlement had been passed with some difficulty and the danger of the Hanoverian option was underlined in 1713 by the Electorate's complaints about Britain's abandonment of an unpopular war by the negotiation of the peace of Utrecht.

The peaceful accession of George I in 1714 was a major disappointment for James, but the consequences were not completely unhelpful for George's policies helped to revive Jacobitism. Whereas both Whigs and Tories had enjoyed favour during Anne's reign and her last leading minister, Robert Harley, Earl of Oxford, had sought to head a mixed ministry, albeit one that centred on the Tories, because of the commitment of most Whigs to the continuation of the War of the Spanish Succession, George I committed himself to the Whigs. This was due both to his hostility to the Tory peace, which had entailed the abandonment of the German princes supporting the Emperor, such as George, and of English subsidies to them, and because he was advised to do so by the Dutch and by his envoy in London. William Bromley, MP for Oxford University, a centre of High-Toryism, wrote on 3 August 1714, two days after the death of Anne, whom he had served as Secretary of State, about the absence of Jacobite action: 'everything has been carried on with the greatest unanimity, all ranks of people expressing their duty to the king, and their satisfaction in our present settlement, so that we have just ground to hope the enemies of our constitution will be discouraged from making any attempts to disturb us'.[3] However, George did not reappoint Bromley, who was a Jacobite in 1713 according to the French and Prussian envoys, Secretary of State, and Bromley was soon speaking in the Commons against the ministry, defending Harley against the charge of high treason in July 1715 and collecting money for the plot

George I by Sir Godfrey Kneller dated 1716

to restore the Stuarts with the help of Sweden. In December 1717 he supported a motion to reduce the army, a theme he returned to in 1720 and 1724, while he opposed the vote of credit for measures against the Swedish threat in April 1717 and the suspension of the Habeus Corpus Act after the discovery of the Atterbury plot. All these were in accordance with traditional 'Country' political themes of opposition to the policies and power of the state, but in the context of George I's reign it is difficult to see them as anything other than Jacobite moves, and they were certainly thus regarded.

It rapidly became clear that Tories would not only be denied patronage but would be dismissed from existing posts, a course that was particularly dangerous to younger sons, but that also pressed hard on a landed society which had been suffering from the dangerous combination of high wartime taxation and an agrarian depression. This party preference exacerbated the normal problems of diminished and altered opportunities that accompanied both demobilization and the accession of a new monarch. In addition, George and the Whig ministers he promoted sought to try the leading Tories as part of a campaign to wreck the party on the charges of having betrayed national interests by the negotiation of Utrecht and of having supported Jacobitism.

If George served the Whigs' purposes by concentrating power and places in their hands, they in return supported his foreign policy. One of the most obvious consequences of the 'Glorious Revolution' had been the wrenching of foreign policy from the generally quiescent, pragmatic policies pursued by Charles II in his last years and by James II, for which both monarchs were accused both then and subsequently of being pro-French, and the commitment of British resources to a lengthy, costly and generally unsuccessful war with France. The policies of the Hanoverians were also unpopular. Jacobite propaganda made much of the Germanic nature of the Hanoverian regime. If Whig publicists could present the Stuart cause as foreign because Catholic, their Jacobite counterparts had no hesitation in proclaiming the alien nature of the Hanoverians. In many senses it was easier to attack them than William III. The latter was both son and husband to Stuart princesses and by the admittedly uncharismatic standards of both George I and II was not without several qualities. William was careful not to proscribe the Tories, a policy followed by Anne. In contrast Georges I and II would accept only the small number of Tory leaders who were prepared to abandon their party, principally Trevor, Harcourt and later Gower. Furthermore, though William was attacked for subordinating English interests to those of his native United Provinces, there was no doubt that his prime commitment was to opposing France. In contrast, there was little doubt that Georges I and II were most interested in Hanover, this preference becoming more apparent during the Anglo-French alliance of 1716–31. This alliance undercut one of the principal criticisms directed against the Stuarts, that they were pro-French. Instead, as a result of British pressure on France, 'James III' was kept south of the Alps. Tory criticism of the foreign policies of Georges I and II was not without reason and force. The more it is realized that 'British' foreign policy was actually that of the king and a small number of ministers and that it was heavily influenced by a desire to defend and aggrandize Hanover, the easier it is to appreciate the hostility that it aroused. Rather than presenting Jacobitism as a disloyal fringe of a loyal population, it is necessary to point out that Jacobitism like Hanoverianism was an option, as well as the product of an ideology, or at least a range of sentiments and beliefs. At times, such as after the fall of Walpole, the Hanoverian option was profoundly unpopular; it was always unpopular with many. The Whig John Perceval observed in January 1715:

> Put the case in the most favourable manner for the Tories, and allow they are not really in the interest of the Pretender, yet they must own they were not so zealous and determined against him as those his Majesty now employs.

He returned to the theme in July 1715:

> If oaths are no security of mens sincerity much less is the bare saying we are for the king to be credited without our behaviour show it, and therefore if men in their several spheres act not freely and above board at this time we must be forgiven if we pronounce them Jacobites. As heavily as the charge may seem it is so natural a consequence of their deportment that it would be a violence to our reason to think otherwise.[4]

The foreign quality of Hanoverian rule was stressed by Jacobite propaganda. *An Address to the Peers of England*, a pamphlet written after the accession of George I, attacked Dutch and German influences and the Huguenots who were declared to be 'armed to cut English throats'. William III was criticized for overturning the church in Scotland, where the Presbyterians had replaced the Episcopalians as the established church; the Nonjurors, Anglican clergy who had been deprived for refusing to accept the legality of William's accession, were praised as 'many of our most pious and learned bishops and clergy'; George was condemned for sending British money to Hanover and the arguments of Whig publicists were challenged:

> ... the partisans of Holland are very busy to cry up that people as Protestant states and Protestant allies, whereas nothing is more absurd, for it is well known religion is the least of their concern ... if we are so fond of Dutch liberty, I would gladly that my countrymen should know, wherein that liberty consists, and by the report of all travellers I have ever conversed with, I find the little finger of Holland to be heavier than the loins of any king I ever heard of ... see how your cruel German king thirsts after English blood. He resolved to cement the foundations of his reign by the blood of English nobles, to make room for German barons, and before he set foot on English soil sold the life of noble Ormonde to the Dutch States, contrary to the example and policy of English kings who begun their reigns with acts of clemency and amnesty, as if he would vie with the example of heathen Rome.

The pamphlet's prescription was clear: the return of James and a Britain 'independent of Dutch politics: we may preserve the dominion of our seas and see our trade flourish, and our religion established in the purity of primitive Christianity'.[5] The role of the Dutch in supporting George during the '15 helped to keep the Jacobite anti-Dutch polemic alive.

During Anne's reign it was possible for Jacobites to hope and scheme for a peaceful Stuart succession but George's accession made it clear that such a possibility no longer existed and that violent action had to be immediate, for there was no longer anything to be gained from delay. Many commentators, including some hostile ones, agreed that sympathy for the Stuarts was widely diffused. In July 1715 Daniel Dering observed 'it is surprising how much the Jacobite spirit has been cultivated all over the kingdom. So much that a great many if not most honest men think it necessary, to increase the size of the army'.[6] Three risings were planned in 1715. James was to follow William III by landing in the south-west of England, where there was to be the major rising, followed by a march on London, while there were also to be risings in the Highlands and the border counties. The rising in the south-west was nipped in the bud in September 1715 as a result of prompt government action on the basis of intelligence and Jacobite indecision. However, on 6 September the Earl of Mar, who realized that he would not receive from George the favour he had received under Anne, raised the Stuart standard at Braemar. Perth was seized and the royal forces, under the Duke of Argyll, heavily outnumbered, for north of the Firth of Forth support for the rebellion was very extensive, but indecision on Mar's part allowed valuable campaigning time to be lost. Argyll should have been engaged as soon as possible so that Scotland could have been a base for assisting the rising of the English Jacobites and Scottish borderers in October.

Mar did not march on Edinburgh until November, and on 13 November he fought Argyll at Sheriffmuir, north of Stirling. Unaware of the dispositions of the other, each general drew up his forces so that their right wings overlapped the other's left. The left wings of both armies were defeated, but Mar failed to exploit his superior force. The indecisive battle was in practice a victory for Argyll as Mar needed a triumph both in order to hold his army together and in order to help the Jacobites in the Borders.

On the same day as Sheriffmuir, the rising in England was coming to an end, as the officers of the outnumbered army surrounded in Preston were negotiating its surrender. The army was the product of three forces: Englishmen from the north-east, under the Earl of Derwentwater and Thomas Forster, MP for Northumberland; Lowlanders from south-west Scotland under Lord Kenmuir; and a unit detached from Mar's army under Mackintosh of Borlum. The small Northumberland rising had failed to make the bold move of seizing Newcastle and it fell back to join the other two forces at Kelso on 22 October 1715. Instead of marching north to help Mar attack Argyll, the Jacobites decided, against the wishes of the Scots, to invade Lancashire, an area with many Catholics whom they hoped to raise. The army, less than 3,000 men, crossed the border on 1 November. Carlisle was judged too strong to attack, as Dumfries and Newcastle had earlier been, but the Jacobites had more success in confronting the militia and the *posse comitatus*, a force drawn from all men over fifteen. This was reported in a letter by Viscount Lonsdale, one of the Deputy Lord Lieutenants for Cumberland, who had assembled the militia on Penrith Fell:

> The *Posse Comitatus* for the county of Cumberland was appointed to meet on Wednesday near Penrith, where I really believe there was near 13,000 men, who by the assistance of some broken officers of General Elliot's regiment (who were extremely diligent) were put in very tolerable order, but as soon as the news came that the rebels were marching towards them, they run off by hundreds, all the means that were possible were tried by several of the gentlemen for keeping the men together but was all to no purpose; when we found that there was no possibility of engaging the rebels in the open field, the officers advised the drawing the men into town, to endeavour to defend that place which we accordingly did, but when we went to put the men upon guard to defend the avenues of the town, there were not a hundred men left, that could be of any defence (excepting two companies of Trained Bands). I don't know whether this revolt proceeded from fear or disaffection, what makes me imagine it was a thing designed is because most of the men came without any manner of arms, and though the rebels knew their number to be so great they did not alter their march at all, which I fancy they would have done, if they had not depended upon a great many friends who did not show themselves. The *posse* for Westmorland was to have met yesterday, but the accounts of what happened in Cumberland the day before so terrified the people, that those who were coming to the place appointed for the rendezvous turned back as soon as they heard the news, and the rest would not stir from home. The country is entirely without defence and I am very much afraid these rebels won't be stopped till they meet with a regular force.

The militia was not only unsatisfactory in Cumbria. The Duke of Manchester, Lord Lieutenant of Huntingdon, was dissatisfied with the state of the county militia, 'those of the Horse that appeared were in no condition of doing any service'.

If the Cumbrians were unable to fight the Jacobites they were also unwilling to

Sword found on the battlefield at Preston. The basket-shaped hilt is associated with those of Scottish design in the eighteenth century

fight for them, the Earl of Carlisle, the Lord Lieutenant, writing 'from the care that my Lord Lonsdale and the rest of the Deputy Lieutenants had taken, not a man of that country joined the rebels as they passed through Cumberland, although their success at the time might have been no little motive for their so doing'. This picture of non-involvement was confirmed by Edward Southwell MP who found Somerset and Gloucestershire 'like to all Wales perfectly indolent which get the better the king or the rebels so as to toss cross or pile', a reference to a game of the period.[7] This situation in England helped the side with the standing army and foreign military assistance, that of George, especially as, thanks to Mar, there was to be no powerful Scottish invasion to alter the military situation, as there had been both before and during the First English Civil War. On 20 October Lord Chancellor Cowper had written of the great danger 'if something be not immediately done ... will infallibly be so many commotions in England that the king will not have troops to attend to all, credit will quite sink, as it is already very near, the Bank [of England] being almost at a stand'.[8] However, though there were Jacobite riots in a number of places, there was no rising to support the invaders of Cumbria and this allowed the royal troops to concentrate on them.

On 9 November 1715 the Jacobites entered Preston but it was to prove as unfortunate for them as it had been for the invading Scots in August 1648. Forster failed to defend the line of the Ribble against the royal troops under generals Carpenter and Wills, though an assault on the town, which had been hastily fortified with barriers, failed on 12 November. However, instead of attacking the besiegers or trying to fight their way out, the Jacobites allowed their enemies to surround the town on the 13th and the weak Forster, who had had no military experience, negotiated an unconditional surrender on 14 November.

The battle of Preston marked the end of the Jacobite rising in England, but Sheriffmuir was not the end of the Scottish rising. Having sailed from Dunkirk, 'James III' arrived in Peterhead on 22 December and Scone on 8 January 1716, where his coronation was planned. However, freed of concern about England, Argyll had now been provided with a far larger army, including 5,000 Dutchmen, and, despite the bitterness of the winter and a Jacobite scorched earth policy, marched on Perth on 21 January. The Jacobite army was already badly affected by loss of morale and desertion and James abandoned Perth, throwing his artillery into the Tay. The army retreated to Montrose, which it prepared to defend, but on 4 February James and Mar sailed from there for France. Abandoned, the Jacobite force dispersed. George had no need of the 3,000 additional troops he had asked the Dutch to hold in readiness.

Had James arrived with a French force comparable to that he had been offered in 1692, 1696 and 1708 or provided with in Ireland in 1689–90 the situation might have been different. However, though there was considerable sympathy in the French court for James, which worried the British envoy, the Earl of Stair, the government was unwilling to risk relations with Britain, especially after the death of Louis XIV on 1 September (new style) 1715. Louis had promised the Jacobites arms but no troops. Jean de Robethon, a Huguenot in George's service as Elector, observed thirteen days earlier, 'If the old gentleman is a going, that will extinguish the hopes of the Pretender better than any of our acts of parliament', while George Bubb, envoy in Madrid, wrote in October of the Jacobites, 'I am surprised to see so large a body of nobility engaged in so foul a case. I do not know how far it may be a mark of their bravery, but sure it is none of their judgment, to have chosen the present season to show themselves'.[9] Stair made it clear to the Duke of Orléans, regent for the infant Louis XV, that good relations would depend on the French refusing to help James.

In December 1715 the Earl of Carlisle wrote from his seat at Castle Howard to Viscount Townshend, one of the Secretaries of State:

> A good conclusion with my Lord Mar and a good treaty of alliance with the Regent will make us all easy and safe, I hope for the remainder of our days. It will be expected from you, since you have now the power in your hands, that you put such an end to this rebellion, that you so entirely subdue this spirit that so barefacedly shows itself in favour of the Pretender that England may be safe and secure for the future. [10]

This was certainly an important objective in the negotiation of the Anglo-French alliance, though that was also designed to serve Hanoverian ends. The French were told the treaty would be impossible unless James was expelled from France,

*Victory medal, struck to commemorate the Hanover-
ian victory at the battle of Preston*

which would make it hard for him to repeat the '15, an episode that had revealed
that the Jacobites were not dependant on foreign military assistance, as the '45
was to do. In August 1716 James Stanhope wrote from Hanover to his fellow
Secretary-of-State Townshend, 'His Majesty is sensible that destroying
Mardyke, removing the Pretender with all his adherents out of France and
dashing thereby the hopes of the Jacobite party, are motives sufficient to induce
England to make a treaty with France',[11] and these were duely achieved in the
treaty signed in Hanover on 9 October (ns) and formally at The Hague on 28
November (ns). A close friendship between Stanhope and Orléans' advisor
Dubois was crucial to the success of the negotiations. Mardyke was near
Dunkirk, the destruction of whose harbour had been specified in the Utrecht
settlement, and it was feared that it would be a substitute for it. British concern
about Dunkirk and nearby harbours, a continuous theme in Anglo-French
diplomacy and British intelligence in the following decades, was one indication
of sensitivity to the prospect of pro-Jacobite activity.

The Anglo-French alliance was made more necessary by the fact that the
situation in Britain was still disturbed. In July 1716 Thomas Erle, the Governor
of Portsmouth, was instructed to take precautions in the light of advice, 'that
there may be some design of an attempt from sea, in concert with some on land,
upon Portsmouth'. The same month Lord Perceval wrote from London, 'I am
sorry to own the civil spirit among the people is very little better than ever, and
that the army is necessary to contain them'. Whigs sent in numerous reports of
Stuart sympathies and Jacobite plottings. George Liddell reported from the
north-east in the spring of 1718 'the rebels meet as publicly as ever'. Adding that
bands of armed men had been seen in Northumberland and that the streets of
Newcastle resounded to cries of 'James Stuart', Liddell wrote:

It is the opinion of all the judicious well affected people both in the county and
Northumberland that we shall have another rebellion and that very speedily unless some
more than ordinary care be taken by the government . . . You may depend upon it we shall in
a very little time have another insurrection in Northumberland if not . . . prevented by the

governments sending a regiment or two of dragoons into Northumberland and a regiment of foot to Newcastle.[12]

Given this domestic unpopularity and the need to establish an unpopular regime, it is surprising that George I did not follow the example of James II, who had essentially abstained from an interventionist foreign policy to avoid creating difficulties while he sought to pursue contentious domestic policies. Instead George, within five years of his accession, was at war with Spain, close to war with Russia and, having divided the Whigs and proscribed the Tories, was seeking to implement a controversial legislative programme. Unlike James, George's response to being in a vulnerable position was to negotiate an alliance with his principal foreign enemy and to fight a power that did not wish to fight him. The need for action, the sense that time was working against the Stuarts, helped to make their cause more significant in international relations. It was likely that the Jacobites would offer support to foreign powers opposed to George and in the late 1710s both Spain and Sweden were to find this analysis correct. Furthermore, George's aggressive foreign policy excused, however, by modern apologists as an attempt to create an early collective security system, combined with his understandable determination to defend his Hanoverian pretensions and his more half-hearted wish to retain British gains under Utrecht, aroused foreign opposition. Foreign powers were also aware that George's policies were not popular in Britain. William and Anne's interventionism, though costly, lengthy and of mixed success, was directed against an unpopular power, France, that many found threatening. In contrast, George's policies struck no resonance with the political experiences and xenophobic traditions of the British political nation.

Thus foreign support for the Jacobites appeared a plausible option. The '15 had failed but it had also revealed that the Jacobites could raise substantial forces and take the field of battle. George's attempt to seize some of Sweden's German possessions led to pro-Jacobite plotting on the part of Sweden. Charles XII had concluded a defensive alliance with James II in 1700. The Jacobites had hoped for Swedish assistance during the '15, but Charles XII was fully engaged in the Great Northern War. Late the following year the English Jacobites offered Swedish diplomats money in return for 12,000 troops and 30,000 arms. The British government, which possessed an excellent spy system, including a formidable deciphering branch in the Post Office, intercepted the correspondence of Count Gyllenborg, the Swedish envoy. In October 1716 Gyllenborg argued that 10,000 Swedes would suffice and that they should be sent in March when easterly winds were prevalent and he claimed that they would be joined by a mass revolt. He was also encouraged by the prospect that the British army would be cut and by divisions among the Whig leaders.[13]

The plot was exposed by the British government in January 1717, Gyllenborg being arrested and his papers seized from the embassy, a clear breach of diplomatic immunity, but that did not prevent a continuation of Jacobite hopes. In March it was falsely reported that the Swedes had sailed with 12,000 men and were to land in Bridlington Bay.[14] That summer the Jacobite MP Charles Caesar pressed Gyllenborg to invade before the winter, arguing that the British army was only 18,000 strong, that it would be nearly a month before a field force of 10,000 could be assembled, that the fear of risings would prevent such a move and that much of the army was disaffected. A pamphlet by the Whig MP Robert Molesworth claimed 'There is scarce a Jacobite school-boy, or poor tradesman's wife about our streets, who has not been instructed how conveniently Norway lies to Scotland, and how much it was for their master's interests that the brave King of Sweden should succeed in his undertakings'. In fact Charles XII's commitment to the Jacobites was limited and motivated in a large part by the desire to raise funds, unsurprisingly so in light of the bitter conflict he was fighting. For Charles, concerned to regain lost Swedish possessions, as for Philip V of Spain, seeking to regain territories lost at Utrecht, helping James regain his patrimony was only worthwhile if it could serve the greater purpose. That the Jacobites were, as Simon Fraser, Lord Lovat noted, 'much sunk with the news of the King of Sweden's death' in December 1718 revealed their willingness to clutch at straws,[15] though it is possible that Charles' invasion of Norway was designed to serve as a springboard for a landing in Scotland rather than, as seems more likely, an advance into Denmark and northern Germany.

The outbreak of Anglo-Spanish hostilities in 1718 offered the prospect of assistance from a new quarter. Amphibious operations were hazardous. Though the Spaniards had successfully invaded Sardinia in 1717 and Sicily the following year, the fleet covering the latter expedition had been destroyed in peacetime by the British off Cape Passaro, a pointed reminder of the play of contingency in international relations. The Spanish first minister Cardinal Alberoni, writing to the Jacobite Duke of Ormonde in December 1718, offered a reflection that was

James Butler, 2nd Duke of Ormonde,
attributed to M. Dahl, dated 1714

not without its point for the Stuart cause in general, 'In great affairs it is necessary to leave some things to chance, though it is also prudent to take reasonable measures'. Alberoni, looking for the opportunity to strike back at George and thus to lessen or prevent British resistance to Spain's Mediterranean plans, was encouraged by reports of the unpopularity of the Hanoverian regime. In March 1719 he sent Ormonde an assessment of the chances of an expedition:

> ... in order to prevent a landing it is necessary to have ships and they take time to arm ... when we have talked of the project we have laid a great stress on speedy expedition but we can't command the winds, we have been constantly assured of the good dispositions of the British and that they will rise when Spain sends you 5,000 regulars and arms ... the British coast is too long to defend effectively ... great enterprises cannot be attempted without major difficulties and only courage and firmness can vanquish them.

Alberoni continued by urging that the invasion be mounted against England not Scotland. The contrast between the successes of the invasions of 1688 and 1745 suggests that his point was a reasonable one, though the military and political circumstances were different, 'only think of Scotland as a last resort because it will be difficult to obtain supplies there, especially as the British government has the means to fill the sea with ships ... to attack England is to attack the heart'. Alberoni suggested that many difficulties came from overestimating enemies and that 'we are in difficulties and possibly England is more than us'. He also warned that failure would wreck the Stuart cause, 'if he misses this occasion that poor prince is lost and he should no longer think of the throne of England'.

Alberoni's analysis is important because it reveals the unpredictability that has been largely lost from sight by those who adopt the long-term perspective and because he exposed the Jacobite dilemma. In March 1719 he informed Ormonde that he supported the idea of a landing in England if it was true that James was very popular and that 10,000 men capable of bearing arms would rise for him.[16] Foreign intervention was therefore conditional on the prospect of domestic support, but the latter was hazardous unless significant foreign aid could be guaranteed. In so far as foreign intervention was likely to be a factor in the 1710s, Dutch support for George, requested again in 1719, suggested that it would not , on balance, necessarily favour the Stuarts. In addition, though more ambigiously, the Anglo-French alliance brought French support for George. The Orléans ministry provided valuable assistance, not least by forwarding information on Stuart and Spanish schemes, for which James Craggs, one of the secretaries of state, thanked them in January 1719. Spanish support for the Jacobites thus fatally entangled them in the kaleidoscopic world of continental rivalries, arousing French opposition. George was able to appeal for Orléans' support on the basis that they were faced by a common enemy, that the international and domestic challenges they each faced were intertwined, an argument that was well founded. In September 1719 Alberoni urged Ormonde to command a Spanish force destined to assist an insurrection in Brittany. Much depended on factional struggles in Paris where Dubois' great rival John Law was pro-Jacobite.

George Keith, 10th Earl Marischal by Pierre Parrocel

The troops whom Ormonde was to command sailed from Cadiz on 7 March 1719 but a violent storm off Cape Finisterre at the end of the month damaged and dispersed the fleet. Two frigates under George Keith, the Earl Marischal, which had sailed separately on 8 March, reached Stornoway but they only carried a diversionary force with 307 Spaniards intended to tie down British troops in Scotland. The Whig Duke of Montrose was to be proved correct when he argued that the invasion would fail, 'sure it cannot hurt us upon the main. If the King of Sweden had lived where should we have been? I would gladly hope that this news would have the effect to make our foolish people expose themselves and run the risk again of being ruined'. He later observed that if the Spaniards landed 'they must soon starve or be ruined'.[17]

The small force moved to the mainland, but its major magazine was destroyed by British frigates. The Earl Marischal advanced towards Inverness but the failure of Ormonde's expedition helped to discourage much of the Highlands from rising. The Jacobites met an advancing royal force under Major-General Wightman in Glenshiel on 10 June 1719. The Jacobites did not charge but rested on the defensive in a good position. However, their morale was low and Wightman, assisted by mortar fire, benefitted from taking the initiative and attacked the Jacobite flanks with success. The Jacobite army disintegrated, the Highlanders retiring to their homes and the Spaniards surrendering.[18]

Glensheil was a minor engagement with possibly 1,850 men confronting 1,100 troops under Wightman. It neither ended Jacobite hopes nor the schemes of Alberoni. One Jacobite reported from London to the Jacobite court at Rome,

The marriage of 'James III' and Maria Clementina Sobieska in 1719, by A. Masucci

'the whole kingdom is running mad for popery and the Pretender and great convulsions in this city' and that there were disturbances in Bristol, Manchester, Newcastle and Norwich. This was an exaggeration, part of the habitual tendency of presenting all discontent as pro-Jacobite. On 7 July 1719 Craggs reported the opinion of the ministers left in London to Stanhope, then with George in Hanover, 'as for tumults at home, they are of opinion that when there is an impossibility of assistance from abroad, they are by no means to be apprehended'. Stanhope had already been pressed on 19 June (ns) by Dubois, the French foreign minister, on the need for Britain to keep enough ships at sea.[19] Had the war gone better for Spain possibly another invasion attempt could have been mounted, but she was faced by Britain, France and Austria, the major military powers in western Europe, while the British navy was clearly superior at sea, even though its strength was lessened by the need to confront Peter the Great in the Baltic. A newsletter sent from London to the Jacobite court at Rome in the spring of 1720 argued that Spain's failure made a Jacobite rising pointless. It portrayed a movement that would be dormant until it received foreign assistance:

After the total disappointment of the invasion intended from Spain last spring his Majesty's friends in England seemed to have nothing to do but to wait events and in the meantime to keep up the spirit of the party and to prevent desertion and it must be owned to their honour no persons of any figure or consideration seemed the least disposed to enter into an opposite

Prince Charles Edward's baptism certificate, showing his full name on the second page

interest. Neither are the commonalty grown better affected than formerly to the present government or less desirous of a thorough change.[20]

Such assertions of Jacobite support were not to be tested, for the international situation continued to deteriorate for James. Alberoni was dismissed and Spain made peace in 1720. The Great Northern War ended in 1721 and, although it was not followed by a resumption of Anglo-Russian diplomatic relations, the Baltic became less tense as in his last years Peter the Great directed his attention to making gains south of the Caspian Sea at the expense of Persia. Alberoni's failure directed Jacobite attention to the prospect of French assistance. In May 1720 Arthur Dillon, the Jacobite envoy in Paris, urged James either to seek a Franco-Spanish understanding or to try to win French support. Two months later James wrote to his half-brother, the Duke of Berwick, a general in the French service, asking him to press Orléans to invade Britain. However, James, in sending his assurances of francophile sentiments to Louis XV and writing to Orléans on 1 January 1721, 'my family regards you as its true help',[21] was simply being polite. He was aware, as Alberoni had been, that, however sympathetic members of the French court might be to his cause, support would only be obtained if the government changed or if there was a major shift in international relations. In April 1721 James wrote to the Earl of Orrery:

... the Duke of Ormonde in Spain and Dillon in France never cease representing the present favourable disposition of England, nor soliciting that help which can alone enable us to profit of it, but till Abbé Dubois be gained of which I see little prospect or till he be removed which I think less unlikely to happen, on account of the universal hatred he has acquired, I see little hopes of our receiving much favour from that government, although I have so many and so considerable friends in France that I should not think it altogether impossible to gain our end by them alone, this particular is not neglected but what success it can or will have, is more than I can yet tell, our hopes from Spain are much more solid.[22]

A sorry comment on the Jacobite position. This was, however, to be the case for the rest of the cause: waiting on foreign powers for them to display sympathy and then finding that it was generally inadequate and complaining accordingly. This certainly remained the position until France proved willing to plan an invasion in 1744. Orrery commented to James in May 1721 on 'the little dependance there is on any effectual friendship almost of any prince'.[23] When in December 1722 the tiny Italian city-state republic of Lucca apologized to the British diplomat John Molesworth because 'James III' had issued a declaration from there, he replied:

... it was indifferent to us what place the Pretender's declaration was dated from and what reception he met with from Lucca; that while he had no better a support than a bad cause, a weak genius and the alms or countenance of Italian princes, we were very little apprehensive of his intrigues especially since the discovery of the late conspiracy which I look on as the last effort of his friends in Great Britain and the destruction of his party there. [24]

A reference to the failure of the Atterbury Plot.

The poor international situation was unfortunate for the Jacobites as 1720–2 were years of political crisis in Britain. The Whigs, who had split in 1717 over Baltic policy and the scramble for places, had been reunited in 1720 as a result of the difficulties that the ministry of James, Viscount Stanhope and Charles, Earl of Sunderland faced in its foreign, domestic and financial policies. However, the reconciliation, which was related to that between George and his son, the future George II, was a superficial one and could not conceal serious rifts. The new ministry was quickly challenged by the bursting of the South Sea Bubble in 1720, the end of a speculative boom that had political consequences because George I and much of the ministry were implicated as beneficiaries of what had basically become a fraudulent financial conspiracy. The search for guilty men was focused on the ministry and the screening of the most prominent individuals involved markedly increased discontent. The situation appeared propitious for the Jacobites, John Menzies writing from Paris in October 1720 'it wants but kindling the train of powder by some strong hand, and a right conduct in placing the train', while James observed in December 1720 that there was no hope of French or Spanish assistance 'which prospect is the more melancholy that matters seem at present to be very ripe in England ... it were to be wished that if no foreign help is to be had one way or another so favourable an opportunity might not be slipped.[25]

Without foreign assistance the Jacobites were forced to rely on developments in Britain, but these became surprisingly more propitious as the result of the rifts within the Whig ministry. Concerned at the prospect that the 1722 general election would be a triumph for his rival, Robert Walpole, the First Lord of the Treasury, and anxious about his fate should the hostile George, Prince of Wales accede, Sunderland negotiated with the Tories and apparently connived at a Jacobite scheme for a rising helped by the Irish regiments in French service and Ormonde from Spain. This conspiracy, known as the Atterbury Plot after Francis Atterbury, the Bishop of Rochester, who was in charge of Jacobite affairs in England and one of the leading plotters, was arguably based on an exaggeration of the extent of Jacobite sympathy in Britain, but militarily the proposal that London should be captured first was a sensible one. It was planned that Lord North would benefit from disaffection in the Guards and cooperation from the City corporation, amongst whose senior ranks were a number of Jacobites, to seize the Tower, the Royal Exchange and the Bank of England. It was then intended to raise disaffected groups of the London population, the Southwark Minters, the Westminster mob and the Thames watermen. Once London fell the counties were to be raised; Ormonde landing in Bristol and Lord Lansdowne in Cornwall. George Tilson, an Under Secretary, noted in London in March 1722 'the ferment runs high here and the Jacobites fancy they have a crisis to exert themselves', but he was sceptical of their chances, writing in May:

> ... the Jacobites abroad were in firm expectation of the great event, and doubted not if the foreign powers would only stand neuter to carry their point. Ormonde and others were beginning to put themselves in motion, and they seemed to depend that it was *un coup seur*, but for my life I can't reason as they do; nor because the mob is poisoned, women and parsons rail, and the grumblers put about libels and ballads, that therefore the whole nation will join and take up arms in favour of the Pretender ... But such are the hopes hot and zealous people encourage one another to.[26]

In mid-April 1722 Sunderland suddenly fell ill of pleurisy. On 19 April, the day of his death, Orléans informed the British government that a *coup* was being planned and that he had been asked for 3,000 troops. Sunderland's death was a major blow to the conspiracy. Lord Lovat wrote from Edinburgh, 'if he had lived by all appearance he had put this island in a terrible confusion. His partisans in our country told openly to all the Jacobites that the Earl of Sunderland their patron was for bringing home the Pretender, and on that supposition many Jacobites joined his creatures'.[27] Whether Sunderland would have supported the plot or not is unclear, but it is certain that his death allowed Walpole and his brother-in-law, Charles, Viscount Townshend, Secretary of State for the Northern Department, to consolidate their power in the ministry and to take firm measures to crush the conspiracy. They had an army camp prepared in Hyde Park, requested Dutch military assistance and summoned troops from Ireland. The Spaniards were persuaded to prohibit the departure of Ormonde and other Irish officers, while Orléans recalled Irish troops from the Channel coast, obtaining British assurances that the alliance would be maintained. The Emperor Charles VI promised George whatever assistance he required. Foreign support gave the ministry confidence, as it was generally agreed that without foreign assistance a Jacobite rising would be foolish. In October 1722 William

Stanhope, the envoy in Madrid reported that 'if any truth is to be given to the most solemn repeated protestations and assurances, together with all other possible appearances of sincerity, this court cannot be engaged in any measures in favour of the Pretender. These assurances the King of Spain has often given me himself', though he added that Spanish financial support for the '15 at a time of official Anglo-Spanish good relations did not encourage him to trust such professions.[28]

Walpole's firm response overawed London, the concentration of troops there making the plans for a revolt inappropriate. The Jacobite leaders in London were placed under surveillance and all foreign mail intercepted at the Post Office. In September the details of the conspiracy were discovered, when a clergyman, Philip Neynoe, was arrested and incriminated the leaders. With the exception of Atterbury, the prominent Jacobites were not prosecuted, presumably because Walpole had taken note of the failure to impeach Oxford successfully in 1715–17 and hoped to cow the Jacobites by making a few examples from the less well-connected conspirators. Whereas no action was taken against North or Orrery, Christopher Layer, a Norfolk lawyer who was North's agent, was possibly tortured and was certainly imprisoned in harsh circumstances before being hung, drawn and quartered for high treason.

North had believed that James might be restored by domestic action alone, but the failure of the plot led to the ruling out of this option by the English Jacobites and by the majority of Jacobites abroad. Atterbury, banished as the result of a parliamentary Act of Pains and Penalties, warned James in November 1723 that until the foreign situation improved 'the wisest way is to lie still' while the following May the Earl of Strafford wrote from England to James, 'it were to

Field Marshal George Wade against a background of his men building the road through the Corrieyairack Pass

be wished your friends here could procure your return home, but since that cannot be you must have recourse to your friends abroad'.[29] The Jacobites appeared defeated, and yet there were hints of weakness in the ministerial position. In January 1722 Thomas Burnet, the debauched son of the famous Whig apologist Gilbert Burnet, wrote to his friend the Whig MP George Duckett of the need to settle:

> ... our affairs upon such a foot, that it may never be in the power of any foreign prince to menace our country with petty invasions. Dear George, is it not highly to our discredit, that not a neighbour of ours can have six or seven men of war in any of the harbours near us and at the same time three or four thousand men, but we must be in danger of the whole, and put ourselves to the charge of a million. We are at present in peace with all Europe. We cannot long be so, therefore it would be worthy the considerations of every honest man to see how that breathing time might be best employed.[30]

The following year a Whig newspaper pinpointed what it saw as the greatest threat to Britain. In an article on the Highlands and Islands of Scotland published on 7 March 1723, the *Flying Post*, known to its opponents as the 'Lying Post', argued that:

> ... these people will never fail to join with foreign Popish powers, to advance the interests they have espoused; so they always have been, and infallibly will be instruments and tools in the hands of those who have a design to enslave or embroil the British nation ... notwithstanding the pains taken by the government to disarm them, they are still well armed, by supplies from abroad, sent them on purpose to put them in case to encourage and support foreign invasions, which it is not possible to prevent by any naval power, because of the wildness of their country, and the many convenient harbours and landing places that are on their coasts.

The newspaper recommended the opening up of the region and the spread of cultivation and education. The advice was only partly followed up and the roads that General Wade built in the Highlands helped the Jacobites during the '45. Had a determined attempt been made to introduce agricultural, tenurial and educational 'reforms' in the 1720s or 1730s the result would probably have been a rebellion. Highland society remained poorly integrated with that of the bulk of the rest of the country, an obvious source of possible support for the Jacobites, though, as the plans for 1715, 1719 and 1722 had shown, the stress was still placed on England, in terms of both disaffection and the prospect of a successful invasion. This was to remain the case for the next two decades and it was only the failure of the '44 that ensured that the '45 was launched in Scotland.

3 Decline and Revival 1723–43

The 1720s and 1730s were bleak years for the Stuart cause, made more so by the failure of states whose relations with Britain deteriorated significantly – Austria in 1725–31, Spain in 1725–9 and again from 1739, France from 1731 – to provide significant assistance. In addition the position of the Jacobites in Britain deteriorated. The failure of their schemes, culminating in that of the Atterbury Plot in 1722, had a demoralizing effect. Furthermore, the Hanoverian regime became less aggressive. The arrogant, costly and contentious interventionism that had characterized George I's foreign policy in the late 1710s was replaced by a more moderate and cautious attitude that culminated in neutrality during the War of the Polish Succession (1733–5). This has been attributed to the influence of Walpole, a leading minister from 1720, First Lord of the Treasury from 1721 and clearly the leading minister from Townshend's resignation in 1730 until his own fall in 1742. Although the minister's role may have been exaggerated, there is little doubt that he must take much of the credit for the abandonment of the ambitious and divisive legislative programme that had typified the Stanhope/Sunderland ministry in the late 1710s. In particular, Walpole was unwilling to continue those ministers' support for an improvement in the legal position of Dissenters, a measure that threatened the position of the Church of England and of its Tory supporters in the localities and was therefore more controversial than the denial of central government patronage to the Tories. Walpole was indubitably corrupt and his ministry a Whig monopoly of power, but his policies were less aggressive and objectionable than those of his predecessors and he caused offence principally to those who took a close interest in politics rather than to the wider political nation, whose position was eased by his generally successful determination to reduce taxation. Once in office Walpole did not increase political uncertainty by toying with the Tories, as Sunderland had done, though when in opposition during the Whig Split of 1717–20 he had sought to cooperate with them in parliament in order to weaken the ministry and thus demonstrate his own indispensability. Walpole's relations with George I were acceptable, though not close, but it was believed that he would fall when the Prince of Wales ascended the throne.

James was reduced to hoping for a change in the international situation, writing in April 1723, 'It is not possible affairs in Europe should long remain in the posture they are in, and we may expect good from any change' a theme he

Thomas Holles, 1st Duke of Newcastle, Secretary of State for the Southern Department during the '45, attributed to Charles Jervais

returned to repeatedly.[1] Changes in continental states, for example in France the majority of Louis XV and the deaths of Dubois and Orléans in 1723, were seen as reasons for optimism,[2] but always without cause. Other Jacobites were less optimistic. In July 1723 the Master of Sinclair, who had risen in the '15, told Molesworth in Italy that he wanted to throw himself on George's mercy, a necessary step if he hoped to benefit from the death of his father Henry, Lord Sinclair in March. Molesworth commented, 'I also find that most of the Pretender's adherents are very much tired of being so; and that impatience, disgust or despair inclines them all to make their peace at home and quit his service'.[3] Sinclair was pardoned in 1726, though not granted the title. British diplomats and ministers were optimistic: William Stanhope reporting from Madrid in 1724 stated, 'the Pretender's affairs seem at present in too low a condition, to deserve any great attention being given to them'. Walpole's brother Horatio, entrusted with the crucial Paris embassy, wrote the same year 'there is not the least reason to suspect at present any design in this court in favour of the Pretender; but that there is and always will be in this nation among the Catholics an inclination towards him, there is no manner of doubt'. The following March the Duke of Newcastle, Secretary of State in the Southern Department, and therefore responsible for relations with France, Spain and the Italian states, from 1724 until 1748, claimed:

> . . . either before or since His Majesty's happy accession, there never was a greater unanimity and zeal in both Houses of Parliament for His Majesty's service, or so universal a satisfaction and tranquility throughout the nation as there is at present; so it is hardly to be imagined that the Jacobites can be mad enough to think of making any disturbance at this time.[4]

The situation appeared to change early in 1725 with the breakdown of good Franco-Spanish relations, when the princess intended for Louis XV was sent back to Spain and he married the daughter of the ex-King of Poland instead, who made up for her relative lack of rank by being ready to bear children: the importance of dynastic considerations ensuring that in regal marital stakes women were in part treated as breeding stock. This blow to Spanish pride played a major role in bringing about the diplomatic revolution of 1725: the reconciliation of Charles VI and Philip V, who had fought for the throne of Spain during the War of the Spanish Succession and for Spain's former Italian territories thereafter. The resulting First Treaty of Vienna led to concern in Britain about rumoured secret articles in favour of James. Jacobite hopes increased, James writing in July 1725, 'the affairs of Europe seem now to be in such a situation as to promise us soon some happy turn in my favour'. Louis XV's former tutor, Bishop Fleury, who was to be his chief minister from 1726 to 1743, warned Horatio Walpole in August 1725:

> . . . that it might be adviseable for His Majesty to have five or six men of war cruising in the Channel to prevent any sudden attempt that might be made in favour of the Pretender. I asked him whether he had any particular reason for it: he said no, but that upon a general consideration of things it was best for us to be upon our guard, that he was persuaded King Philip was in his heart for the Pretender.[5]

Fortunately for George the new alignment led to the consolidation of the Anglo-French alliance, which had been weakened since 1720 by better Franco-Spanish relations. Philip V's claim to be the successor to his nephew Louis XV, despite his renunciation of his rights at Utrecht as demanded by Britain to ease fears of the union of the crowns of France and Spain, was opposed by the French ministry and in September 1725 France, Britain and Prussia signed the Treaty of Hanover guaranteeing each other's territories and rights and clearly aimed at the Treaty of Vienna. This thwarted Jacobite hopes of a Catholic league against Britain, but the new situation ensured that there were powers willing to consider the Jacobite option. Horatio Walpole was concerned about the prospect of Spanish support and the possibility that the Jacobites would start a rebellion if war broke out. James, who believed that 'nothing but a foreign force can do the work effectually', appealed for Austrian and Spanish support. The Duke of Wharton was sent to Vienna where he assured the Austrian government that London was pro James as were most of the soldiers and many officers. He added that if Britain was invaded the government would not be able to assemble a force of 3,000 men in any place, except near London where 5,000 could be marshalled, but only if the rest of the kingdom was left unprotected. In May 1726 'Sir' John Graeme, the Jacobite envoy in Vienna, presented a memorandum to the Austrian minister Prince Eugene, the Duke of Marlborough's battle-companion during the War of the Spanish Succession, arguing that Jacobite strength in Britain presented Austria with an opportunity to attack her. He asked for 6,000 troops only, claiming that they would animate the Jacobites. Graeme pointed out that it was only a short trip from Ostend, the principal port in the Austrian Netherlands, to Britain, claiming that only fishing boats and small ships would be required and that, because a major naval expedition was not necessary, the element of surprise would ensure success. He added that as many British ships had already sailed to the Mediterranean and the West Indies, there were insufficient left to prevent an invasion, that the voyage would take a few hours only, that there were many ports in Britain of which only a few were guarded, that it was possible to cross by night, that Spain was ready to invade the west of England with a similar number of troops, thus dividing the British response, and that an invasion would be met by a general rising.[6]

The Austrian government was unimpressed and made it clear that they would provide assistance only in the event of an outbreak of hostilities with Britain. Britain, largely thanks to pressure from her French ally, was careful to avoid a transition from cold war to full hostilities, thus thwarting the Jacobites rather as her neutrality in the next European war, that of the Polish Succession (1733–5), was to do. Hostilities were confined to an unsuccessful Spanish siege of Gibraltar in early 1727, an episode to which the Jacobites contributed in the form of the drunken Wharton, who was wounded in the foot by the bursting of a grenade. Even had she been willing, Spain was in no position to mount an invasion. The British navy dominated Spanish waters, though concern about the possibility of an attack led Newcastle in March 1727 to press for a French invasion of north-western Spain, in order to overrun likely invasion bases. The French had already been pressed to prevent Jacobite preparations in Brittany and to move their Irish regiments away from the Channel.[7]

Unluckily for the Jacobites a preliminary settlement of international differences, postponing most of them until a peace conference could be held, was reached at Paris in May 1727. Twenty-two days later George I died at Osnabrück on the way to his beloved Hanover. James's attempt to exploit the situation was unsuccessful. He set off from his court in the papal town of Bologna, hoping that by the time he reached the Channel an uprising would have broken out in Britain. However, both France and Austria refused assistance, the Austrian Chancellor Count Sinzendorf declaring that there would be no help unless there was war and that Austria was bound by the preliminary peace terms. James' half-nephew, the Duke of Liria, Berwick's son, a Spanish diplomat, wrote to him from Vienna that Austrian support would not be forthcoming unless James could show himself 'at the head of a good party', and that the Austrians would not let themselves be persuaded that Britain would declare for James. The Austrians were to be proved correct, for in 1727 the accession of George II passed without disturbance, a marked contrast to the Tory demonstrations that had followed that of George I. Most of the Tory peers who had not been to court for years paid their respects to George II, though Charles Caesar informed James that some did so 'hoping to so lull the government asleep that they would disband some of their forces',[8] while others did not want to split the Tory party, and those who had hoped for royal favour were swiftly disabused. However, whereas the monopolization of royal favour by the Whigs in 1714 and the proscription of the Tories had helped to provoke the '15, there was no comparable response to the continuation of the same situation under George II The English Jacobites acted as if they accepted proscription

George II on the eve of the Jacobite rising,
by T. Hudson, dated 1744

and were unprepared to run the risks of a rising unless assured of considerable foreign assistance. Ireland was quiet, as it had been since the surrender of Limerick. Those who might have provided the Jacobite cause with leadership had emigrated, Catholic political power was broken and the bulk of the British army was based in Ireland both in order that the Irish taxpayer should pay and in response to traditional fears of the Irish. Charles Delafaye, one of Newcastle's under secretaries, observed in 1725 'I can have no notion of a scheme of our enemies upon Ireland where there is an army, and where all the Protestants (in whose hands is the wealth and power) bad as they are, are so nearly concerned in point of private interest to resist such an attempt'.[9] In Scotland the attempt to apply the malt tax to Scotland led to riots in Glasgow, a Whig town, in 1725 but the Jacobites were not able to exploit the crisis, while government fears of Russian military assistance to them that year proved mistaken. Russian ships bound for Spain had arrived at the island of Lewis, but they did not bear an invasion force, though they did show that warships could reach the Scottish islands without opposition.

Thus the accession of George II proved a disappointment, as the Alliance of

Vienna, the Glasgow riots and a Whig split had done in 1725. Future promising developments – the Anglo-French break of 1731, the Spanish mobilization of 1732 and the outbreak of the War of the Polish Succession – did not break the stability of the Hanoverian regime and Walpole ministry as had been anticipated. James' proposal in 1728 to deliver a memorandum to the international peace congress at Soissons, 'in which my right might be set forth, and arguments brought to prove that my restoration can be the only solid basis of an universal peace, and that no one power has any true interest to oppose it',[10] appears unrealistic and it is easy to find examples of governmental correspondence in which the Jacobites were dismissed as inconsequential. In July 1732 George Tilson, an Under Secretary in the Northern Department, wrote to James, Earl Waldegrave, grandson of James II (after whom he was named) by his mistress Arabella Churchill, a former Jacobite and George II's envoy in Paris, dismissively of Jacobite moves:

> Her Grace of Buckingham has been said to have fallen ill at Boulogne. The Jacobites have affected very mysterious airs in this juncture. The Duke of Ormonde is another apparition and if we believe the gazettes at Rome, they pray there for the success of the Pretender. Soft and fair and keep quiet and these swarms will pass over.[11]

And yet the failure of the non-Jacobite opposition to bring about the fall of Walpole in parliament or at general elections during the 1720s and 1730s does not lead scholars to write it off as inconsequential. If success was the criterion for study then such opponents of Walpole as Bolingbroke and the 'Patriots' would not receive the attention that has been, and continues to be, devoted to them. Just as the failure of the opposition to overthrow Walpole did not prevent them from influencing ministerial policy and threatening the government, so the Stuart cause was not without its influence. There is no single source that can provide a measurement of government concern about Jacobitism. If it played little part in diplomatic relations with the states in the Northern Department (Russia, Turkey, Austria, Scandinavia, the German states and the Dutch), especially in the 1730s, the situation was different in the Southern. Scepticism was expressed by contemporaries and has been displayed since about the degree to which the Walpole ministry was concerned and it has been argued that it was employed as a polemical tool designed to rally Whig support and divide and discredit the opposition. Presenting British politics in the guise of a tale, 'The History of the Norfolk Steward' (Walpole was a Norfolk man), the leading opposition newspaper, the *Craftsman*, argued in its issue of 2 September 1727 that the steward used Squire Welsh (James) to frighten the people. Walpole certainly dwelled on the Jacobite threat in parliament, as in the Commons' debate on the Address in response to the King's Speech opening parliament in January 1727. However, this political exploitation was not incompatible with genuine concern and there is little doubt that, even when confident, the Walpole ministry felt it necessary to take precautions. A week before Tilson wrote the letter cited above his superior, Lord Harrington, informed the Duke of Newcastle of the concern of Britain's Dutch ally that Spanish military preparations might be intended to support the Stuarts:

... though they have not the least suspicion of its being designed against any of His Majesty's dominions, they approve however extremely the orders given for fitting out a squadron of ships, not only as a prudent measure, but such a one as would have been impardonable in the ministers not to have advised in the present conjuncture.[12]

Though it did not lead to any military assistance for the Jacobites for over a decade, the international situation became far more threatening for the Hanoverian regime from the spring of 1731. The negotiation of an Anglo-Austrian alliance, the Second Treaty of Vienna, in March 1731, brought to an end the confrontation that had begun in 1725 and destroyed the Anglo-French alliance. This had occurred not so much because Britain had taken the initiative without consulting her ally, a common move in the secretive diplomacy of the period, but because the terms of the treaty were unacceptable to France. The Emperor, Charles VI, ruler of the Habsburg territories, which are collectively though inaccurately known for convenience as Austria, had no sons and he had decided on the Pragmatic Sanction, the undivided inheritance of his dominions by his eldest daughter Maria Theresa. Britain guaranteed the Pragmatic in 1731, whereas France hoped to exploit Charles' death, when it occurred, to weaken Austria. The collapse in Anglo-French relations was matched by concern about possible Jacobite action. The British ministry noted an upsurge of Jacobite activity and received reports that James had travelled secretly to France and met Louis and Fleury. Fears were expressed that France would support the Jacobites. Newcastle complained of the French envoy Count Broglie 'having more than once said, talking of his own court, upon what has lately happened, that they only had to use the Pretender'. British envoys were ordered to keep a close watch on Jacobite activities, Newcastle writing to Waldegrave 'It is certain the Jacobites begin to conceive hopes of France and therefore the greatest attention imaginable should be given to that'. Waldegrave was sceptical about the possibility of French aid for the Jacobites, a scepticism that was to lead to subsequent accusations of disloyalty, but his doubts had little effect upon Newcastle. Though James, who had been forced by British-inspired French diplomatic pressure to leave first Lorraine and then Avignon for Italy after the failure of his dash to the Channel in 1727, did leave Rome, it was in order to visit Naples and Waldegrave was able to assure Newcastle in June 1731 that Fleury had refused a Jacobite request for James to be given permission to visit France.

Nevertheless, concern about possible Bourbon support for the Jacobites helped to increase ministerial anxiety about European developments and, in particular, about Bourbon naval preparations and this remained the case from 1731 until the failure of the '45. In June 1731 both Britain and France became suspicious of each other's naval preparations. Fears of a British attack on Dunkirk, which was in fact reported without reason in the London press, led to French forces being sent there, which in turn led the British ministry to take precautions against an apparently intended invasion.[13] The crisis was defused but it indicated the depths to which relations had fallen so rapidly and the sensitivity of the Walpole ministry about possible invasion preparations. Much of the army was deployed along the Kent and Sussex coasts and steps were taken to obtain military assistance from Austria, the Dutch and British forces in Ireland.

*Princess Maria Clementina Sobieska,
mother of Charles Edward, married
'James III' in 1719, artist unknown*

The breakdown in Anglo-French relations was followed by a revival of Jacobite activity, now focussed on the prospect of French help. Other French commitments, French hesitation about actively sponsoring the Jacobites and their refusal to offer assistance unless they were certain of the support of the divided and often elusive English Jacobites made this help unattainable, but there is no sign in the correspondence or actions of the Jacobites in 1731–5 that they regarded the movement as spent. The Jacobites were unfortunate. The logic of the Anglo-Austrian alliance suggested that Britain would support Austria in any war with France and thus the situation seemed especially propitious in late 1733 when, in response to the invasion of Poland by Austria's ally Russia, France, Spain and Sardinia attacked Austria. However, Britain, disenchanted by the course of Anglo-Austrian relations in 1732–3 and con-cerned about the likely political and financial consequences of a war that might include greater opportunities for the Jacobites, chose not to intervene militarily, but rather to offer its good offices to mediate in the conflict. This diplomatic position was supported by a massive naval mobilization that led to the deployment of a fleet easily outnumbering that of France, while in April 1734 the Lord Lieutenant of Ireland was instructed to move troops to England and Scotland. The Bourbons were fully committed against Austria and not in a military position to assist the Jacobites even had they felt that to be necessary. The Earl of Chesterfield told the Lords in 1734:

> We are certainly in greater danger of being suddenly invaded by our neighbours, when they have their troops unemployed and quartered upon the sea coasts, than when all their troops

Henry Stuart, Cardinal Duke of York, second son of 'James III', later 'Henry IX', by L.G. Blanchet, dated 1738

are marched many hundred miles from their sea coast, and employed against another enemy; and surely they may more suddenly fit out a fleet proper for that purpose, when none of their ships of war are employed elsewhere, than when they were obliged to keep many of them in seas very far distant from this island.[14]

Prior to the outbreak of the war in the autumn of 1733 the Jacobites had sought French assistance arguing that Britain was disaffected, a claim that appeared to be justified by the outcry against Walpole's financial legislation in the spring of 1733, the Excise Crisis. The French were not averse to engaging in discussions about a possible invasion, but for them the Jacobite option was but one card in their international hand. If anything war in 1733 made it less likely that they would play it, as it engaged their military forces elsewhere without provoking British intervention. However, the Jacobites were to find the situation discouraging when peace returned in late 1735. It is clear that both before and after the war plans to support the Jacobites, though sponsored by Chavigny, the actively anti-Walpolean French envoy in London, and Chauvelin, the foreign minister, were unwelcome to Fleury, who was far more cautious and recognized the imponderable consequences of such action. The inability to take advantage of the collapse of Anglo-French relations and of the international crisis of 1733–5 combined with the success of the Walpole ministry in weathering the crisis of 1733 and in winning the general election of 1734, demoralized the British Jacobites. It was but part of a wider failure of the domestic opposition to Walpole in these years which left him stronger than is generally appreciated. Bolingbroke's attempt to create a 'Country' platform to unite Tories and opposition Whigs in a loyal non-Jacobite opposition failed and he retired to France in 1735. Opposition unity splintered in 1734–7 over foreign policy, the rights of Protestant nonconformists and the position of Frederick, Prince of Wales, who had followed what was to become a Hanoverian pattern by falling out with his father and seeking opposition political support. The opposition of the heir to the throne and the expectation that George, born in 1683, and still more Walpole, born in 1676, would not live for ever challenged the apparent stability of the ministry, but it was far from clear that the Jacobites would benefit from this challenge. In July 1733 Delafaye had smugly written 'Jacobitism must, in the nature of things, be rooted out by the long continuance of a government under which no man can say that he has been injured in his liberty or property',[15] and, although his claims on behalf of the ministry can be doubted, it was true that the long continuance of the Hanoverian regime encouraged even those who disliked it to adapt to it and in many cases regard it as inevitable. The Jacobites were seeking a second Stuart restoration, but whereas that of 1660 had followed a rejection of royal power of less than two decades, by 1733 most people had grown to political consciousness during a period when the Jacobites were a defeated and proscribed movement.

There was, however, to be a revival of Jacobite activity from the end of the 1730s. This reflected two developments, a change in the international situation and the sense of a ministry under strain that helped to produce an increasingly volatile political atmosphere from 1738. The strength of the Jacobites in this period, as ever, is open to debate. The problem is that it was in everyone's interest to either exaggerate it or diminish it. The ministry stressed the danger presented by Jacobitism in order to rally Whig support, undermine attempts to unite opposition Whigs and Tories and discourage pressure for reckless foreign policy moves that might lead to Bourbon support for James. 'Take away the Jacobites and there will you find a Tory', wrote Charles Hanbury-Williams in October 1739, though he accepted that others disagreed with this view. In contrast, opposition Whigs and Tories who wished to cooperate with them claimed that Jacobites were few and the Tories loyal, understandably so as the position of the opposition Whigs was weakened if they were seen to act with the Jacobites. In November 1739 the Earl of Winchilsea, an opposition Whig, informing the Lords that Tories and opposition Whigs were united, declared 'the Jacobite party is now ... entirely broke'. The following year other opposition speakers informed the Commons that the Jacobite threat had been exaggerated. It was certainly true that scepticism about the strength and dedication of the English Jacobites was expressed by emissaries sent by their continental counterparts and by France.[16]

On the other hand directions sent from James in September 1741 helped to ensure sufficient Tory parliamentary support for the cause of a united opposition to help precipitate Walpole's fall the following February. Chesterfield, a leading opposition Whig, had felt it important to visit Ormonde in Avignon in 1741 in order to obtain Jacobite support to that end. There had already been signs of a revival of activity in Scotland. In early 1738 Gordon of Glenbucket, who had made the journey from Scotland to Rome and said that he was empowered to speak for the Highland chiefs, urged James to come to Scotland, promising that Scotland would rise, after which England could be invaded. In February William Hay was sent by James to Scotland to assess the situation. The response to this initiative was discouraging. Colonel Cecil, the agent in London, argued that if the Scots acted alone the English Jacobites would be arrested and the Scots crushed by the army, and that a Scottish rebellion could only succeed if an invasion force of 8–10,000 men landed in England at the same time. Hay reported that the Lowland gentry also wanted a foreign force, because they feared the military strength of the army and did not have the inaccessible refuge of the Highlands.[17]

Foreign support was therefore crucial. The breakdown of Anglo-Spanish relations over vigorous Spanish policing of what they claimed was illegal British trade with their Caribbean possessions, symbolized by the furore over Captain Jenkins' alleged lost ear, brought the two powers close to war in 1738. The Queen of Spain then said that if Britain forced 'her to a war, she can raise such troubles in England, as will make us sick of it'. A compromise, the Convention of the Pardo, was agreed to and pushed through parliament by the government majorities in early 1739, but disagreements over its implementation, the restricted room for manoeuvre of the Walpole ministry due to ministerial disagreements and domestic opposition and fundamental differences over the issues at stake led to war in 1739. The Jacobites had already sought Spanish assistance in 1736 when O'Brien, their agent in Paris, had suggested to Trevino, the Spanish envoy, that Spain prepare an expedition ostensibly for Italy that could be diverted to attack Britain, which he claimed was disorganized by

Henry Stuart, Duke of York, as a boy, by Jean Marc Nattier

domestic strife. Fleury, however, told O'Brien that Spain could not afford such an enterprise and that the collapse of Franco-Spanish good relations caused by the French abandonment of her allies in 1735 when she made peace with Austria precluded any Spanish action. In 1737 the Jacobites sought Spanish help in exploiting the Scottish discontent manifested in the Porteous riots in Edinburgh the previous year, and in January 1738 Spain was asked for 10 to 12,000 men. The situation was not then propitious, Spain being neither at war with Britain nor sure of French assistance, but the outbreak of hostilities appeared to alter the situation. In June 1739 Waldegrave reported from Paris on Fleury's views:

I do not believe the Cardinal, unless we were at open war with England, would give in to all the trifling schemes the Court of Spain might be proposing to him, but I am firmly of the opinion, from the knowledge I have of His Eminence's way of thinking, that nobody would go to greater lengths to help the Pretender than the Cardinal, were he satisfied of a probability of success; but he does not imagine it could be compassed at once, he foresees the opposition a French invasion would meet with in England and fears a union of the Protestant powers and the Empire.

On 3 July Horatio Walpole wrote to Edward Weston, an under secretary in the Northern Department, 'I do not think that the conjecture of an embarkation from the Groyne [near Corunna in north-western Spain] for Ireland is extremely out of the way' while that November François de Bussy, a senior French foreign office official who was also the British agent 101, reported that Spain 'meant to play the Pretender on them and that France did not discourage it'.[18] At the beginning of 1740 Ormonde was ordered to go at once to Corunna where an expeditionary force was allegedly being assembled for an invasion of England and that March the Duke of Devonshire, Lord Lieutenant of Ireland, expressed concern about a possible Spanish landing in Galway or Mayo, where the Catholics outnumbered the Protestants, 'the west side of Ireland is the properest for the Spaniards if they attempt to make a descent on Ireland because they may sail wide of the Channel in the Western Ocean and so avoid the British fleets'. In May 1740 Ormonde forwarded a report to the Duke of Montemar, the Spanish minister of war, of an agent recently returned from England, and writing of 'friends who only require the help described in the report to join me and risk their lives and property to free themselves from the tyranny that oppresses the nation', expressed optimism about the chances of an expedition. The report declared that a force of 12–15,000 men would be sufficient to win England, while, in addition, Montemar was informed that the Scots had offered to raise 14,000 men and that an invasion force of 6,000 would win Scotland.[19]

However, for Spain the crucial military objective was Minorca, captured by Britain in 1708 during the War of the Spanish Succession and granted to her at Utrecht, while she also sought to prevent British gains in the West Indies. By February 1740 James was certain that the armament at Corunna was a feint, information conveyed to the British government via Bussy and the Dutch envoy in Spain. Bussy reported that the Spanish ministers said 'that their design in sending for the late Duke of Ormonde and Lord Marischal into Spain and their making encampments in Galicia and Catalonia, was only to create fears in

Prince Charles Edward's silver travelling canteen, made in 1740–1 possibly for the prince's twenty-first birthday on 31 December 1741

England and to slacken their ardour for America'. Spanish support for the Stuarts was little different from the intimidation and brinkmanship that constituted such an important part of the international relations of the period. Aside from providing a surrogate force and a potentially debilitating weapon, support for the Stuarts could also be used as a diplomatic ploy. Thus, in June 1738 Guy Dickens, British envoy in Berlin, reported:

> Mr Grumbkow and Thulemeyer, speaking to me of the provisional possession proposal in favour of the Prince of Sultzbach told me that if the king our master gave his guaranty for maintaining that possession they look upon it in no other light than they supposed His Majesty would do if they gave theirs to the Pretender, for the crown of England.[20]

Spanish action alone had been unsuccessful in 1719, and in 1725–9 Spain had done nothing to assist James, not least because of British naval superiority. In 1739 the Spanish navy was not large enough to confront that of Britain and it was generally agreed that the situation could alter only as a result of French cooperation. In 1739 a French agent visited London and walked from London to the sea as part of his research for a memoir arguing that it would be easy for France to invade the Thames estuary. He reported that the fort at Tilbury would fall easily and based on his trip suggested in 1756, when an invasion was considered, that if a French force could occupy one of the banks of the river below Gravesend Britain would be dealt tremendous harm. In January 1740 the Sardinian envoy in Spain dined with George Keith, exiled Earl Marischal of Scotland, who predicted that France would join the war on Spain's side and that an invasion would then be possible. Six months later Arthur Villettes, British envoy in Turin, wrote to Horace Mann, his counterpart at Florence, about Charles Edward Stuart:

> I am persuaded as you are that a journey was really intended or rather that this family is a tool in the hands of some people and made to believe great things in agitation in their behalf, when those or the like bruits can serve their ends. I am still of the opinion that unless another power should join with Spain in the present war against us, little or nothing is to be apprehended from that side, however one cannot be too cautious in the present circumstances, and the trusting to outward appearances and one's own conjectures in a matter of this importance is what no prudent man and truely zealous in the service of his prince could forgive himself should things turn out contrary to his surmises.

The French position was crucial, as Mann wrote to Waldegrave in February 1740, 'unless France should take part in the present war, nothing will be undertaken in their favour'.[21] However, Fleury's attitude was ambivalent. He wanted to prevent Britain from seizing any important base in the Spanish empire by intimidation, but he did not want war. Although willing to discuss matters with the Jacobites, he would not provide support, and from late 1740 his attention was diverted from the prospect of war with Britain by the death of Charles VI. The British government received contradictory reports about French intentions and Newcastle trusted neither Fleury nor Bussy. It was easier for Fleury to threaten George by sending a fleet to the West Indies in 1740 and moving troops into Westphalia and towards Hanover in 1741. An invasion of

Britain was too drastic a step for Fleury in 1740. Fleury told Waldegrave that action in favour of the Jacobites would unite Britain. It might also call into play the defensive clauses of Britain's alliances, particularly that with the United Provinces, which Fleury wished to avoid. In addition, Fleury's trust in Spanish intentions was severely limited. Unimpressed by Jacobite accounts of their strength in Britain, Fleury insisted on sending an agent of his own to assess the situation. He deliberately sent a friend of Bolingbroke, who had rejected Jacobitism, in order to obtain a negative report. In the autumn of 1740 Fleury promised to support the Jacobites, offered the use of the Irish regiments and suggested several projects to Philip V, including sending arms to the Scots, but the gap between what Fleury promised and what he did was such that sceptical Jacobites were entitled to their belief that he was interested in them only as a possible weapon if Anglo-French hostilities broke out. Thus, 1740 closed with little prospect of Bourbon support for James and, although the remarks were motivated by the British political debate over foreign policy, it is easy to grasp the force of the description of him by William Pulteney, leader of the opposition Whigs in the Commons:

> ... Pretender is an unhappy fugitive, driven in his infancy from this country, and by consequence without any personal interest; that he is supported by the charity of a prince whose name is hated almost by every inhabitant of the kingdom; that he has neither sovereignty, nor money, nor alliances, nor reputation in war, nor skill in policy; that all his actions are watched by British spies ... What could a wise man conceive of a nation held in continual alarms by an enemy like this; of a nation always watchful against an invasion from a man who has neither dominions to supply, nor money to hire a single regiment; from a man whose title all the neighbouring princes disown, and who is at such a distance from them, that he cannot be assisted by them without open preparations, of which we cannot fail of having intelligence, and which may be defeated, without danger, by the vessels regularly stationed on our coasts?

In private, however, Pulteney wrote in 1741 that the Tories meant 'nothing but Jacobitism'.[22] In 1730 James had urged his parliamentary supporters to take measures that might promote an Anglo-French misunderstanding. The failure of France to support him once the Anglo-French alliance had collapsed was a surprise, but the correctness of this approach was displayed in 1742 for the ministry that replaced Walpole's was aggressively anti-French and provoked the shift in French policy that led France to support the Jacobites, though other developments, especially the death of Fleury in 1743 and the rise of more pro-Stuart ministers, were important. Walpole fell because in the aftermath of the, for him disappointing, 1741 general election his opponents united to overthrow him in parliament. However, the subsequent reconstitution of the ministry did not benefit all the opponents. A large number of the 'Old Corps' Whigs, Walpole's supporters, remained in office, including the Duke of Newcastle, still Secretary of State for the Southern Department. A number of the leading opposition Whigs joined the ministry, including Pulteney and Lord Carteret, who became Northern Secretary and effectively directed foreign policy until his fall in 1744. The Tories were excluded from office, thanks to the determination of George II and the Old Corps, and a number of prominent opposition Whigs, led by the Duke of Argyll, declined office because of the refusal to take in the Tories. The opposition Whigs who accepted office abandoned most of their former policies, especially their hostility to placemen and pensioners (politicians in receipt of government pensions) sitting in parliament. This betrayal of principles aroused outrage among many and helped to discredit the 'Country' platform and the idea of a loyal opposition of Tories and opposition Whigs. The new ministry was far from popular and it was soon to become less so as a result of its willingness to support the hiring of Hanoverian troops.

The major effect of the new ministry was in foreign policy. The death of Charles VI in 1740 had been followed first by the attack of Frederick II (the Great) of Prussia on his daughter Maria Theresa and then by the attacks of

Horace Walpole, third son of Sir Robert Walpole, 4th Earl of Orford, by John Giles Eccardt, dated 1754

other claimants on the Habsburg succession, including Bavaria and Spain, all sponsored by France, whose armies crossed the Rhine in the summer of 1741. The British response had been pro-Austrian. Parliament voted money for Maria Theresa and British envoys sought to rally diplomatic support for her. However, these attempts were discredited in the autumn of 1741 when the advance of a French force under Marshal Maillebois on Hanover led George II to sign an ignominious neutrality convention by which he agreed to vote for Charles Albert of Bavaria, the French candidate for emperor, rather than Maria Theresa's husband Francis of Lorraine. Though British diplomats disclaimed any connection between British and Hanoverian policy, inaccurate rumours that Britain was no longer to oppose Bourbon designs on Austria helped to undermine the credibility of the British government, both domestically and internationally. The ease with which George had been intimidated encouraged some Jacobites. In January 1726 George Lockhart had advanced a scheme for the Jacobites to seize Hanover with the assistance of Austrian troops and hold it until George I abandoned Britain. In December 1741 Horace Walpole reported from Florence that the Jacobites were claiming that the French would not evacuate Hanover 'but on conditions very advantageous to the Pretender's family . . . which they interpret to be the dismembering Scotland from England, and settling themselves there'.[23] Fleury of course had no such thoughts. These ideas were both impracticable, greatly exaggerating the extent of royal power in Britain, and ignored the French desire to present themselves in the Empire (Germany) as exponents of a legal style of diplomacy. Furthermore, while France could successfully pressurize George II by threatening Hanover there was little need to commit herself to supporting the Jacobites. An army sent to Westphalia could simultaneously threaten Hanover and the Dutch, influence Prussian conduct and affect military operations throughout the Empire. In contrast, a force kept on the Channel coast waiting whatever unpredictable and unlikely opportunity, winds and British naval power would provide for an invasion was of little other military value especially while the Austrian Netherlands were neutral, as they had been in 1733–5 and were to be in 1741–4.

By 1744 the French were less able to threaten Hanover. Their military position in the Empire collapsed in 1742 and they failed to revive it in 1743, while the Carteret ministry proved itself unwilling to have British policy determined by the position of Hanover: in early 1742 George II was obliged to abandon the Hanoverian neutrality, though Carteret, if not his colleagues, was very influenced by Hanoverian interests. It was clear that if France wanted to stop Britain she would have to invade her. In 1742, after the resignation of Walpole, the British moved troops into the Austrian Netherlands and their commander, the Earl of Stair, considered plans for an invasion of France. There were no hostilities that year, but in 1743 the British army, commanded by George II, moved into the Empire and at Dettingen (16/27 June 1743) defeated a French force, though not decisively, George being the last British king to command in battle. In negotiations aimed at detaching him from France, Carteret encouraged Charles Albert of Bavaria to look for territorial gains not at the expense of Austria, but at that of France in Alsace and Lorraine. It was not surprising that the French decided to show more favour to Jacobite proposals and to invade England. This also owed much to the discrediting of ministers who had advocated a concentration of effort on campaigning in Germany and the rise of the secretaries of state, who viewed the Jacobite option with more favour.[24] On 10 February 1744 the Duke of Noailles, then the most influential advocate of the German strategy, sent Louis XV a memoir arguing that in both Britain and the United Provinces there were war and peace parties and that France needed to conduct herself so as to help the peace parties, hinder their rivals and deny the latter pretexts for war.[25] Such advice was already too late. The French Brest fleet was by then sailing up the Channel.

4 The '44 and the Background to the '45

Certain news that the French intend a descent, and the Brest squadron is reported to be now in the Downs, and they intended to come up the river, had got many pilots . . . We are very bare of soldiers, cannot collect 7,000 in a fortnight.

Diary of Dudley Ryder, Attorney General, 12 February 1744[1]

The desire to strike back at George combined with the more receptive atmosphere in Versailles towards glowing reports of the strength of Jacobitism that followed the death of Fleury led Louis XV, impressed by the Welsh Jacobite Sir Watkin Williams Wynn who he had received in May 1743, to send James Butler, his master of horse and an illegitimate son of Ormonde, to England in August 1743 in order to investigate the strength of the movement. He met many of the leading Tories, both in the London corporation and among the landowners. He returned in October with an optimistic assessment of Jacobite strength in England which encouraged Louis to determine upon supporting James, a decision that was officially communicated to the Jacobite envoy in Paris in November and to Philip V in December. In 1725 Louis had written, with regard to the Duke of Holstein-Gottorp, that the crown of France was known as the protector of unfortunate princes.[2] Eighteen years later it looked as though this was to be forcefully demonstrated. The English Jacobites requested an invasion force of 10,000 and arms for that number. Control of London was presented as the crucial objective and Maldon was selected as the landing place because it would allow a march on London without crossing the Weald, the Downs and the Thames, Essex was reputedly relatively favourable and the British fleet did not patrol that coast. They also asked for Maurice of Saxe (Saxony), a Protestant who was to be the finest French general of the pre-revolutionary eighteenth century, as their commander and for a separate French expedition to Scotland. France agreed with the exception of the Scottish expedition. In December 1743 Saxe reconnoitred the situation in England.

Recalling the attempt to elicit Austrian support in 1726, Lord Barrymore suggested that the French come over in fishing boats, but the French wanted naval protection. The French force consisted of 10,029 troops, compared to the British army of 11,550 in England and 2,800 in Scotland. The French plan was to send the Brest fleet to sea to cruise off the Isle of Wight in order to prevent the British fleet, under Sir John Norris, from leaving Spithead or, if he did, to engage him in the western Channel. Five of the Brest ships were to sail to Dunkirk to escort the troops to the mouth of the Thames. The French fleet was not ready to sail on 9 January as originally planned; it did not leave Brest until 10 February. Four days later on 30 January (old style, 10 February new) Carteret instructed Robert Trevor, the envoy at The Hague, to inform the Dutch that Charles Edward had left Italy for France and it was feared that the Brest fleet would be used for an invasion. He added that the Dutch would soon be asked to march 6,000 troops to a port preparatory to their transportation to England, a statement that reflected British confidence in their command of the sea. On 2 February Ryder recorded in his diary:

> News came that the Brest squadron of 21 sails were come within the chop of the Channel, and seemed to be sailing northwards and had 30,000 spare arms. Intelligence also came that the Pretender's eldest was gone from Italy and suspected he was gone to Brest. But Solicitor [General] thought not, and that the French would not send into Scotland where he said there were no families of consequence would join the Pretender. Sir John Norris sent to our ships at Portsmouth.

In Weymouth two days later Richard Tucker noted the report that the Brest squadron was sailing for Ireland with 30,000 soldiers, while Sir James Lowther MP commented on widespread unease about the movements of the squadron and the difficulty the British Admiralty was encountering in raising seamen. On the 9th William Ponsonby MP, Viscount Duncannon, wrote to his father-in-law, the Duke of Devonshire, that Newcastle had told him that Charles Edward was not on the French fleet.[3] Charles Edward had left Rome at 3 a.m. on 9 January, arrived at Antibes on the evening of the 23rd, having dodged two British ships that sought to intercept his boat, and reached Paris on 8 February. The prince's early arrival, the result of his impetuous desire to be where the action was, had not been sought by the French who feared, correctly, that it would increase British suspicions, though they were not to know that in return for £2,000 Bussy would reveal the entire invasion plan to the Duke of Newcastle.

His report was decyphered on 14/25 February. On that day Carteret formally requested 6,000 Dutch troops and asked for Dutch warships to convoy the transports to the Thames. Amelot, the French foreign minister, blamed Charles Edward's early departure for tipping the British off and this view, however exaggerated, helped to increase French ministerial hesitation about entrusting the Jacobites with the details of plans. On 15/26 February parliament agreed to an address expressing its detestation of the plan for an invasion and its resolution to defend George. Two days later Carteret wrote to Lord Tyrawly, the envoy in Russia, of:

> ... there being no manner of doubt but that whatever diversity of sentiments may happen in matters of less consequence, any attempt to disturb the peace of His Majesty's reign, and to

force a popish Pretender upon this Protestant nation will produce an universal resentment against the authors and abettors of such a design and at once unite all His Majesty's people in the defence of his person and government . . .

but in fact that was no mass demonstration of popular enthusiasm for the Hanoverian regime and the ministry preferred to rely on force. Jacobite leaders were arrested and Habeus Corpus suspended. Lord Barrymore and Colonel Cecil were arrested on suspicion of high treason though no charges were pressed and no one was brought to trial. George Bowes MP, who offered to raise a troop of horse at his own expense against the invasion, found it incredible that someone of Barrymore's immense fortune should 'engage in such a desperate cause which has been so long justly neglected'. British troops were summoned from Ireland and the Austrian Netherlands, and units already in southern England marched to the coast. Lord John Sackville, who had recently faced the anger of his parents for making Lady Frances Leveson Gower pregnant and been obliged to marry her two days after she gave birth, had the less heroic task of marching with the 2nd Foot Guards, of which he was Lieutenant Colonel, to Rochester. Norris was ordered to attack the French fleet.[4]

By the time Roquefeuil reached Spithead Norris had left it in order to follow his instructions to take up position on the Downs to intercept any invasion force. The two fleets came in sight of each other off Dungeness on 24 February/ 7 March. They anchored, Norris preparing to engage the next day, but a strong gale that night drove most of the British ships out to sea, while the smaller French fleet was able to run before the wind to Brest. The British lost more ships and seamen in the storm than the French. The same storm hit Dunkirk where Saxe's force had begun embarking on 22 February/5 March. On 15/26 February Saxe claimed that he should have already landed in England, but that neither the promised detachment from Roquefeuil's fleet nor the pilots promised by the English Jacobites to guide him to the landfall they had switched to from Maldon, Blackwall near London, had arrived. The storm destroyed many transports and much of the stockpiled supplies. Ryder recorded in his diary:

> Sir John Norris was ready to attack the French fleet lying at Dungeness, waiting for the tide, but the French slipped their cables in the night and run away in a high storm. The same night the French fleet of transports were got out of Dunkirk, coming over to England, but the storm dispersed them, cast several away, disabled others, and put an end to the invasion.

Ryder exaggerated the effects of the storm which many, such as Colonel Ellison, saw as the work of providence, but there was little doubt that the British ministry had been fortunate, especially in light of the earlier failure to predict French intentions which was widely criticized by parliamentarians such as Sir Henry Liddell and John Tucker.[5] Their good fortune was to be underlined on 11 March when a second storm caused further damage at Dunkirk, destroying more transports and leaving the fleet without cables and anchors. That day Saxe wrote to Charles Edward at nearby Gravelines to tell him that the expedition had been abandoned.

On 2 March 1744 Chavigny, then French envoy to Charles Albert of Bavaria, a ruler who military misfortune had driven from his dominions as his father Max Emmanuel had been during the War of the Spanish Succession, but who, like his father and unlike the Stuarts, was to be restored as part of a peace settlement, wrote to Amelot, the foreign minister, suggesting that the wisdom of the French invasion attempt could only be judged by its fate.[6] Various views were advanced as to the value of the '44 to France. It was seen as an attempt that would, even if unsuccessful, lessen British military involvement on the continent and when British troops in the Austrian Netherlands were ordered to prepare to embark for England Amelot claimed that this demonstrated the value to France of alarming Britain. Trevor had suggested on 14/25 February, 'perhaps this uneasiness is all that France at present aims at; and if she could but augment it enough to make us weaken Flanders, she would strike a home blow on that side . . . I have no idea of an invasion; though the news from Dunkirk and all along that coast are suspicious'. John Tucker MP wrote to his brother on 1 March, 'abundance of people treat the notion of an intended invasion in favour of the Pretender as a political piece of cunning in the French to amuse us and prevent any succours going either to Mathews [in the Mediterranean] or to Flanders and if that be their aim they have done it effectively'.[7] On 25 February/8 March the opposition London newspaper, *Old England*, urged the recall of British troops from the continent, and also provided a good illustration of the freedom to criticize government policy that the press continued to enjoy in wartime:

> We are, at this instant, alarmed with the old ministerial cry of France and the Pretender; of armies and transports, incog., at Dunkirk; of invincible armadas from Brest . . . either true or false. If true; how will our all-sufficient statesman excuse himself for having treated France as a contemptible power, from which so little was to be feared, that we had nothing to do, but to draw the sword, and carve out its dominions into what shreds and fritters we pleased? Where was the intelligence which ought to be the fruit of all those mighty sums which are said to be annually expended in secret service? How can he keep himself in countenance for having embroiled us in his rash and ridiculous measures abroad and thereby drawn upon us this shocking insult at home? That the French were able to put a formidable squadron of ships to sea is now self-evident: that till the very instant, almost, of their sailing, we were ignorant alike of their strength and their preparations, seems to be highly probable . . . the affair of Dettingen might have convinced us that she would not stand upon ceremonies when revenge was in her power.

Militarily the alarm might have been valuable to France but this should not be exaggerated. The first Channel storm led the Admiralty to conclude that the danger was past and Norris was ordered to send several ships to reinforce Admiral Thomas Mathews in the Mediterranean. On 11/22 February Mathews had attacked the combined Franco-Spanish fleet which had left Toulon the previous day, fearing that it might seek to join the Brest fleet and thus affect operations in the Channel. Although the British fleet was superior the battle was indecisive and the British did not cover themselves in glory. Norris was very angry about the decision to reinforce Mathews and consequently resigned, but the most interesting feature of the episode was the willingness to detach ships from the Channel. As in 1692, when the Toulon ships had not arrived by the time that Barfleur was fought, and 1759, when the Brest and Toulon fleets were defeated separately at Quibéron and Lagos, the French suffered in 1744 by the division of their naval forces. They were always called two fleets, Ponant and Levant, not one. In addition the French and Spaniards did not coordinate their operations in the Atlantic as they did in the Mediterranean. Such cooperation was not to be achieved until the Bourbon invasion attempt of 1779 during the War of American Independence when the British navy lost her control of the Channel, only to be rescued by the delays and disease that affected the Bourbon fleet. The Trafalgar campaign of 1805 was to provide another warning of the danger of Franco-Spanish naval cooperation.

However, in 1744 the situation was very different. Whereas during the American War of Independence the defeat of Britain was the clear Bourbon priority and in 1805 Napoleon provided united direction to the same end, during the War of Austrian Succession (1740–8) the conflict with Britain that had broken out the previous year, the War of Jenkins' Ear, took second place in Spain's objectives to gains at Austrian expense in Italy. In 1700 the Spanish dominions, the largest empire in the world, had included the islands of Sardinia and Sicily, the Kingdom of Naples (southern Italy) and the Duchy of Milan (Lombardy). All had been lost in the War of the Spanish Succession, but in 1734–5 Philip V had gained Naples and Sicily for Don Carlos, his eldest son by his influential second wife, Elizabeth Farnese, and he now hoped to make fresh Italian gains, including a settlement for Carlos' younger brother, Philip. There is a tendency when writing on Jacobitism to forget the wider international angle and the fact that there were other, generally more attractive, options for potential supporters. Throughout the war Spain was more interested in Italy. Indeed it is all too easy when concentrating on the '45 to lose sight of the fact that one of the most dramatic developments of 1745 was the march of a French army along the Genoese Riviera, its crossing of the Ligurian Alps and the Franco-Spanish defeat of Britain's ally Charles Emmanuel III of Sardinia at Bassignano on 27 September. On 17 November Asti, less than 30 miles from Turin, fell and this was followed by the Bourbon capture of Casale, the Montferrat and, on 16 December, the city of Milan. Charles Emmanuel signed a secret armistice, though the kaleidoscopic nature of eighteenth-century warfare and diplomacy had Sardinian troops surprise Asti on 5 March 1746 and recapture Casale. Don Philip evacuated Milan and on 16 June 1746 the Franco-Spanish army was defeated at Piacenza by Austro-Sardinian forces. This battle ended Bourbon hopes of overruning northern Italy and set the territorial pattern of the peninsula until the Revolutionary Wars. In its way it was as decisive as Culloden. Similarly, the failure of the French under Richelieu to mount an invasion of England in the winter of 1745–6 to assist Charles Edward was compensated for by Saxe's surprise attack on Brussels, which fell on 20 February 1746, a campaign eased by the recall of British forces to England.

In judging the failure of the '44 it has to be seen in the wider context. When the experienced British diplomat Thomas Robinson wrote from Vienna on 4 March 1744, 'It is likewise advised from Paris that the Brest fleet had been seen in the Channel, going as was thought to Dunkirk to take in troops. This would be the expedition of 1708',[8] he was unconsciously glancing at the repetition of the strategic relationship between Jacobitism and operations in the Low Countries. France's Bavarian ally urged her to concentrate on the war in the Empire[9] and drew attention, as did her other German allies, to the international implications of assisting Jacobitism. Prussia and Hesse-Cassel, both Protestant, warned of a revival of Protestant unity, Chavigny countering by presenting support for the Stuarts as a response to British plans to invade eastern France and dispose of it like the objects in the garden of Herrenhausen, George II's palace outside Hanover. He added that a misunderstood notion of the Protestant interest could not stop France. Amelot also explained French support for the Jacobites as a reply to British policy towards France.[10] It was also an attempt by the secretaries of state to free themselves from the influence of courtiers, such as Noailles, in the Council of State.

The criticisms that the attempt would simply unite Britain behind George and that it was more effective to strike at him through Hanover were more pointed. Charles Albert of Bavaria, the Emperor Charles VII, made the former point, as did the Hessian and Prussian envoys at his court who both pressed Chavigny to undo the effect by having Charles Edward sent back to Italy. Chavigny decried the value of the Jacobites in a report to Louis XV. He stood for a German policy and was closely linked to a ministerial group who advocated this forcefully.

Suggestions were made that the invasion attempt would and did increase loyalty to the Hanoverian regime and lessen internal divisions, though these are impossible to prove. Trevor argued that French support for the Jacobites 'gives a flat lie to the boasted moderation and innocence of her views; and must convince every subject of the Republic, as well as of England, that not only the possessions of the House of Austria and the balance of power, but even our own liberties and religion, are struck at by that ambitious power'. There was an upsurge of loyalist activity. The Northumberland landowner Lancelot Allgood wrote to the Lord Lieutenant, the Earl of Tankerville, on 15 March 1744, 'Your Lordship may be assured that the gentlemen, clergy and freeholders in this part of our county retain a just impression in their minds of the fatal consequences of any invasion or rebellion, wherefore His Majesty may be fully satisfied of our inviolable attachment to his sacred person and government'. He described how in response to a letter from Tankerville the JPs had called a meeting at Hexham at which the local gentry, clergy and freeholders signed a loyal address, how the statutes against Catholics had been put into effect and how instructions had been issued to seize arms and horses in their possessions. George Bowes commented on how 'addresses are flying up to town from all parts of the nation', but, of course, they always did. On 10 March Richard Tucker supplied a superb account of 'Establishment' propaganda in action in Weymouth when he reported on the Grand Inquest:

> Mr Clark the Judge who gave the charge I believe had studied good part of it, which was visibly calculated to work upon the passions of his auditors:– there was a great deal said of the excellency of our Religion Laws and government and a long enconium upon the former branch and then much of the lenity of our government touching Roman Catholics whom though our laws do not permit them to enjoy the use of their religion yet the connivance of the government has been almost equal to the toleration allowed by law to Protestant Dissenters and therefore 'tis the more extraordinary that any of them should ever think of disturbing the peace of a Government so indulgent but it is notorious to all the world and he was not afraid to say that it had ever been the restless principle of France to promote and encourage factions here as well as in all the country in Europe to carry on their own perfidious schemes, upon

which topic he flourished away with great oratory and instanced their mischievous stratagems from East to West from North to South – said a great deal of the necessity in this time of public danger to be vigilant in putting the laws in execution against Papists but that he knew His Majesty's clemency and goodness was such that the most tender method this could be done in would be most agreeable to him and this also he said would be most consistent with the religion we profess and might tend to make proselytes of the most considerable and rational among them – there was also much said about the established character of our national faith, and how assuredly, our allies always trust in them and that . . . several parts of the kingdom had already found the good effects of their manufactures (as he hoped it was and would be also soon in the West of England) by the French having been obliged of late to draw of great number of their manufacturers for soldiers and sailors . . . he expatiated upon the excellency of our government when compared with any of the neighboring ones.

The judge also dwelt on the dangerous consequences if the Pretender became king, 'one of them was, that as the family have been supported and bred up at the charity of France and nursed in the politics of that country they will be under such obligations there that this nation must become a Province of France'.[11]

The British ministry was aware of the argument that it would be more effective for France to attack Hanover, Carteret writing to Robinson on 27 March 1744 to request Austrian military assistance for the defence of the Electorate not Britain:

The king having intelligence from different parts that the French court, full of rage and disappointment upon the providential miscarriage of their late infamous design of invading His Majesty's British dominions in time of full peace, in favour of the pretender to his crown, whose son they had before received into the dominions of the French king, contrary to the obligations of all their treaties, are now preparing to revenge themselves in another shape upon His Majesty by falling upon his Electorate.[12]

The wisdom of the '44 was and can thus be questioned not least by considering the alternatives. Though Saxe did not march on Hanover, as was feared, French operations in the Low Countries were to be successful from their commencement in 1744 until the end of the war. On 3 May 1744 Louis XV left Versailles for the army in Flanders and in May and June Furnes, Menin and Ypres fell to the French. The conquests made were to be returned as part of the Peace of Aix-la-Chapelle in 1748 but they gave France the diplomatic and military initiative for the rest of the war, compensating for defeats elsewhere, especially at sea in 1747 at the hands of the British, and provided gains that could be traded as part of the peace settlement. The decision to campaign in the Low Countries where, by 1747, France had invaded the United Provinces, storming the major fortress of Bergen-op-Zoom, fits better with the established view of pre-Revolutionary eighteenth-century warfare as limited in its methods and objectives. In such a perspective French support for the Jacobites can be seen as an aberration, not so much because of the amphibious strategy that it dictated, as because it was far from limited in its goal. In most eighteenth-century conflicts hostilities were accompanied by negotiations and the War of Austrian Succession was no exception. France negotiated with Austria and Sardinia, Britain with Spain. French support for the Jacobites made Anglo-French negotiations, such as occurred in early 1742 and the summer of 1745, more difficult and thus lessened the diplomatic options of both powers. It also brought to an end the ambiguous state of undeclared war between the two powers. British and French forces had fought in 1743 as auxiliaries of Austria and Bavaria respectively but on 15 March, after the failure of the '44, France declared war.

However, rather than seeing the '44 as an aberration and, therefore, regarding the initially unsupported '45 as the more 'natural' or 'inevitable' type of Jacobite enterprise, it is reasonable to point out both that all eighteenth-century warfare and diplomacy were not limited and that there were good reasons for France to seek to overthrow George II. The attempts to partition the Swedish and Austrian empires during the Great Northern War and the War of the Austrian Succession respectively, the boldness of the plans for partitioning the Spanish empire, the proposals to partition Prussia during the Seven Years War (1756–63) and the discussion during the Wars of the Spanish and Austrian Succession of schemes for pushing back France's eastern frontier reveal the willingness of rulers and ministers to consider major changes. Support for rebels was not rare, nor had it been earlier in the sixteenth and seventeenth centuries. In the first two decades of the eighteenth century France backed the Hungarians against their Habsburg rulers during the War of the Spanish Succession, Sweden supported the Ukrainians during the Great Northern War and Russia and Austria both sought Balkan assistance against the Turks. In this context French support for the Jacobites did not appear exceptional. The British role in engineering and sustaining European hostility to France was considerable, especially once the importance of British subsidies was taken into account.

After the failure of the '44 France concentrated on the new front in the Austrian Netherlands, but the British ministry remained concerned about the possibility of another invasion. In late June 1744 reports were received of a build up of French forces at Dunkirk and, as the Brest squadron was at sea at the time, there was concern about an invasion, which obliged the British navy to take defensive moves. At the same time the French advance in the Austrian Netherlands aroused fears. One Privy Councillor, Stephen Poyntz, observed on 26 June 1744, 'If Ostend falls next, the outworks of England are gone . . . If at the same time the Toulon and Brest squadrons get the better of ours . . .' The following month Thomas Grenville, a naval captain, noted, 'New alarms of the French squadron have brought us back to Spithead'. There was renewed concern about 'something extraordinary brewing at Dunkirk' in November.[13] However, though Charles Edward pressed the French to send an expedition, the French government, under the influence of the Duke of Noailles, preferred to concentrate on campaigning in the Austrian Netherlands and persuading Frederick II to attack Austria again. The English Jacobites sought to gain French assistance. Lord Barrymore pressed for an invasion, while in October 1744 Sir Watkin Williams Wynn travelled to Versailles to seek Louis XV's support. In July 1744 Charles Edward wrote to Louis, arguing that the dispatch of English troops to the Continent had made England vulnerable and seeking support. The English Jacobites believed that for any invasion to be effective it had to be directed at England. Murray of Broughton, sent by Charles Edward to London in August 1744, was told that a Scottish expedition would be pointless

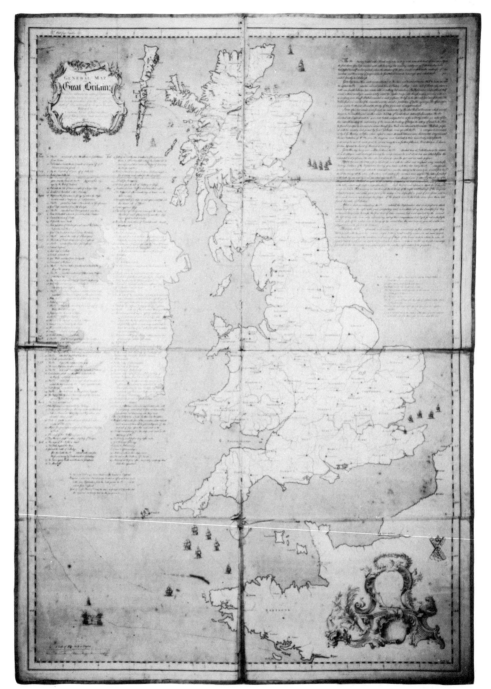

John Finlayson's map of the '45, which, although geographically inaccurate, is of great interest as a contemporary document and for its pro-Jacobite decoration

unless there was also a simultaneous landing near London as it would leave the English Jacobites vulnerable, George II in control of London, the army and the fleet and Charles Edward a long way from London. James agreed. In January 1745 the English Jacobites pressed again for an invasion of England. The French had other ideas and the English Jacobites were unable to prevent the attempting of the Scottish option.

Disappointed with the French response and feeling ill-treated, a characteristic of his unstable personality which became paranoid when things went badly, Charles Edward began to display greater interest in two subjects, a Scottish rising and the idea that he should go alone without French assistance. Initially he sought French troops, including the Irish brigade, arms and money. In October 1744 Louis was pressed to provide 3,000 troops for a Scottish expedition. French unwillingness led Charles Edward to advance the idea that the French could be encouraged to intervene militarily if a rising had already broken out. This was despite the fact that the Scottish Jacobites believed that the prince should come only if accompanied by a sizeable force. Without French support, Charles Edward needed to find funds for the arms that would be required by the Highlanders and transportation to get himself and his supplies thither. He did so from the network of expatriate Irish and Scottish bankers and shipowners in France, especially a group of Irish shipowners based at Nantes and St Malo. They were motivated by their Jacobite sympathies and the hope that they would benefit personally. As Charles Edward made his preparations, Britain and France began exploratory probings towards a peace that would certainly have ignored his interests. The British were affected not by the prince's preparations, of which they knew nothing, but by French successes in the Austrian Netherlands, where on 11 May 1745 Saxe had won a major engagement at Fontenoy before obtaining the capitulations of Ghent (15 July), Bruges (19 July) and Ostend (23 August). The news of the fall of Ghent led Carteret's successor Harrington to write on 20 July to Newcastle from Hanover about the need to prevent an embarkation from the French coast.[14] Meanwhile, while the ministers left in London when George went to Hanover were discussing the dispatch of reinforcements to Ostend, the prince, keeping his movements secret, both from the French and from James, travelled to Nantes and on 22 June/3 July embarked at St Nazaire on a frigate, the *Doutelle*. The '45 had begun.

5 From the Western Isles to the Enterprise of England

General Cope had made his dispositions to receive them from the west but next morning by day-break they wheeled and attacked our army on the south-east side; by which means they in a great measure marred the effect of his artillery. And before he had fully finished the proper alterations of his disposition, they began the attack and with so much fury that they disordered the horse which turned the foot into confusion. This advantage the Highlanders immediately took hold of, and after their first fire rushed in upon them sword in hand . . . I hope the cause of religion and liberty will yet find friends to espouse. And although our country must now be branded with disaffection yet I'm sure the government has friends enough amongst us to have prevented things coming this length, if the Disarming Act had not bound up their hands and both deprived them of arms and warrant to use them. Edinburgh has been basely betrayed into the rebels hands which has contributed not a little to the rout of our army for the Highlanders wanted both arms and ammunition till they were provided there.

Bailiff of Jedburgh, 23 September 1745[1]

As befits one of the most dramatic and heroic episodes in British history, the tale of the '45 has often been told. Naturally enough, attention has centred on Charles Edward, on his conquest of Scotland, the invasion of England, the decision to turn back at Derby, the course of events that led to defeat at Culloden and the subsequent flight through the heather. The recent bicentenary of the prince's death in 1788 saw the appearance of a number of biographies that accentuated this trend. In contrast, the governmental response has never been studied so fully, though there is a useful recent book by W.A. Speck on the Duke of Cumberland, the younger son of George II who commanded the royal forces at Culloden, and the suppression of the '45. The account that follows,

An impression of the fight between the Lion *and the* Elisabeth *on 9 July 1745. While the two men of war engaged, the frigate* Le du Teillay, *carrying the Young Pretender and the 'Seven Men of Moidart' to Scotland, looked on, probably from a much safer distance than in this reconstruction.*

concentrating as it does on the military aspects of the '45, seeks to present the situation from both points of view in order to cast light on the question of how near Charles Edward came to success.

British naval power nearly scotched the scheme at the outset. Initially the prince had been delayed by contrary winds at the mouth of the Loire and it was not until 1/12 July that the *Doutelle* made her rendezvous with the *Elisabeth*, a 64-gun warship, carrying arms and 700 men of the Irish brigade, which was ostensibly prepared for a privateering mission in Scottish waters. The two ships sailed for Scotland on the 5/16th, but on 9/20 July, 100 miles west of the Lizard, they encountered HMS *Lion*, a 60-gunner under Percy Brett. The action between the *Lion* and the *Elisabeth* lasted from 5 p.m. until 9 p.m. by which time the *Lion* was a dismasted wreck with 45 killed and 107 wounded out of a complement of 400. The *Lion* was obliged to return to Plymouth but the *Elisabeth* had also been badly damaged and was neither in a state to continue the voyage nor to heave to and transfer the 1,500 muskets and 1,800 broadswords she carried to the *Doutelle*. Just as serious was the loss of the soldiers who would have provided a solid trained core for the Jacobite army that would not melt away when the situation appeared unpromising.

The *Doutelle* had not taken part in the engagement, which was the closest that it came to being taken, though on the 11/22nd it had to outsail pursuing warships. On 23 July/3 August the prince reached Eriksay in the Western Isles.

Monument at Glenfinnan where the standard was raised; the monument itself was erected a hundred years later

By 17 September Edinburgh had fallen. The route from the smokey hovels of windswept Eriksay to Holyrood Palace was not, however, without severe problems. The first was the reluctance of much of Scotland to join the rising. The '45 is usually seen as a Highland rising that enjoyed only patchy support in the Lowlands. In fact the Highlands were deeply divided. Several of the most important and relatively wealthy clans supported the government, which could count on the Campbells, Mackays, Munros and Sutherlands. Other clans were divided. More worrying for Charles Edward was the fact that several Jacobite clans provided no support for him, while those that did commonly hedged their bets to a certain extent. This most frequently took the form of the refusal of the clan leader to commit himself, so that the clan support for the prince was generally led by a kinsman of the leader. Many of the Jacobites had made the

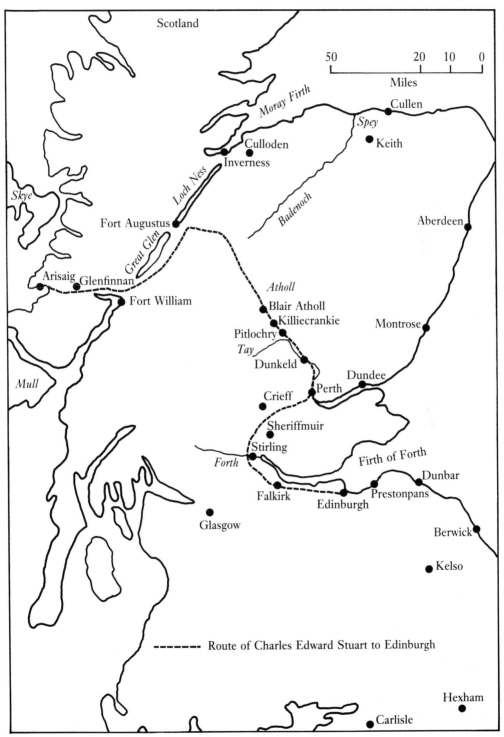

Scotland

50   20   10   0

Miles

Moray Firth

Cullen

Spey

Culloden

Keith

Inverness

Skye

Loch Ness

Badenoch

Fort Augustus

Aberdeen

Great Glen

Arisaig

Glenfinnan

Atholl

Fort William

Blair Atholl

Killiecrankie

Pitlochry

Montrose

Tay

Dunkeld

Mull

Dundee

Crieff

Perth

Sheriffmuir

Stirling

Forth

Firth of Forth

Dunbar

Falkirk

Prestonpans

Edinburgh

Glasgow

Berwick

Kelso

- - - - - - - Route of Charles Edward Stuart to Edinburgh

Hexham

Carlisle

Charles Edward's advance to Edinburgh

arrival of a French force a pre-condition for rebellion, and it was on those grounds that the prince was informed the day after his arrival that the two major Skye chiefs, Norman MacLeod and Sir Alexander MacDonald of Sleat would not rise and was advised to return to the Continent.

While the sounding of Highland chiefs took place, the prince, anxious to avoid the British navy, sailed to the mainland where on 25 July he anchored at Lochailort in Arisaig. Despite the refusal of more chiefs to 'come out', the prince landed the arms and ammunition from the *Doutelle* before persuading several chiefs to rise, not least with the argument that the French would send troops once they saw that the Jacobites had risen. Hostilities began on 14 August when a party of soldiers on their way to reinforce Fort William, the fort in the Great Glen nearest Arisaig, were taken prisoner by the Jacobites, a larger group being captured two days later. On 19 August the royal standard was raised at Glenfinnan, where Charles made a speech in which he declared that he had come to Scotland to make his subjects happy, a claim that may have sounded somewhat strange to some of his listeners who had been raised only by the threat from their clan leader that otherwise their dwellings would be burnt over their heads.

At the Jacobite war council held at Glenfinnan on 19 August it was wisely decided to attack the royal army under Sir John Cope as soon as the Jacobite force was prepared. This was sensible. Manoeuvring without engaging in a decisive battle, which was the key to the Highlanders' type of war, had been fatal to Mar during the '15, while a siege of a fort such as Fort William would take time and be difficult, perhaps impossible, without artillery and storming, a method sometimes used by regular forces, might be expensive in casualties and, if unsuccessful, doom the rebellion. To attack Fort William, or the other two garrisons in the Great Glen, Fort Augustus at the southern end of Loch Ness, and Fort George at Inverness, would be to do precisely what the Hanoverian regime wanted rebellious Highlanders to do: attack a fortified position that maximized the strength of the defence, especially its fire-power. Reinforcements could be sent to the garrison along the network of military roads constructed by General George Wade, Commander-in-Chief in Scotland from 1724 until 1740. If a fort fell it would provide an obvious target for a counter-attack that besieging artillery would probably make successful. Having gained the fort the Jacobites would risk not only losing it but having to weaken their forces by providing a garrison. Fort William was therefore bypassed. The Jacobites soon discovered that they might get the battle they sought sooner than expected. Cope, who had left Edinburgh on 19 August and Stirling on the 21st, was marching towards Fort Augustus, to near where the prince had advanced.

The British government began to make the preparations that would enable them to counter Charles Edward before he had even landed in the Western Isles. They did so not because they had any intelligence of his journey, though he was believed to be on one of the ships that had escaped the *Lion*, and a proclamation offering a reward for his capture in case he landed in Britain was issued on 1/12 August, but because they believed that the French would follow up their successes in the Austrian Netherlands by an invasion of England. This course of action was indeed urged on the French by the English Jacobites in

August 1745 when they asked for 10,000 men and 3,000 arms to be landed near Maldon in Essex and promised to rise if this happened. On 9/20 July Harrington wrote from Hanover to George II's younger son, the Duke of Cumberland, then commanding the British forces in the Austrian Netherlands, ordering him to be ready to send troops to England immediately. Six days later he wrote again:

> I prepared your Royal Highness in my last for the possibility of the French court's being induced by their late successes to meditate some attempt on His Majesty's British dominions. What we then only foresaw as a thing that might happen is now but too much verified, for the king has certain and infallible intelligence, and I am ordered to acquaint you in the utmost confidence that the resolution is actually formed at the court of France to execute immediately such an invasion.

Cumberland was instructed to prepare to send over a detachment from his army if circumstances made this necessary. Newcastle was ordered to prepare transports to bring Cumberland's troops over and informed, 'the scheme of a new invasion by France upon England . . . does now appear to be a fixed and settled design for which everything is in earnest preparing . . . in resentment for the general stand he [George] has made in the defence of the liberties of Europe'. In explanation of these instructions, Harrington sent a copy of a letter from Frederick II to the Prussian envoy in Paris, Chambrier and another from the Danish envoy Bernstorff to Christian VI. Both testified to the excellence of the Hanoverian interception and deciphering system and its value to the British, for the Electorate lay athwart the postal routes between Paris and northern Europe. Frederick's letter referred to information Chambrier had received from the pro-Jacobite French minister Cardinal Tencin that France was thinking of an invasion of England, while Bernstorff wrote that he did not think that the French would support the Jacobites.

Nevertheless, the option clearly existed and on 26 July/6 August Newcastle replied that many ships had been recalled from the Mediterranean and that most of the army in England had been ordered to march towards London. He also suggested the move of Austrian troops from the Rhine to the Austrian Netherlands, which would obviously free British forces. Four days later Newcastle pressed for the return of George from Hanover and on 2/13 August he reported that there were seventeen ships of the line in France's western ports and that the French were talking of moving the Brest fleet to Ostend, where it would be well placed to cover an invasion. A week later he added an ominous note about disaffection in Britain, which is an interesting comment not so much on the credibility of Jacobite hopes but on the notion that the bulk of the nation was, as in 1715 and arguably 1688, scarcely committed to either side, 'the ill humours and dissatisfaction that are rising here . . . they are confirmed from many parts of the nation, and the best-intentioned, and the best-affected, are under the greatest alarm and apprehension'. On 22 July/2 August Henry Pelham, the First Lord of the Treasury, wrote to Henry Fox, one of the Lords of the Treasury, mentioning his fear of French naval preparations at Brest, adding 'we have not left troops enough in this country to mount guard at the royal palaces, nor to quell an insurrection or smuggling party of one hundred men'.[2]

Intelligence was not only obtained from postal interception. On 23 July/ 3 August, the day the prince reached Eriksay, Andrew Stone, one of Newcastle's two under secretaries, received a report from Richard Wolters, the royal agent at Rotterdam who ran a network that provided information on French naval preparations. Wolters wrote 'it is more than probable that the French have some great design against England' and suggested that they might land in Ireland with Charles Edward or sail up the Thames to Gravesend. A copy of the report was sent to the Admiralty the following day. On 1/12 August, before information of the landing at Eriksay had been presented to them, the Lord Justices, the ministers who had responsibility for government while George was away, ordered the dispatch of 5,000 stand of arms to Scotland with the instruction that Archibald, 3rd Duke of Argyll should have as many of them as he wanted.[3]

In fact the French were not preparing to invade, though concern about a Bourbon invasion remained strong. On 2/13 August Stone wrote to Edward Weston, an under secretary in the Northern Department, 'We hope we shall soon have a pretty strong squadron in the Channel: But I know too well, the great delays and uncertainties that service is liable to, to depend very much upon it'. On the same day Harrington warned Newcastle that Charles Edward had probably already landed in Scotland and that 6,000 Spaniards and a squadron of warships had been assembled at Ferrol, in north-western Spain, probably to support an invasion. On 22 August/2 September the Lord Justices expressed their fear about the possibility of an invasion from Dunkirk or Ostend.[4] The importance of these fears is two-fold. First, the British government was clearly looking to its security *before* news of the prince's landing arrived and the vital military move, the transfer of troops from the Continent, was already being prepared. This was arguably of some importance in the response to the prince's subsequent invasion of England. In falling back in the Austrian Netherlands, Cumberland was instructed to secure Antwerp and thus to maintain links with England that would permit a rapid transfer of troops. Secondly, these fears explain the nature of the military response to the prince's movements. From the outset, *before* the build up of French forces near the Channel ports following the decision to proceed with an invasion that was taken at the meeting of the royal council on 4/15 October, the British ministry was concerned about the prospect of an invasion of southern England. Had the decision been taken as soon as news of the prince's landing reached London to send most of the troops in England to Scotland this might well have affected operations there, but in London the security of southern England seemed paramount. In part this view can be criticized, as the likely success of Charles Edward was certainly underestimated, but the events of 1745–6 revealed that control of southern England was crucial, whereas that of Scotland could be reversed. On 13/24 August 1745 Newcastle received an express from the Duke of Argyll sent from Rosneath, between Glasgow and Inverary on the 7/18th with information from his steward in Mull and Morvern concerning the prince's landing. The account exaggerated Charles Edward's force, saying that he had landed with about 2 to 3,000 men and 2,000 stands of arms. Newcastle credited the report because the description of the boat corresponded with the ship that had avoided the *Lion*. The royal government was aware that Charles Edward had been on that ship. As a result of Argyll's report, orders were sent that day to Sir John Cope, the Commander-in-Chief in Scotland, to march on Charles Edward and attack whatever rendezvous had been arranged for the rising. Newcastle wrote to Cumberland on the 13/24th informing him of Charles Edward's arrival and that troops might speedily be required from Flanders. On the same day William Pulteney, Earl of Bath, a privy councillor, wrote from London to Sir John Rushout, a supporter:

> We have so many concurrent intelligences to persuade us to the belief of the Pretender's son, being actually landed in Scotland, that there is no room to doubt the truth of it, as romantic and chimerical as it may seem to be, but nobody believes the push is to be made in that kingdom, but as a large squadron of ships is getting ready at Ferrol, and an embarkation of troops is actually making there, and that the French talk at the same time of sending a large force from Dunkirk, and have at least eleven ships of war, in Brest and other ports, we are under the greatest alarms . . . . The Duke of Argyle who was in Scotland, and going to his estate in Argyllshire, was forced speedily to return to Edinburgh from whence he sent an express to the Regency to inform them of the affair. General Cope is ordered immediately to march, with such troops as he can get together, to the place where the Pretender is supposed to have landed . . . possibly the French may finish in Flanders with the taking this place [Ostend], and then it is likely they may wish to transfer the seat of the war to this place . . . should it happen I own I am in no great fears about the success of it, since as discontented as the nation may be in some respects, I really think that very few mean to submit to the Pretender introduced by a French force amongst us.

On the same day Stone was more pessimistic. He wrote of the prince's plans 'The undertaking, in its present appearance, seems, (as it is the fashion to call it), rash and desperate: But I cannot think it is altogether to be despised. We are so naked of troops, that, if a body of men was to be flung over, no one can say what may be the consequence',[5] a view the historian might take notice of. The sense of relative unconcern in some circles in London about events in Scotland can be gauged from the correspondence thence of a Scottish military expert, the 2nd Earl of Stair, who was linked to Carteret rather than to his political rivals, Newcastle, Henry Pelham and Hardwicke. On 17 August he wrote to the 4th Earl of Loudoun, another loyal Scottish peer, 'I think it is impossible to make a better disposition than Sir John Cope has made. When that is put in execution and a chain secured from Inverness to Inverlochy I think it highly improbable if not impossible that the enterprise of the younger Pretender should come to anything'. Five days later Stair expressed optimism about Scotland, adding 'we are in much greater danger God knows on this side', especially as the French did not allow the Ostend garrison to sail to England as part of the capitulation agreement, and hoped that 'we shall not allow the enemy to profit of any advantage they may have over us by their situation, and from the few troops that we have in this country'. On 26 August Stair added a postscript:

> . . . one has little to fear from irregular troops . . . what I mean by a right disposition of our troops, is to put them into such a situation as to make them support one another by their fire and not to put them into a position, where the Highlanders by making an impression upon one part, may divide them from one another and so take them in flank.

Many ministers were also inclined to doubt positive reports of the prince's progress. On 27 August the Earl of Sandwich, one of the Lords of the Admiralty, reported to the Duke of Bedford, the First Lord, a conversation he had had with the secretary of war, 'There is this day a report that one or two of the disaffected clans are up in arms and that the landing of the Pretender's son is confirmed; this account I had from Sir William Yonge, I know not how far his authority is to be depended on'.[6] In contrast, the danger of a Bourbon invasion still seemed more pressing. Wade, now a Field-Marshal and the Commander-in-Chief in England, told Newcastle on 14 August that he had no doubt that the French would invade England as soon as Ostend had fallen. Two days later the Duke of Richmond wrote to his fellow Sussex Whig grandee Newcastle that he did not fear Charles Edward but a French invasion and he returned to the theme of pulling troops back from the Continent on 25 August. Newcastle wrote to Cumberland on 20 August:

> It is not to be imagined that the court of France do not at present intend to support this attempt. That must either be done by an embarkation from Ostend and Dunkirk, or from Ferrol and Brest, or from both; and the haste they were in to be masters of Ostend, and their not sending any considerable reinforcements to the Rhine, looks extremely as if they intended to employ some part of their army in Flanders for this purpose . . . all true friends of the government are extremely alarmed.

Cumberland was instructed to send the British troops that had garrisoned Ostend, which had surrendered on 13/24 August, to England. Newcastle urged Cumberland, whom he thought excessively concerned about the situation in the Low Countries, to take the danger of an invasion more seriously and on 27 August he conveyed to Harrington advice from the Lord Justices for the movement of troops to Britain. Cumberland replied to Newcastle's letter of the 13/24th three days later, 'I am surprised to see this romantic expedition revived again, that it has taken place as far as the landing of any troops in Great Britain. But I don't doubt but that Sir John Cope will be able to put a stop immediately to this affair'. He expressed his opposition to sending any of his troops to Britain. Cumberland sent Lieutenant-General John Ligonier to meet George II on his way from Hanover to London at Utrecht and to press him on the dangerous situation in the Austrian Netherlands. Ligonier succeeded, George deferring the transfer of the British troops and deciding to rely upon the 6,000 men that the Dutch were obliged to provide by the Anglo-Dutch defensive treaty. The Dutch chose men from the garrison of Tournai which had surrendered after a feeble resistance on 20 June. The capitulation agreement stipulated that they were not to serve against the French until 1 January 1747. The decision to send the Dutch did not encourage all commentators. The diplomat and MP Benjamin Keene, wrote from London on 3 September:

> The Pretender's son is in Scotland with near 3,000 rebels with new arms and French louis d'ors. We have not above 1,500 men under Sir John Cope, and not a clan has risen to join him though he has marched two-thirds of the kingdom . . . I confess this affair in Scotland taken by itself gives me no great terror, but when I look upon it only as a branch of a more extensive and pernicious project, connected with the Spanish embarkation from Ferrol and contrived by France, who now has it in her power to invade us, void of troops and defense at present, from Ostend, Dunkirk, Brest and where not, I cannot but wish for the return of the

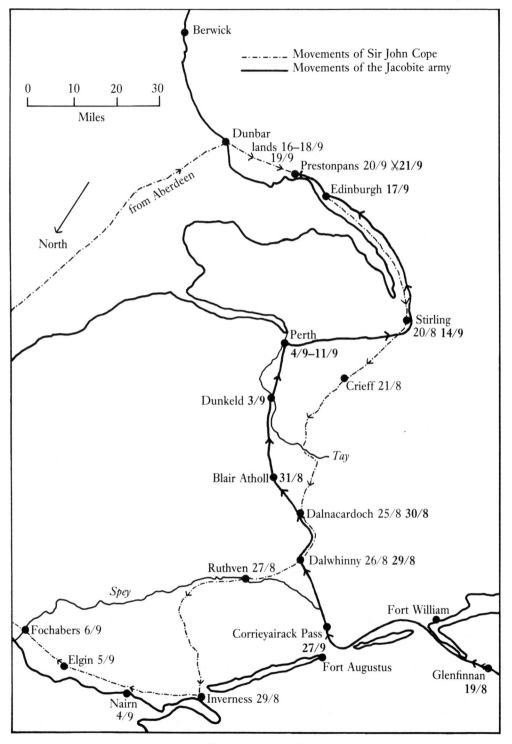

Berwick

-·-·-·-·- Movements of Sir John Cope
———— Movements of the Jacobite army

0   10   20   30
Miles

from Aberdeen

North

Dunbar
lands 16–18/9
19/9
Prestonpans 20/9 X 21/9
Edinburgh **17/9**

Stirling
20/8 **14/9**

Perth
4/9–11/9

Crieff 21/8

Dunkeld 3/9

Tay

Blair Atholl 31/8

Dalnacardoch 25/8 **30/8**

Dalwhinny 26/8 **29/8**

Ruthven 27/8

Spey

Fort William

Fochabers 6/9

Corrieyairack Pass
27/9

Elgin 5/9

Fort Augustus

Glenfinnan
19/8

Nairn
4/9

Inverness 29/8

Cope outmanoeuvred

Duke of Cumberland and the forces, at least 10,000, under his command, without which I am certain we do not sleep in whole skins. Our danger is near and immediate, all our defence at a distance. You can not well imagine the concern all people are in . . . I am thoroughly convinced we shall be invaded from Flanders. And the 6,000 Dutch that are to come over will do nothing without 10,000 of our own people to fight our own battles. I bewilder myself in scenes of misery to come, unless providentially prevented.[7]

The news had not yet reached London that Sir John Cope, the Commander-in-Chief in Scotland, had failed to confine Charles Edward to the western Highlands. On 27 August the prince blocked Cope's route towards the Great Glen by seizing the head of Corrieyairack Pass but Cope, who had told Glenorchy that he would meet the Jacobites there on the 28th, changed his mind about an engagement when he reached the pass. Fearing an ambush there, he decided not to attempt the pass. His force was small, because he had left troops to strengthen the garrisons of Edinburgh, Glasgow and Stirling and because the pro-Hanoverian clansmen he had looked to for reinforcements did not arrive, a fact he subsequently employed to account for his failure. Neither the Duke of Atholl nor Lord Glenorchy were at the agreed meeting place at Crieff with the force Cope had expected, a disappointment that is suggestive of the possible response of loyal English aristocrats at a moment of crisis. Cope had taken 1,000 weapons with him for reinforcements that never came. Glenorchy wrote to the Secretary of State for Scotland, the Marquess of Tweeddale, on 1 September excusing his failure, 'I was sorry to see this country useless for want of arms . . . I was informed, from very good hands, that it is doubtful how far arms can be made use of by law, which made me lay aside all thoughts of raising the country, which indeed would have been extremely difficult, though the law had permitted it, from the great scarcity of meal and the mortality amongst the cattle'. He was surprised to be told by Cope that he had brought arms for his use, as he had no prior warning 'and your Lordship knows people are not to be assembled at a whistle'. Glenorchy was forced to devote his efforts to preventing his followers from joining the prince, writing 'I'm sorry to find too many have still a leaning to that side, which was general not many years ago'.

Totalling less than 1,400, Cope's force was an illustration of the discrepancy between field forces and army size that should be borne in mind when subsequently considering the possible military response to the Jacobites in England. The army in Scotland was in theory nearly 4,000 strong. Worried about the terrain and believing himself greatly outnumbered, Cope retreated towards Inverness, a port in a region of pro-Hanoverian feeling, which he reached on 29 August, encamping to give his troops 'necessary rest, after so many successive fatiguing marches'. Without adequate supplies, a result of the refusal of local officials to provide horses to pull the baggage, Cope could not hold his position on the defensive, and even if he had sought to do so the Highlanders would have been able to outflank him. Cope had no wish to retreat the way he had come through unfriendly territory. An army was always most vulnerable in retreat and it was less hazardous to fall back on the relatively nearby fortresses in Badenoch and at Inverness, rather than to retreat to Stirling. It is possible the Cope's small force would indeed have been defeated at the

Corrieyairack had there been an engagement, given the nature of the terrain and the Highlanders' superior mobility. It would have been difficult to draw it up so as to take advantage of its firepower and the terrain was favourable for a Highland charge upon a strung-out army. On 26 August the senior judicial officer Andrew Fletcher, Lord Milton had already, in a letter which referred to desertions among the loyal Highlanders who Loudoun was assembling (desertion affected both sides), written of the mobility of Highlanders, describing them as 'really a sort of foot hussars who have it in their power to go round regular troops and attack where they see advantage and when beat off cannot lose much in the pursuit, and are apt to attack in the right time'.[8]

Charles Edward did not pursue Cope, a wise move as that would have forced him to attack defended strongholds, always a risky tactic for irregular forces, as was illustrated by the failure of a detachment sent to capture the barracks at Ruthven after Cope's retreat, and the earlier failure against Dunkeld in 1689 after the victory of Killiecrankie. Instead, in 1745 the prince, marched towards lowland Scotland reaching Blair Castle on 31 August and Dunkeld on 3 September, before entering Perth on the 4th, where he proclaimed his father king. Duncan Forbes, the Lord President of the Court of Sessions, warned Tweeddale on 1 September that Cope's retreat had exposed the Lowlands to the

A blank Commission for a Lieutenancy in Cluny MacPherson's regiment. The seal is important as it shows that Charles was using the Royal Arms quartered for England and France surrounded by the Collar of the Order of the Thistle

Lord George Murray, Lieutenant-General in the Jacobite army

Jacobites, 'as there is no body of forces in their way to oppose them, it is to be feared that their reputation will grow, and with it their numbers'. The prince stayed at Perth until the 10th, receiving recruits, including Lord George Murray, whom he made a lieutenant-general, and raising funds by collecting public money. Murray, a brother of the Duke of Atholl, had taken part in the '15 and the '19, been pardoned in 1725 and in 1745 was Deputy Sheriff of Perthshire. Meanwhile, the ministry in London was having to face the prospect not only of the loss of Scotland, but also of an invasion of England. Cope's retreat put the prince nearer to Perth and Edinburgh than were his forces. It settled the issue of the recall of British troops from Flanders for George II now appreciated the seriousness of the situation in Britain. On 4 September orders were sent for the immediate dispatch of the ten best battalions under Ligonier. The troops, who sailed from Willemstad, reached Gravesend on 23 September/3 October. The machinery of local government was put into motion to deal with any potential support for Charles Edward. On 5 September a proclamation 'for putting the laws in execution against Papists and Nonjurors' was issued. Catholics were ordered to leave London and its environs. Those who refused to take the Oaths of Allegiance and Supremacy and the Test Act Declaration were to have their horses and arms confiscated. Orders in Council were sent to the Lord Lieutenants in order to implement the proclamation. On

5 September, for example, the Privy Council wrote to the Earl of Hertford, as *Custos Rotulorum* (head of the county's Commission of the Peace) of Wiltshire, about the precautions to be taken, informing him that 'there is the greatest reason to apprehend that those wicked attempts have been encouraged and maybe supported by a foreign force', and instructing him to order the JPs to disarm disloyal Catholics. On the same day other Lord Lieutenants, such as Lord Hobart in Norfolk, were ordered to raise troops, while Newcastle sent an important letter to Viscount Lonsdale, the Lord Lieutenant of Cumberland and Westmorland, warning him of the danger that Charles Edward and his force of allegedly 3,000 would take Perth or Edinburgh or both:

> . . . it will give them great hold in Scotland and encourage the French and Spaniards to make attempts in favour of the Pretender, which undoubtedly they must have engaged to do, when the Pretender's son determined to come to Scotland. We had an account last Tuesday that there are at present above thirty ships at Dunkirk, capable of bringing over 7 or 8,000 men, and some men-of-war, that the Irish regiments and officers are all quartered upon the coast, that their seamen are all sent to Dunkirk, that there is an embargo laid on the ships on the River Charente, and we have reason to think for some time that there are French and Spanish men-of-war of the line near thirty, at Ferrol and in the western ports of France. All these circumstances make it much to be apprehended that we shall soon have some attempt from abroad. I wish we were in a better condition to oppose it, than I am afraid we are. However, we have a very considerable squadron of great and small ships in the Downs under the command of Admiral Vernon, and Admiral Martin will have fourteen or fifteen sail, I think of the line, with him cruising off the Lizard to watch the ships from Brest etc. Last night orders were sent to the Duke of Cumberland to send over hither with the utmost expedition ten of the best regiments of foot from his army and Sir John Ligonier to come with them. The Dutch are sending hither 6,000 men . . . as we have hardly any regular force between Berwick and London, it has been thought proper to direct the Lord Lieutenants of the four northern counties to have the militia in readiness. I hope we may send some northwards, if there is occasion, but at present by what I understand, there are not in all England of all kinds 6,000 men, guards included. I must own I have been for some time under great apprehensions, I think people begin now to be alarmed, I heartily wish they had been so a little sooner.[9]

Newcastle's view that the rising would not have occurred but for a promise of Bourbon support was clearly an established view in ministerial circles. Viscount Duncannon MP, the son-in-law of the Duke of Devonshire, had already warned an Irish official of this on 19 August.[10] However, a number of ministers played down the initial danger of the situation, because they did not want Britain to weaken her military commitment to the continent. This was certainly the position of Carteret, now Earl Granville and still influential with the king though no longer Secretary of State, and his ally the Marquess of Tweeddale, the Secretary of State for Scotland. They initially cast doubts on reports of the prince's landing and subsequently on his success, Ryder recording in his diary on 15 September that Tweeddale and his allies were claiming that the Jacobites were deserting and would soon be suppressed. It was not generally appreciated that Charles Edward's mission was very much a personal one, not even approved by his father let alone the Bourbons. However, the prince certainly hoped to obtain Bourbon assistance through success in Scotland. Indeed rumours already circulated that the Bourbons had landed. On 15 September Cumberland's former governor, Stephen Poyntz, wrote from his seat at Midgham in Berkshire,

'A fellow pretty well dressed passed through Newbury on Thursday last, their market day, and published that he was sent express to London with news of the French being landed at Poole in Dorset; but as he did not take post-horses and was thirty miles southward of the direct road no credit was given to him'.[11] Tension was certainly rising in London. On 4 September Harrington wrote to Cumberland that it was 'absolutely necessary to demand an immediate embarkation of British troops from Flanders' and six days later he told the Hessian envoy Alt that the 6,000 Dutch troops requested in mid-August were impatiently expected. It was feared that the Jacobites might bypass Edinburgh and march directly into England. The government decided to send troops northwards when the Dutch and British reinforcements from the Low Countries had arrived. These forces were to be supplemented by the raising under the authority of the Lord Lieutenants of companies of volunteers. Three Dutch regiments arrived in the Thames on 14 September.[12]

Further north Charles Edward was just about to advance from Perth. On 13 September he crossed the Forth at the Fords of Frew and the following day marched past Stirling, fired on by the castle's cannon. On 16 September the surrender of Edinburgh was demanded. The town could have been defended: the successful Genoese rising against occupying Austrian troops in December 1746 showed what determined volunteers operating in their own surroundings were capable of, but there was no such determination in Edinburgh, despite the presence of a garrison in the castle and of a town wall. The events in Edinburgh suggest what might have been the fate of towns in England. On 2 September Robert Craigie, the Lord Advocate, reported to Tweeddale:

> I have this moment a deputation from the Magistrates and Council of this city informing me that they were sure that the well affected inhabitants would levy and pay for three months one thousand men for the defence of the Government and desiring that I would write to your Lordship for a proper authority from the King or the Justices for this purpose.

Sixteen days later he wrote from Dunbar of the fall of the city which he blamed on an absence of resistance, 'It was carried in Council that no opposition should be made to the Rebels, thereupon the volunteers delivered in their arms to the Castle and the cannon mounted on the city wall were defaced'.

The ignominious retreat of two regiments of royal dragoons to Dunbar after an exchange of fire with the Highlanders west of Edinburgh had pushed the magistrates towards surrender. However, on the evening of the 16th news reached Edinburgh that Cope, who had marched from Inverness to Aberdeen before sailing from there, had arrived at Dunbar. His movement was a consequence of British control of the sea for, without this, he would have had to march on from Aberdeen, finding the crossing of the Tay at Perth in Jacobite hands and the Highlanders between him and Edinburgh. Despite Cope's speed he was not operating on internal lines, as was Charles Edward, an advantage which, when coupled with superior Jacobite mobility, gave Charles Edward several options. William Hogg, an Edinburgh correspondent of Matthew Ridley, the Mayor of Newcastle, noted on 14 September that Cope was criticized by many for delay, so that the country was left open to the Highlanders. The delays

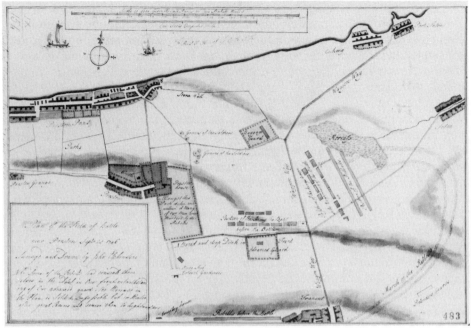

Map of the battle of Prestonpans

Cope encountered illustrated some of the disadvantages of transport by sea: embarking, contrary winds and disembarking. Though he reached Aberdeen on 11 September he was not able to sail until the 15th and, having landed his men, he had to rest them and land the artillery.

While the magistrates dithered, the Jacobites took advantage of an open gate to enter Edinburgh on the morning of the 17th, the Provost secretly helping. The regular forces retreated to the castle as James III was proclaimed. Newcastle responded to the fall of Edinburgh by informing Richmond that 'The Pretender has now got possession of Scotland'. Although it was hoped that Cope would defeat Charles Edward, a force under General Wentworth was ordered to march 'towards Lancashire, or to any other place in England, where he shall hear the rebels are', while two Dutch regiments were sent by sea to secure Newcastle. Sir Henry Liddell MP, a County Durham coal-mine owner, observed on 21 September, on the news of Edinburgh's fall, 'If this be true that affair begins to look serious, and whatever my duty to my country may call me to, probably my duty to wife and family will make me soon think of removing them from hence', an honest response that may provide a clue as to how many prominent Whigs would have responded to a Jacobite advance. On the same day George Bowes and John Hedworth, the two MPs for County Durham, wrote to the Duke of Newcastle stating their conviction that Cope would be unable to prevent an invasion of England and expressing their confidence that George II would send immediate orders 'to protect this unarmed part of the world who have hearts sincerely attached to his Majesty and are willing to serve him to the utmost of our power'. Newcastle had already concluded, before the news of Prestonpans, that 'it is possible that the rebels may proceed into England'.[13]

Having obtained much-needed supplies in the city, Charles Edward left it on 19 September to confront Cope, who was advancing on Edinburgh with a roughly similar force of 2,400. On the 20th Cope reached Prestonpans, a flat, marshy battle ground that was completely different to the Corrieyairack. He was protected by the Firth of Forth to the north and a deep morass to the south whose potential as an obstruction was enhanced by ditches. Cope drew up his men facing west, the direction of Edinburgh and the Jacobite forces. However, the Jacobites, who had planned a night march around the morass and falling on Cope's flank at dawn, were informed of a track across the morass which they accordingly crossed before dawn on the 21st, arriving to the east of Cope's flank. Cope had altered his dispositions during the 20th as he discovered that the Jacobites were south of his position, and in conventional military terms he had a more balanced force than Charles Edward with dragoons and six cannon, whereas the prince had no guns and only forty horsemen. However, neither arm was of much value to Cope. The nautical gunners fled and their untrained army replacements did little damage before they were overrun, while most of the dragoons refused to charge. Some attempted to do so, but they were met by Highlanders slashing at their mounts. A Highland charge, the formation unbroken by the fire of Cope's infantry, led the infantry to flee in panic a few minutes after the first impact of the charge. The speed of the Jacobite victory was referred to in a Newcastle item in the *Caledonian Mercury* of 16 October 1745:

> Poor Sm——h was apprehended and imprisoned yesterday, for saying over a bottle, that the Dutch auxiliaries here would find an infinite odds between pluffing at the *petit Maitres* before Tournay or Fontenoy, and encountering with the desperate Highlander's trusty broadsword and targe, headed by a person who can lie on straw, eat a dry crust, dine in five minutes and gain a battle in four.

The Jacobite broadswords caused most of the casualties and inflicted many hideous wounds. The Jacobites lost about 25 men, Cope about 300, but Cope's army was destroyed, with at least 1,500 men taken prisoner and Cope himself fled to Berwick. Most of the casualties occurred during the retreat, for infantry formations that lost their order in retreat were particularly vulnerable to pursuing infantry, as at Prestonpans, or cavalry, as at Culloden. The royal forces only fired one round of ammunition and apparently not one bayonet was stained with blood. William Hogg wrote from Edinburgh on 24 September that Cope was 'much reflected on on all hands', that the Jacobites 'did most execution with their broadswords' and that the wounded were so numerous that it was bad to be in the infirmary. Cope never commanded a unit in battle again. The council of officers appointed to inquire into his conduct unanimously absolved him of all blame, deciding fairly that he 'did his duty as an officer, both before and after the action; and his personal behaviour was without reproach'. Instead they blamed the defeat on 'the shameful behaviour of the private men', an unfair verdict as the infantry had not been trained for such conflict and cavalry units were not accustomed to being attacked by infantry. Even the veterans of continental warfare proved unable to stand up to the Highland charge. Robert Craigie wrote on 23 September from Berwick:

> . . . the action or rather the rout . . . The officers in the general condemn the soldiers and in a particular manner the dragoons who they say did not strike one blow before they fled and neither they nor the foot could be prevailed upon to rally. We think this accounts for the defeat without any other reason either the attacks being early in the morning or the bravery or number of the Highlanders.
>   One thing is certain that this defeat will make it a dangerous experiment for His Majesty's troops to engage the rebels a second time without a visible superiority. This has raised their contempt of the regular troops and I own I have a great doubt but that His Majesty's troops will have a diffidence of one another especially of their leaders though they have come safe off in this action.

When on 9 July 1755 General Braddock's force of regulars was defeated near Fort Duquesne by the French and their (Red) Indian allies, the blame was similarly allocated by Lieutenant-Colonel Thomas Gage, who took part in the battle, ' . . . this shameful affair . . . no officers ever behaved better, or men worse'. However, as at Prestonpans, where the troops had had no prior experience of or training to withstand a Highland charge, so, a decade later, Braddock's men were unused to being fired on by an enemy they could not see. Horatio Sharp, the Governor of Maryland, wrote 'the novelty of such fighting struck our troops with amazement and terror. They found themselves destroyed by an invisible enemy, and were soon thrown into the greatest consternation'.[14]

Prestonpans marked the end of effective royal opposition in Scotland with the important exception of a number of Lowland and Highland fortifications including the castles of Dumbarton, Edinburgh and Stirling, and Fort Augustus and Fort William. These could not be taken without siege guns and large besieging forces, but in the absence of an army the garrisons could not uphold George II's position in Scotland to any significant extent. The situation was to alter when Charles Edward left for England, because the basis of a Hanoverian recovery existed: garrisons in a number of strategic spots; loyal aristocrats, clans and ministers willing to act in a number of areas, especially the Argyll country and around Inverness; and the control of the sea that would enable the ministry to send reinforcements.

The battle had an electric effect in England. On 13 September Alt noted assurances that Cope would crush everything, though adding that there was concern because there were so few troops in England. Poyntz complained on 24 September, before he had received the news of the battle:

> That a nation like Scotland which makes the strictest profession of the Protestant Religion and values itself on respecting the sanctity of an oath should suffer the Pretender's son with a handful of rabble to walk the Protestant Succession out of that kingdom, without lifting up a single weapon or hand against him, is astonishing to the last degree, and fills one with dreadful apprehensions for the behaviour of England, where a dissolute indifference for everything sacred and serious, and a luxurious impatience of dangers and hardships more generally prevails. Had the town of Edinburgh made good the professions of their address, they might easily have destroyed such an undisciplined crew from the windows of their high stone houses, but how far it may now be in Sir J^n Copes power to dislodge them, or how far it

may be practicable for him with his handful of men to engage them now they are strengthened with the gatherings of a disaffected capital, I tremble to think. The unhappy mistakes which have been made about the destination of the Dutch, and the present impossibility (as I imagine) of calling home the remainder of our army, without sacrificing the sixteen remaining provinces of the Netherlands will make it very late before a sufficient force can be assembled in the North; and if the Pretender and his other son should land, one of them in Ireland and the other in the West of England, a new set of Principles must be formed amongst us before we can hope to repel such divided attempts against our constitution . . . I have seen the Bp of Salisbury's Circular to his Clergy which is a very good one, and produced an honest discourse from Mr Spackman our minister last Sunday, who among other things left this short apophthegm on the minds of his Parishioners that if the Pretender got the better, their only option would be *Turn* or *Burn*.

The following day Henry Fox MP wrote to his brother Stephen that Harrington was certain that the French intended to invade that year, adding:

. . . our inability to resist is plain enough, so you will not wonder at those who wished for some of our army home . . . [Field Marshal] Wade swears that England is for the first comer, and if 6,000 French land before these Dutch *and English* are here, that London is theirs as soon as they can march to it, and that they may march to it from any part of the kingdom without the least opposition . . . that the Pretender's son can hardly come thus without assurance of foreign support, is the thing that frightens me most, and considered as part of a scheme only, his coming has succeeded beyond expectation.[15]

The situation was viewed with alarm by many. Ryder recorded in his diary on 26 September, 'Mrs Stone talked of the probable success of the Pretender, which she supposes from the general dissatisfaction of the people and the ill-usage the king gives his friends', though he also wrote:

My fear is for want of a good head to conduct the spirit there is in the people in support of the king, rather than that there is not affection enough in the bulk of the people.

On the 26th Thomas Sherlock, Bishop of Salisbury also wrote of the bad news from Scotland:

I have lived in great fear of this event; and could never understand why our forces were to be exposed piecemeal to the rebels . . . the credit given to the rebels will, I doubt not, bring many of their secret friends into action, and be attended probably with new commotions in England.

Prestonpans finally settled the debate about recalling troops from the Austrian Netherlands. On 24 September Robert Ellison remarked 'our People are now I believe going to act with vigour' and he expressed the hope that with the assistance of the troops from Flanders it would be possible to stop the Jacobites.[16] Two days later Cumberland was ordered to dispatch eight more battalions and nine squadrons to England immediately. Both Cumberland and the Dutch, who wanted the troops they were obliged to provide by treaty regarded as a substitute for the recall of Cumberland's men, feared that the dispatch of British troops would wreck both the crumbling defence of the region and the anti-French alliance. There was particular anxiety that it might encourage Austria, then at war with Prussia in the Second Silesian War, to neglect the conflict with France and that it might encourage already powerful neutralist tendencies in the United Provinces. These fears continued after the recall of troops had been decided upon and carried out, but from late September the strategic and political issues confronting British policy had altered. In place of the question as to whether forces should be brought back to southern England to face a likely Bourbon invasion or be retained in the Low Countries to prevent the French from overrunning the Austrian Netherlands, the prime strategic problem was now that of deciding how many troops to retain in southern England and how many to send north against Charles Edward. The major political question was no longer how the anti-French alliance could be kept together at a time of bad war news, French peace initiatives and disputes as to whether to concentrate efforts against France or Prussia, but whether Britain would be able to remain a member of such an alliance. There was little doubt in London that Charles Edward would follow up the conquest of Scotland, which was regarded as in effect completed by Cope's defeat, by invading England. This invasion would not be a mere border excursion or a campaign that culminated in a siege, for example of Berwick, Carlisle or Newcastle, as would have been the case in most conventional military operations, but would instead be a rapid advance designed to seize London and one in which the Jacobites would not be averse to a battle. Cope's failure was scarcely auspicious and the speed with which his units had been routed, less than fifteen minutes, was especially frightening. It was assumed that Charles Edward would invade because the Stuarts wanted to be restored in England as well, Scotland always being a secondary objective for the prince, a means to an end, because such an invasion was essential for the protection of the Jacobite position in Scotland and because this was assumed to be part of the strategy coordinated with the Bourbons. However, the very fact that Jacobite operations and the response to them were both regarded as part of a wider strategic picture, made the response more difficult. If too many men were sent north the Bourbons might be tempted to invade. If the concentration of forces developing in southern England was divided then it could be defeated or outmanoeuvred in detail. Prestonpans had revealed that equality of forces would not be sufficient to defeat the Jacobites. Edinburgh indicated that towns with fortifications would perhaps offer no resistance and that the presence of a royal garrison might be of slight military significance.

However, to send no troops to the north would be foolish. Prior to Charles Edward's invasion of lowland Scotland it was possible to argue that Cope and the loyal Scots would be able to defeat Charles Edward or at least prevent him from overrunning all Scotland. It was therefore plausible to present the strategic question as southern England or the Low Countries. After Prestonpans this was no longer possible. Cope had not simply been defeated. His army could not be regrouped. It had been destroyed, its morale shattered and many of its members had become casualties, prisoners or deserters. A new force would have to be of regulars, sent from southern England or the Low Countries. To leave northern England defenceless might in theory have been the more sensible military course as it would have kept the army together, strong enough to dissuade the Bourbons from invading and powerful enough to defeat the Scots if they marched too near London. Nevertheless, such a course of action was neither militarily nor politically practical. Surrendering northern England would provide the Jacobite army with many sources of supply, including the Yorkshire clothing

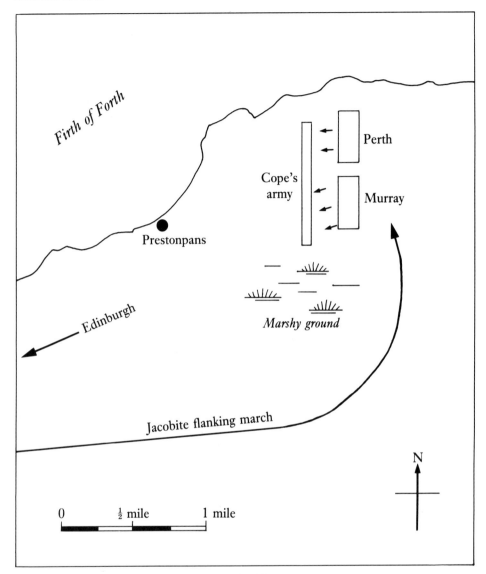

Plan of the battle of Prestonpans

industry. More seriously it would enable them to raise recruits, especially in Lancashire, an area where Catholics were relatively common, it would discourage loyalists in Scotland, whose activities would be necessary to divert Jacobite strength, and it would create a crisis of confidence throughout England and probably Ireland in the Hanoverian regime. What form this would take was unclear, but that did not make the danger any less pressing. Therefore, it would be necessary to defend northern England but that in itself posed problems. Geographically the region was split in two by the Pennines and routes were north–south, rather than east–west. England is narrowest between the Solway Firth and the Tyne estuary, but, though the Tyne valley offered a route into Northumberland, there was no good road through to Carlisle. If therefore a forward defence policy was to be followed it was clear that the ministry would have to choose whether to concentrate its forces sent north east or west of the Pennines. The rendezvous selected for the troops sent to the north was Doncaster, chosen so that they could proceed to Tyneside or Lancashire, but Doncaster covered the eastern route south more effectively than that west of the Pennines. Wade moved on from there to Newcastle and the troops sent by sea to Newcastle further strengthened the eastern orientation. The decision for the east was probably inevitable. The North Sea was the major axis of communications, indeed the nexus of the anti-French alliance and the Hanoverian polity as it had earlier been of William III's personal combination of powers. London looked to Newcastle, Hull, Amsterdam and Hamburg as it did not really look to Carlisle or Liverpool, Belfast or Dublin. The world of the Irish Sea was a different one. It was more influenced by Catholicism and by old loyalties and traditions of political hostility to London, now including Jacobitism, though the Episcopalian north-east of Scotland was a hotbed of Jacobitism. Centres of commercial activity, Bristol, Liverpool, Whitehaven and Glasgow, looked to Ireland, Iberia and the Mediterranean and North America, not to London and north-western Europe.

These were essentially subconscious pulls. More important in 1745, when speed appeared to be of the essence in combating the fast-moving Charles Edward, was the fact that it would be easier to move troops from the Low Countries or the Home Counties to Yorkshire and Newcastle than to Lancashire and Carlisle. Once they reached their destination it would be quicker to move them back to southern England if the Bourbons invaded or, in the case of the Dutch, to the Low Countries. Falling back to shield London would be easier if the army was concentrated east of the Pennines. On 25 September the Duke of Newcastle replied to Bowes and Hedworth's letter of the 21st, taking note of the subsequent news of Prestonpans, which, as he wrote, had to change the ministry's plans. He informed the MPs that Wade would march north with 10,000 men, some of whom had already set off, and a large artillery train, to wherever Wade thought best. He would be joined by two regiments from Dublin, who would arrive via Chester, and by the remains of Cope's force currently at Berwick. In addition, ten British regiments as well as Dutch auxiliaries from Willemstad would defend London. The MPs were told that George II would do all in his power to protect those areas most threatened by the Jacobites and would act immediately to suppress the rebellion. On the same day the duke wrote to the Duke of Devonshire informing him that Wade would march to near Mansfield, 'that the army may take either way, according to the motions of the Rebels', to the west or east of the Pennines. On 26 September Thomas Ramsden, one of Newcastle's under secretaries, wrote to Viscount Lonsdale, who was quickly gaining a new prominence as Lord Lieutenant in Cumbria, from Whitehall:

... the Cabinet having sat this night till past twelve have at last come to a resolution to send for eight regiments of foot to be immediately sent from Flanders to Newcastle, as also three regiments of dragoons will be ordered to come forthwith, but as the proper transports for them are not ready, it may possibly be some time before they can be here . . . . There has been a little run upon the Bank, yesterday and this day, but no considerable merchants are concerned in it, and I hear they have declared, that they are ready and willing to take Bank Bills in payment, which must retrieve the sinking credit, and ease people's minds. The rendezvous is now altered to Doncaster; where the troops will be more at hand to go either to Lancashire or directly northwards as the rebels may go . . . everything continues quiet in England.

On 28 September the Duke of Newcastle expressed his conviction of the utmost importance of the security of Newcastle, but added that as the preservation of Berwick was also crucial, in order to deny the Jacobites free passage into England, Cope and the dragoon regiments in Berwick had been ordered to remain there. The duke reported the inaccurate news that the Jacobites were going to call a convention of the state of Scotland at Edinburgh, which he hoped would delay their march south, giving the government time to strengthen itself and for Wade to march north. He was correct to argue that the Jacobite delay in moving south gave the ministry the opportunity to prepare to defend England, though paradoxically it ensured that there would be more troops with Wade at Newcastle and thus that the Jacobites would bypass a larger force by invading rapidly through Cumbria. The failure to hold an assembly at Edinburgh can be seen as detrimental to the Jacobites in terms of public relations, though the repudiation of the Act of Union which might have been called for to satisfy Scottish opinion did not accord with the Stuart determination to keep England and Scotland united, while Charles' position in such an assembly would have been contentious, not least because he had no authority to act on behalf of his father.[17]

Though the run on the Bank of England was stemmed, confidence in the stability of the regime was precarious in late September and early October as the successive shocks of the bypassing of Cope, the Jacobite entry into the Lowlands, the fall of Edinburgh without resistance and Prestonpans were digested. On 19/30 September Robert Trevor wrote to Robinson from The Hague about the dispatch of troops to Britain, 'My private letters represent their presense as but too necessary; and it is apprehended by some good sensible Whigs that the indifferency and lukewarmness of the many is more dangerous than the activity of the few'.[18] With little understanding of the formidable Jacobite logistical and other problems, a speedy invasion of England was anticipated. An advertisement for the sale of county maps in the *London Evening Post* of 3 October 1745 noted 'As there is at present a great demand for the northern counties . . . a considerable part of them are printed'. Rumours of a French invasion circulated, Dudley Ryder recording in his diary on 1 October 'a letter found in the road by two women that imported a notification that the French would land near Poole'. On 7 October Thomas White of Bruton in Somerset wrote to the Duke of Bedford, a major landowner in Devon who was raising an infantry regiment, 'We are much concerned here with the apprehensions of a French invasion either at Lyme or Torbay'. He added, 'I am informed your Lordship do design to head your country gentlemen against those rebellious thieves that threaten us'.[19] However, it was not until a council meeting on 3/14 October that the French government decided to invade and the preparations took a considerable time. The London newspaper *Old England* claimed on 19 October 'had they thrown in ten thousand men in time, we may tremble to think what would have been the consequence: France would soon have seen all the western world her own'. Nevertheless, while unclear about French intentions, the government in London was provided with what appeared to be a window of opportunity by the delay in French moves. Stair, a member of the military committee formed in London to draw up a plan of operations, wrote on 2 October, 'We are persuaded that the enemy does intend to make an invasion upon us from abroad, but we cannot perceive that they are as yet ready in any one place, to put those designs in execution suddenly and in the meantime more troops are ordered from Flanders'. The following day Poyntz noted 'our affairs look so black in all quarters that I have not the heart to write about them; yet the Duke of St Albans showed me a letter from Lord Vere assuring him that by the freshest accounts there was no embarkation going on at Dunkirk or Ostend'. Newcastle informed Lonsdale on 3 October:

> We have an account that there is an embargo laid on all ships etc. at Dunkirk; but, at present, there are no considerable number of ships for transports or any men of war of force. Some large privateers there are at St Malo and a number of large ships at Brest; which however we are told, are not yet ready for the sea. For my own part I can scarce believe France will neglect this opportunity; when they undoubtedly set this young Pretender to work; who, from such fatal accidents, mismanagements, misunderstandings and infatuations has succeeded beyond what the most sanguine of his party could never have expected; but I hope in God, if our troops come in time, his success will soon be at an end. There is a great zeal almost universal in your northern counties; and I hope, and believe, that example will be followed by most of the Midland counties and some of the maritime ones; but I doubt the western counties and the Welsh counties will not behave so well . . . Admiral Martin is cruising off the Lizard with a very considerable squadron. Admiral Vernon continues in the Downs; and we have a great number of small ships in different parts of the Channel.

The previous day Tweeddale had informed William Forrester, Moderator at Dumfries, 'The King has ordered a large body of troops to march directly to Scotland', which Tweeddale hoped would end the rebellion. By 11 October, when he wrote to the Duke of Devonshire, Newcastle was less optimistic, 'The French army is gone into winter quarters . . . we have nothing more to fear in Flanders, but an embarkation from thence, which may very possibly happen sooner than we imagine'. He added information from the Duke of Cumberland that the Irish Brigade in French service was marching towards Dunkirk in order to embark for England.[20]

The degree of support that could be expected from the population was clearly of growing importance for if Charles Edward invaded northern England the strength of his force would depend on his ability to attract volunteers, while the capacity of the royal forces to respond would be affected by the degree to which their strength was diverted by risings by the English Jacobites. English Jacobites had shown that they were willing to rise in the '15 in the north, where they joined the Scots, though not in the south-west, where the leaders were arrested, and several of the ministers prominent in 1745 had been in office during the Atterbury Plot. Newcastle had raised a troop for service during the '15, while his brother Henry Pelham had served as a volunteer at the battle of Preston. William Stanhope, Earl of Harrington, Secretary of State during the '45, had been a colonel during the '15. The decision to supplement the army by allowing selected loyal aristocrats, such as the Earl of Halifax, to raise regiments and the warrants sent to the Lord Lieutenants and selected mayors and town magistracies empowering them to form their own companies and battalions threw the attitude of the population into greater prominence, as did the likely role of the militia. Newcastle noted on 21 September 'the difficulties that there are in calling out the militia; and the little use, that, it is apprehended, would arise from it; have induced some of the Lords Lieutenant to propose, that particular authorities should be given to them for raising men within their respective counties'. Efforts were made to encourage loyal feelings and to direct them to practical effect. The press warned about the consequences of a Catholic government. On 9 November the *Cambridge Journal* carried a letter urging the printing of Fox's *Book of Martyrs*, and three week's later a report of how Highlanders had looted Carlisle and assaulted young women there. Associations were formed for the defence of crown, country and church. Subscriptions were raised, volunteer units formed. On 2 October 1745 £3,895 16s. were subscribed at Chester. The Bristol subscription, launched on 11 October, had reached nearly £36,000 by 16 November and over £38,000 by 23 November. Ireland was quiet, though not without anxiety. On 1 October the Bishop of Down wrote from Dublin to Robert Wilmot, the Secretary to the Lord Lieutenant, complaining both that the disarming of Catholics, for which he had pressed, had not been carried out, and that the militia lacked arms, 'the arms in the hands of private gentlemen are inconsiderable, and arraying without arming will only show our enemies our weakness ... the whole county of Antrim joining in a hearty subscription, the attempt I find was ridiculed by the people in power here and very lately we have been in a state of inactivity'. Another Dublin correspondent reported on 24 October 'There has not been the least disturbance here, nor any likely to be. The Papists of property are afraid of a commotion as what may cause only present confusion, in which they'll suffer and be made the cat's paw of France' and again on 16 November 'everything is quiet here and likely to continue so; the people in the north have been unreasonably alarmed with the fear of an invasion from the rebels, who they apprehended would get boats and land about Belfast and Carrickfergus'.[21] There were also reports of loyal activity in England, including 'an uncommon ardour among the people ... to learn the art of war' in Bristol and reassuring comments to British diplomats, Ramsden writing on 18 October 'every county in England continues in perfect peace and there is not the least riot or rising' and on 5 November 'I believe so general a spirit throughout the whole nation ... has not at any time appeared in this kingdom'. On 22 October a London tradesman, Richard Finch, sent a merchant with whom he had dealings a letter that revealed rising confidence in loyalist circles in London as the shock of September's events in Scotland wore off:

The rebels have continued at and about Edinburgh ever since ... and after several fruitless attempts and artifices to get the castle into their hands, seem to be somewhat disheartened, especially as their friends the French have not as yet been able to land a body of troops to second and strengthen the rebellion. We have now on their march for the North of England near 15,000 regular troops, which in about a week will be joined by about 5,000 more, and the whole will proceed to Scotland as fast as possible to seek the rebels; in case they do not march into England and meet our troops. A native of London who went abroad before this rebellion began and knew the discontents of the people before would scarce credit the zeal, affection and loyalty, which appears every where all over the nation, on behalf of the king, and the Protestant religion; to the degree that smaller matters seem to be cancelled; the newspapers every day full of pathetic incitements to fight for our king and our liberties; and the pamphlet shops crowded with entire new books on the same important subjects. Our most gracious king and our excellent constitution were never so greatly the love and delight of all ranks and orders of men as at this time.

Four days later Jane Ellison expressed Whig confidence in divine support, 'we shall have numbers of the traitors heads on Temple Bar, for as it pleased God that they lost their opportunity after Cope's being defeated, I take it as a favourable symptom that God Almighty only suffered that to open our eyes'. On 16 November Stephen Weston, Registrar of the Exeter diocese, wrote from Exeter 'all in these parts continues very quiet' adding a comment on the willingness of aristocrats to raise units, among whom he singled out the Tory Lord Gower, who had joined the government in December 1744, 'it gives me pleasure to see so much virtue left in our nobility as it must necessarily diffuse itself into all ranks of orders below them; but I think Lord Gower's example is of inestimable value at this time, as the Tories will be influenced by it sooner than by that of any one man's in England'.[22]

However, notes of scepticism were struck, while the response of the militia in the north-west to Charles Edward's invasion was scarcely that of enthusiastic defenders of George II against an invading force of irregulars. Newcastle wrote to Devonshire on 11 October, 'The western part of the Kingdom is necessarily without troops: If the French should fling in a number of troops anywhere there, it would create a great deal of trouble. For, I am much afraid, those counties are by no means, so well affected, as the northern ones'. In Yorkshire the Tory MPs for York, George Fox and Godfrey Wentworth, were among the gentry and merchants of both parties who followed the active lead of Archbishop Herring and agreed on a loyal address 'in which each pledged himself to the other to defend the existing order' and to raise £20,000. However, neither MP emulated the Whig William Thornton, who raised a company of foot at his own expense to oppose Charles Edward and took part in the battle of Falkirk. This contrast was to be highlighted by Whig propaganda in York during the election campaign which led to the election of Thornton in 1747.[23] Herring was sceptical about the value of Tory subscriptions to the association and it is unclear what would have happened had the Jacobites invaded Yorkshire. Possibly they would have received even fewer volunteers than in Cumbria but, equally, there might have been as little activity in support of George. In other counties, such as Dorset, there was less enthusiasm for an association and in some, such as Oxford, the Tories refused to subscribe. On 10 October Lord Herbert wrote to the Duke of Devonshire about the meeting held at Shrewsbury to launch a county association, ' . . . public notice was given to People of all Parties without Distinction.

Our Friends only appeared'. There was opposition in Bristol to the association formed to raise troops and refusals to subscribe. The granting of commissions raised 'jealousies and discontents', it was argued that the troops could not serve outside the town, and by 23 November only twenty-two men had enlisted. Recruits were still coming in 'very slowly' a month later.

The situation in Durham was not encouraging. On 17 September the Bishop, Edward Chandler, wrote to Bowes expressing concern about the legality of drawing out the militia and the lack of enthusiasm shown by Henry Vane MP, a prominent local landlord, and mentioned the possibility of a county association. Bowes agreed but on 27 September he reported to Chandler that the turnout at the meeting he had called at Durham had been very poor and that he had been struck by 'the absence of some and the coolness of others'. 'Strong resolutions in regard to the Roman Catholics', a safe target, were taken and Bowes expressed the hope that the association would be able to raise a force of 200 cavalry within a few days, while noting that the rebels were no longer expected almost hourly. He also informed Chandler, then ill in London, that he had approached several gentlemen to take commands in the militia, but all had refused. Chandler replied on 3 October stating that no arms could be sent from the Tower of London but that as Newcastle would be well provided for that should ensure the safety of County Durham. He reminded Bowes how in 1640 in the Bishops' War the invading Scots under Alexander Leslie had entered the county by crossing the Tyne at a ford, bypassing Newcastle, and 'like locusts continued to graze there till nothing green was left'. In mid-November Bowes wrote to Chandler complaining of a great shortage of arms, the unwillingness of the government to remedy it, the lack of support from some of the gentry and the failure of all but one of the Deputy Lieutenants to turn up at a recent meeting, which he reported was a great check to the spirit that ought to be shown. His fellow county MP, John Hedworth, who was over sixty and was to die in 1747, was laid low by a cold and gout in the stomach and bowels. On 21 November Bowes claimed that his regiment was nearly 170 strong and would have been complete could arms have been procured. However, the force was soon dissolved when the militia was raised. In retrospect both Bowes and Chandler regretted the failure to support the association effectually, Bowes writing that the cause 'has been too long looked on with indifference'.

Chester was a walled city and contained a castle, but there was doubt about its ability to resist attack. On 16 November the 3rd Earl of Cholmondeley, Governor of the castle and Lord Lieutenant of the county, reported to Newcastle that he was strengthening the town walls and gates, and that 'the castle's walls are in very good order', but the following day he complained that he would not be able to do much with his 'handful of raw men' and was concerned about the 'dispositions of great numbers within the place'.

It was claimed that the new units would not be able to stand up to a Highland charge. Units from Earl Gower's regiment arrived in Chester in November, but they were short of arms and mutinous.[24] There were complaints about a lack of enthusiasm. 'Agricola', writing in *Old England* on 9 November 1745, complained that a failure to take the Jacobite invasion seriously had been one of the major causes of its success. He blamed inaccurate newspaper reports of cowardice, desertions, poor discipline and mutinies among Charles Edward's forces for a false sense of security, a theme the paper returned to on 22 March 1746.

Popular hostility was generally only a scant impediment to a successful invading force, as Frederick II had recently demonstrated in Silesia. In the case of England in 1745 it is by no means clear how extensive this hostility was. Charles Edward did not benefit, as William III had done in 1688, from a deliberately fostered confusion about his objectives. There was no doubt that the violent overthrow of George II was sought, nor that the consequence would be sweeping political changes. Concern about the religious implications helped to rally support for the king. Though George I and II were Lutherans and had sponsored a number of bishops with beliefs that were generally regarded as heterodox, they were not seen as threats to the Church of England as compared to that presented by the Catholic Stuarts. John Tucker, an MP who had opposed the ministry, wrote to his brother on 7 September, 'I think this nation will never submit to a Popish yoke again, but will all join to keep out this biggotted race'.[25] The theme of religious danger was taken up by caricatures produced in this period, such as *The Procession or the Pope's Nursling riding in Triumph*.[26] A mass of anti-Jacobite material appeared in print, much of it centring on the supposed threat of the forcible introduction of Catholicism. *Great Britain's Memorial against the Pretender and Popery* by the London nonconformist minister Samuel Chandler went through ten editions. *The French Expedition or the Lamentation of Louis*, a broadsheet published on 8 October that supposedly set out Louis XV's objectives, promised the introduction of the Inquisition and declared, 'we will make them kneel down before our altars and they shall worship pictures and wooden images. And behold we will send cardinals and priests of all sorts, so that they shall swarm all over the land, and they shall bring down all the people, from the highest unto the lowest'.[27] In fact when he occupied Edinburgh Charles Edward assured the Presbyterian clergy of religious toleration. The Stuarts had made frequent declarations of their support for the Church of England and had pledged not to repeal the Test Act since 1702, but the impact of these was probably vitiated by the limited circulation of the declarations and the general conviction that Catholics could not be trusted in such matters and that they would indeed deliberately employ deceit. Stuart support for the religious rights of individual members of the Church of England did not amount to a conviction that they collectively constituted a viable church. It is easy to appreciate why on a number of occasions English Jacobites had pressed the political value of the conversion of James or Charles to Anglicanism. Anti-Catholicism was possibly the major ideological commitment in England, a perspective that did not preclude friendship for individual Catholics, but that encompassed political, cultural and religious fears and offered a way in which both British history and the contemporary world could be viewed. Catholics were seen collectively as constituting a sort of 'fifth column'. There was no comparison to the situation in Scotland where the post-1688 disestablishment of the Episcopalians had created a substantial disaffected group accustomed, through recent Scottish history, to the idea that the situation could be altered by armed struggle and ready to provide an ideological kernel for Jacobite activity. The Episcopalians in Scotland were more important than the less numerous

Catholics. In England many of the Catholics had adapted to their exclusion from the public world. The policy of the Widdrington family is instructive. William, 4th Lord Widdrington (1678–1743) played a prominent role in the '15 in Northumberland and was attainted as a result. His eldest son Henry was careful to demonstrate his loyalty during the '45. On 24 September the latter's wife wrote to George Bowes asking for his protection for 'my little man . . . as he never will be concerned in any thing of that kind'. By mid-October Henry had handed over nine horses and nine guns to Bowes. On 28 November Henry wrote to Bowes concerning the sudden and mysterious departure of a servant which, he feared, might excite suspicion after he had taken every step necessary to take away any distrust of him. He noted that he was 'tied both by my word and honour to neither meddle nor make directly nor indirectly', while Bowes had given his 'word and honour' for him.[28] The Nonjurors in England were less significant politically than the Scottish Episcopalians. The principal group denied a full share of civil privileges in England was Protestant as in Scotland, but the nonconformists did not look to the Stuarts. Their position had been eased since 1688 and though the Old Corps Whigs had not brought them the rights they had sought, much of the legislation against them had been circumscribed or suspended. In addition Anglican discontent was less marked than in 1689–1720, not least because the leading forum for the expression of clerical views, the Convocation of Canterbury, had been suspended in 1717. The 1740s were not years of new rights for nonconformists and there was no debate akin to that of Bangorian controversy to suggest that heterodox notions and clerics were being promoted. Whereas in late 1709 the cry of the 'Church in Danger' had been raised against the Whigs in response to Sacheverell's sermon *In Perils among False Brethren*, in 1745 it could only be directed against the Jacobites.

However, the coherence of anti-Stuart propaganda was countered in part by a number of other factors including anti-Hanoverianism and criticism of the government. These did not necessarily lead to support for the Jacobites in England, though their effect was greater in Scotland where hostility to the Union focussed political tension, but they tempered loyalty to the Hanoverian regime. The official Whig response can be measured in ministerial pronouncements, but not the Jacobite one. Cotton and Wynn who led the Tories in the Commons and Beaufort who led them in the Lords had answered for the Tories wanting a Stuart restoration and it can be presumed that they were best placed to know the views of the rank and file. The ministers in London had little doubt that they would have to depend on the regulars. Reports reaching them in late September certainly encouraged this attitude. On 18 September Charles Areskine wrote to Tweeddale from Dumfries, 'The body of the people in this country where I am, and in the Stewartry of Kirkcudbright, are extremely hearty in the common cause, but without arms, without officers, and without advice of any kind from any of the officers of the Crown as if Government for some time had fallen into an apoplectick fit'.[29] If the army was defeated or out-manoeuvred it was unclear how far the English Jacobites would rise or rather how many Jacobites there would be in practice, but it was likely that most cities would offer no more resistance than Edinburgh had done. The fall of Carlisle, whose keys were presented to Charles Edward, Lancaster, Preston, Manchester and Derby in November and December 1745 justified such fears. After Carlisle had been recaptured, the Duke of Cumberland advocated making an example of it because of its initial surrender, 'I have taken upon myself to seize both the Mayor and the Town Clerk of Carlisle, upon information, that they both met the Pretender' son, and proclaimed his father, whether they did it out of fear or disaffection seems to me to be of the same bad consequence; they both of them own the fact'.[30] As the duke pointed out, fear and disaffection had the same effect: to open the path to Charles Edward's invasion.

William Augustus, Duke of Cumberland 1721–65, painted about 1748–9 by an artist of the school of Morier

6 The Invasion of England

The march of the rebels to the south is a very fortunate event, as it will inevitably hasten their destruction.

General John Murray, 2nd Earl of Dunmore, Antwerp, 18/29 November

Marshal Wade's returning to Newcastle and the rebels continuing their march with such rapidity has struck a general terror.

Thomas Anson, 25 November

I have the pleasure to find a general good disposition in this country and a general desire and zeal to do everything that may be most for the king's service.

Duke of Cumberland, Lichfield, 28 November[1]

Like many observers, Stephen Poyntz reacted to the news of Prestonpans by assuming that Charles Edward would invade England at once:

> I have a letter from Durham with the same good account of the spirits and disposition of that country as of York; but I tremble to think what progress and havoc the rebels may make before Wade and Wentworth can face them. If the Dutch battalion from Bridlington . . . be got into Berwick and the Newcastle colliers take a right turn, I imagine the rebels, leaving a proper strength at Edinburgh may reduce Glasgow and stretch for Lancashire through Cumberland.[2]

Returning to Edinburgh from Prestonpans on 22 September, the prince certainly wanted to invade at once. He was, however, told by his officers that his army was too weak and tired to pursue Cope to Berwick.[3] Many eighteenth-century victories were not followed up because the defeated army was still a powerful force, its formation unbroken. That was not the case with Prestonpans, but Charles Edward had little over 2,000 men, some of whom he would have to leave in Edinburgh, which otherwise might be retaken by the castle garrison.

Berwick was a fortress, where extensive works had taken place as recently as 1717–21. To advance on it without having made preparations to tackle its defences would have been foolish and might have led to an ignominious retreat. Instead, the prince was persuaded to consolidate his position in Scotland and to press the French to send troops. The strength of a fortified position held with determination was amply demonstrated in Edinburgh. The Jacobites tried to starve the castle garrison into submission but failed. It is difficult to reconstruct exactly what happened in the castle initially and there is a suggestion that the divided command and counsels that were to help cause the surrender of Carlisle, both town and castle, to the prince in November were not without influence in Edinburgh. Lieutenant-General Joshua Guest, the octogenarian lieutenant-governor of the castle, who had served in Scotland during the '15, was reputed both to have rejected a Jacobite bribe to surrender the castle and to have proposed its surrender at the council of war held after Prestonpans, on the grounds that the garrison was too weak. According to the latter story, his predecessor, George Preston, another octogenarian, who had, as a captain in the Dutch army, accompanied William III in 1688, and had been in command at Edinburgh during the '15, blocked Guest's proposal. During the '45 Preston, who had remained as a volunteer, helped to keep the guards alert by regular inspections, wheeled round in an armchair. Preston replied to the Jacobite blockade by threatening to use his cannon to wreak destruction in Edinburgh. Charles Edward threatened reprisals, but the cannon opened fire and the prince felt obliged to raise the blockade.

Unable to subdue Edinburgh Castle, Charles Edward had less success than he had anticipated in raising the men and money necessary for the planned invasion of England. Encouragement was derived from signs of French support. Between 9 and 19 October four ships from France with artillery and stores reached Montrose and Stonehaven, illustrating an important defect in British sea power: it was not comprehensive or fast-moving enough to prevent the passage of individual ships that could be crucial for communications and supplies. As the Jacobite forces gradually swelled in size, it became necessary to confront the problem of whether England would be invaded and what, if anything, would be done before winter. As the Jacobite army was not a force with more than a few horsemen, unlike all regular armies and many continental irregular forces, they would not have to wait until the grass started growing again in the spring to provide the horses with forage, in order to begin operations in 1746. However, December–March were commonly poor campaigning months anyway, and the routes into northern England might well be blocked by snow then. It would be a formidable task to dig trenches which would probably fill with water and rivers might be difficult to ford. Therefore, having spent October in Edinburgh, it was necessary to decide where to act the following month. The decision was taken at Holyrood on 30 October at a meeting of the permanent cabinet or Grand Council set up by Charles Edward after Prestonpans. The meeting was an acrimonious one and indeed divided counsels were to characterize Jacobite military operations during the invasion of England. In contrast, the divergent political, diplomatic and military views that had embodied governmental policy during the summer of 1745 were replaced by a coherent

The order book of the Stewarts of Appin Regiment, containing orders from 11 October 1745 to 18 January 1746

Receipt for £100 lent by Lady Cunyngham to Prince Charles Edward at Holyrood and united military response, symbolized by the return of the Duke of Cumberland from Flanders and his appointment to command the army that had been built up in the Midlands. This unity of military purpose was Cumberland's most important contribution to the suppression of the '45 and it contrasted with the political disunity in London in early 1746 which culminated in George II's unsuccessful attempt to replace the Pelhams (Henry Pelham and his brother Newcastle) by Granville and Bath, who he believed would be more sympathetic to his views, especially in foreign policy. Clear agreement over objectives, a united command and a responsive command structure were crucial to those facing superior forces and the Jacobites were to suffer from their lack of them.

On 30 October Charles Edward argued that the momentum of the rebellion, threatened as it was by desertion among Highlanders who were no longer carried along by the euphoria of continual success, excitement and prospects, depended on a new victory. This would further secure Scotland and, he claimed, encourage French intervention. In contrast, Lord George Murray and the clan chieftains pressed for a retreat to the Highlands. They claimed that their small army had little prospect of defeating the larger royal forces and they were sceptical about the amount of assistance France would provide. Instead they pressed for a determined attempt to defeat the pro-Hanoverian clans and to overawe those that had hitherto refused to commit themselves. This would secure the Highlands, discourage desertion and permit the settling of old scores. The idea was not without value. Indeed on 26 September Poyntz had written to Weston:

> If the rebels should march southward, and the castle of Edinburgh holds out, a small force landed in the Forth might I should think recover the town, where the government has many friends. An old officer of Wade's regiment tells me that if the small garrisons of Inverness, Fort Augustus and Fort William were ordered immediately to lay waste the cottages and possessions of the Highlanders who are marched southward, they would meet with no opposition, and that they will certainly occasion a desertion from the Pretender's army.[4]

It did not require service in the '45 to advocate a harsh approach to the Highlanders. A basis for the revival of pro-governmental activity in the Highlands was provided by the return of John Campbell, 4th Earl of Loudoun. He had fled to England after Prestonpans, but then sailed north on a warship with arms and funds, arriving at Inverness on 14 October. He took over the men Lord President Duncan Forbes had been raising in the area and within six weeks had a force of over 2,000, which in early December relieved Fort Augustus. Loudoun's activity was but part of the revival of governmental fortunes that occurred in October, while the Jacobites remained in Edinburgh. To a considerable extent the Jacobites then lost the initiative, and neither of their hoped for allies, the French or the English Jacobites, took it. Murray and the clan leaders were sceptical about the prospect of support from the English Jacobites. As was to be shown during the invasion, this was a reasonable doubt, but it was less pertinent as a criticism of what was, in fact, proposed; an advance on Newcastle and an attack on Wade. For Charles Edward, though not for the Scots, many of whom hoped for the reversal of the Union, the conquest of England was the logical sequence to that of Scotland, but there was also the sense that some action was necessary in order to regain the initiative.

Charles Edward won the debate over invading England, though by only one vote. This narrowest of margins was scarcely a good omen for subsequent agreement during the course of the invasion. The prince was, however, unsuccessful when he pressed for an advance on Newcastle. He claimed that Wade's army, which had arrived there from Doncaster on the 29th, would be exhausted by the march, but that, if it was not defeated, it would threaten the Jacobite position in Scotland. Murray argued that by marching south from Edinburgh and entering north-west England (Carlisle is south of Edinburgh not, as is sometimes imagined, south-west of it) the Jacobites would attack a more vulnerable target: Carlisle rather than Newcastle. The combination of Newcastle's defences and Wade's army would present a formidable challenge, while one of the routes to the town, that along the coast which would be the one least affected by poor weather, was defended by Berwick, one of the best-fortified towns in England, and one whose population included many Dissenters. On 17 September Berwick had a garrison of 300 and fifteen companies of 50 men, formed by John Watson, the Mayor, under royal commission. By 23 September there were another 700 Dutch and 500 dragoons in the town, as well as Cope. On 25 October Edward Weston reported, 'Wade is to be at Newcastle next Tuesday. Lord Albemarle is already landed there, so there will be an army of 12 or 13,000, the rebels by our best accounts not exceeding 7 or 8,000'. A 'Return of the Rebels Army', dated Edinburgh 29 October gave the Jacobite force as 7,287 infantry and 300 cavalry.[5] If an attack on Newcastle was unsuccessful, the retreating Jacobites would be vulnerable. Carlisle, in contrast, though walled, lacked a force of regular troops, and if Wade marched to its assistance he would have to face inhospitable terrain and would be exposed to Jacobite attack. Murray also claimed that an invasion of north-west England would give the French an opportunity to act, and that it would keep the government uncertain as to the Jacobites intended final destination: London or Wales.

The decision can be assessed in a number of ways. It has been argued that by avoiding an engagement with Wade, the Jacobites lost the chance of a victory that would have led their English supporters to rise.[6] Conversely, it might be pointed out that if London is seen as the prize and reaching it with as large a force as possible an important military objective, then the Jacobites did manage, thanks to the Pennines and Wade's slowness, to avoid Wade's army both on the march south and during the retreat. Furthermore, from Murray's point of view, if by invading through Carlisle the response of the English Jacobites and the French were tested, and found wanting, it would be without engaging the prince's forces in a battle on unfavourable terms. Wade's army, reinforced by British and Dutch troops that had come to Newcastle by sea, was far larger than that of the Jacobites, and thus the military challenge was greater than that posed by Cope at the Corrieyairack and at Prestonpans. According to an Edinburgh item in the *Newcastle Courant* of 21 September, 'The young Chevalier much effects the example of Charles the 12th of Sweden'. That young monarch (1697–1718), born in 1682, made his military reputation during the Great Northern War (1700–21) through bold attacks on superior Russian forces, which brought him victory at Narva (1700) and defeat at Poltava (1709). Charles

An authentic portrait of Prince Charles Edward during his time in Scotland. Engraved by Sir Robert Strange during the prince's stay at Holyrood

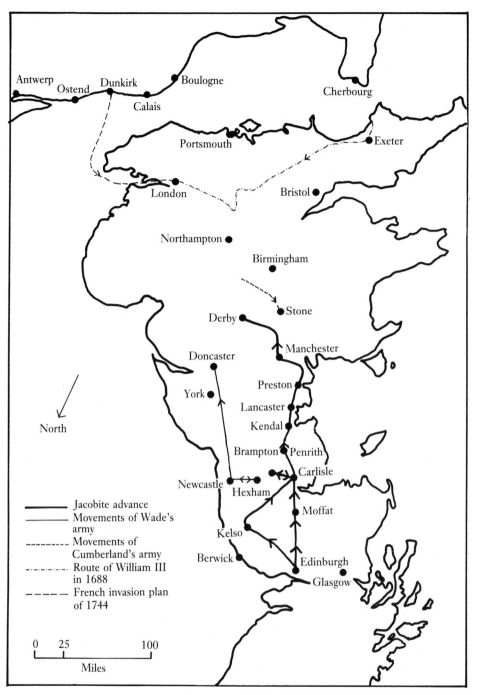

The invasion of England

was supported by trained and well-disciplined troops, though, like Charles Edward, he knew that it would be difficult to replace his casualties. It is not altogether fruitless to speculate as to what would have happened if the prince had advanced on Newcastle. Contemporaries considering the '45, including most crucially generals, had to probe options. Wade, born in 1673, had little vigour and his cautious generalship the previous year in the Austrian Netherlands, his first experience of commanding an army in the field, had brought no success. Henry Pelham observed in August 1744, 'The poor old man does the best he can', but the Dutch politican Bentinck accused him that October of blocking all proposals and claimed that he was so old and infirm that he required two days to recover from the fatigue of four hours on horseback.

Mobility was to be crucial in the '45 and it was already seen as important prior to Prestonpans. Writing on 10 September 1745, Pelham had regarded the decisive problem as one of forcing the Jacobites to an engagement:

> I heartily wish the troops were arrived both Dutch and English, for though I look upon these Highland rebels as a sort of rabble, yet if there is no force to oppose 'em, they may come in time to be considerable. We have scarce any regular troops in the country, and between you and I, I don't find that zeal to venture purses and lives that I formerly remember. I don't care to look out for the reasons. I suppose you have heard the rebels have passed Sir John Cope . . . They pay for everything they want, but are many of them but indifferently armed; so that if a regiment or two with good officers at their head could but come at 'em, this affair would soon end in smoke.[7]

Prestonpans had shown that tactical skills could overcome the advantages of a good defensive position and the Highland charge could break the resistance of an army of equal strength, but, if Wade chose to fight at Newcastle, he would have the advantage of a defended site. However, if his men were placed in a defended position outside the walls or blocking the Jacobite advance on Tyneside, then it is possible that a bold and determined attack on part of the position could have led to Wade's collapse, especially if his response was unimaginative or slow.

On 31 October, the day on which Lord Hartington noted the London report that the prince had fled to Dunkirk and that 'letters from the North represent the Rebels not so strong as was imagined and . . . in great confusion', the Jacobite council decided to attack Carlisle. This was to be covered by a feint to Kelso, suggesting that the army intended to march to Newcastle via Wooler, while the rest of the force marched via Moffat. On 5 November Hartington wrote from London 'it is the general opinion here that the Rebels will retire as soon as Marshal Wade gets into Scotland'. In fact, the Jacobite army, about 5,500 strong, crossed into England, fording the Esk, on 8 November. The march to the Esk had not been as successful as anticipated. Though public money and horses were collected, there was no rising of Lowland support, while desertion from the army had been considerable. On the 9th the Jacobites reached Carlisle, whose inadequate defences reflected the limited efforts expended on English fortifications over the previous half-century and the absence of the clear command structures that would have existed in a more militarized society. Lieutenant-Colonel James Durand, who commanded the castle in the absence of the governor, quarrelled with the town officials over defensive preparations, while confusion over the operation of the militia laws exacerbated the situation. Some 580 citizens of Carlisle volunteered for service, submitting a loyal address to George II which in the words of Thomas Pattinson, the deputy mayor, informed him, 'we are not only ready to serve cheerfully our most gracious sovereign, but we do more, we sincerely love him'. They were formed into companies and supplied with guns from the castle storekeeper. About 210 men from the local militia, which had been summoned by Lonsdale on 9 September, entered Carlisle in early October, mostly armed with old and inadequate guns, supplementing the castle garrison of 83 invalids and 38 of Cope's men who had fled after Prestonpans, a battle that affected morale in the town. The defences of both the castle and the city were in a weak state. In contrast to recent fortifications, the walls were not covered by a system of outworks designed to keep the trenches and artillery of besiegers at a distance. Ten guns were obtained from Whitehaven but there was a shortage of trained gunners. Durand pressed for reinforcements from Ireland, but without success, though the rest of the county militia arrived in late October, only to be charged high prices for accommodation and supplies. Had the town been well-defended it might have been bypassed, as in 1715, for the Jacobites lacked sufficient numbers to blockade it effectively, adequate artillery to bombard it and experience in siegecraft.[8]

   It was clear that Carlisle could only be saved by Wade, who indeed marched to its relief. Informed of Wade's intentions, Charles Edward left Carlisle on the 11th, where operations had begun the previous day to march on Brampton where he had decided to give battle. Wade's delay led the Jacobites to return to Carlisle on the 13th, but unseasonal snow made the siege unpleasant. However, their return from Brampton and the news that Wade would not arrive soon demoralized Carlisle's defenders. The Jacobite trenches came steadily nearer. Fears of a storming led the militia, which was affected by desertion, and the citizens to urge Durand to surrender on the 14th. The besiegers insisted that they would not accept the surrender of the town, without that of the castle, whither Durand had retired in order to continue the resistance, and on 15 November a Council of War, affected by the weakness of the castle, local demoralization, the unwillingness of the militia to fight and the absence of Wade, agreed to capitulate. Wade did not set out from Newcastle until the following day. His advance was disastrous. The army, already affected by dysentry, low morale and fear of the Highlanders, were now faced by snow, hard ground on which they could not pitch their tents, bad roads and inadequate rations. They reached Hexham on the 17th where news arrived that Carlisle had fallen. On the 18th an officer wrote from Hexham 'arrived here last night after a very fatiguing march the weather and roads being so bad that we were twelve hours each day on the march with the army. We have had all the assistance we could possibly have from the gentlemen of this neighbourhood and there is plenty of provisions for the men'. Major-General John Huske, who had served in the '15, added in a postscript that 'as the castle of Carlisle has submitted it's thought our army can not subsist to go on any farther' and that he expected to return to Newcastle. On the 19th Brigadier-General James

Cholmondeley MP, the colonel of the 34th Foot wrote to his brother the Earl about the march:[9]

> ... miserable roads, terrible frost and snow. We did not get to our grounds till near 8 and as my quarters were five miles off I did not get there till 11, almost starved to death with cold and hunger, but revived by a pipe and a little good wine. Next morning we found some of the poor fellows frozen to death for they could get nothing to eat after marching 13 hours. The next day we marched to this place [Hexham]. Roads and weather the same. Got to camp about eight. Nothing for the men . . . it strikes me to the heart to see the distress of the poor fellows borne without murmuring. I do everything in my power to assist them, every morning I fill my pockets with sixpences which I give to the men and keep an open table for the subs: this is some relief although but a mite considering our numbers. Our men fall sick apace.[9]

Lack of provisions and problems with transportation led the Council of War that met on the 19th to unanimously decide to retreat to Newcastle, which was reached on the 22nd. By then the Jacobites were in Kendal.

On 18 November the Jacobite Council met to consider what to do now that Carlisle had fallen. Lord George Murray opposed any further advance into England, pointing to the small size of the army, which would be diminished by the garrison left in Carlisle, and to the absence of any English rising or French landing. However, claims by Charles Edward that he had letters from English supporters promising to join him at Preston, the revelation by the French agent, the Marquis d'Eguilles, that he was supposed to report on Jacobite strength in Scotland and England and the argument that the English Jacobites would not rise without an invasion prevailed. The Jacobite advance guard reached Penrith that afternoon, and successfully demanded hay and oats from all but one of the local great houses. Exaggerating the strength of their army, they demanded billets for 8,000 men. From the outset the ministers in London found it difficult to obtain accurate information about Jacobite moves. On 9 November Pelham wrote to Lord Hartington reporting that:

> Wade had stopt his march, on account of the rumour that the Rebels had marched to Kelso, some said to Carlisle and Lancashire, others to meet the Marshal and give him battle. Which to believe we don't know, for we have had different reports every day, yesterday an express from Handasyde said they were actually at Wooler on this side the Tweed, and today we have had that partly contradicted by an express from Lord Lonsdale, whose intelligence says a great party of them were at Moffat on their way to Carlisle, on the 5th the same day Mr Handasyde said they were at Wooler and just now an express is arrived from General Handasyde and Mr Wade with intelligence that the young Pretender at the head of 4,000 men was marching for Jedburgh . . . and that their artillery was going for Dumfries. What all this means no one here can tell, whether they are determined at all events to push on their way to England, or whether this is a feint to amuse and disconcert our army is to me doubtful, but, be it as it will, the Marshal has determined to stay at Newcastle, until he is more certainly informed which way they bend, to get his army together, and then I presume follow them wherever they go. Ligonier is making all the haste he can to put his troops in motion, but I fear it will be some time before he can get all the necessarys for so long a march.

In fact there was no advance through Wooler or move of the artillery to Dumfries.

The government was unclear which way the prince would advance. If he marched south through Lancashire he would eventually have to face the army under Sir John Ligonier intended to block such a move, but if the Jacobites crossed the Pennines into Yorkshire, the situation would apparently be far less under control, as Wade could be bypassed and Ligonier avoided. However, the prince both pressed south and moved with a speed that thwarted governmental plans to have their troops in southern Lancashire first. Henry Pelham informed the Duke of Devonshire on 19 November that Ligonier's force would not be able to rendezvous at Warrington until the first week in December. The Duke of Richmond, who had been appointed to command the cavalry in Ligonier's army, wrote from Coventry on 21 November, 'they can and certainly will gett to the Mercy [Mersey] before us'. The local resistance was proving as weak as that at Carlisle had been. The Lancashire militia was disbanded on the 22nd. If Charles Edward received few recruits, a failure ministerial supporters were well aware of, he also met no real obstacle. When the Jacobite advance guard reached Lancaster on 24 November the magistrates wisely abandoned their plan to defend the castle.[10]

The ministry received many conflicting rumours of Jacobite intentions, including advances on North Wales, Shrewsbury and the West Riding of Yorkshire. It was reported, for example, that when Lockhart of Carnwath was told at Penrith that Wade had 15,000 men and Ligonier 10,000, he replied 'they would march with all speed into Wales where they were sure of 4,000 men ready to join them'. Fearing that the Jacobites would reach Durham on the evening of 19 November, Thomas Vane persuaded his brother not to risk his life among such a 'merciless crew'. The extent of the panic in the West Riding can be gauged from Jessop's diary. On 23 November he recorded the most common of the Jacobite atrocity stories then circulating and added an account of the feeling in Leeds and Wakefield:

> They say that the rebels in Carlisle took the women and children and bound them hand and foot and chained them together and set them in the forefront of the castle so that they could not shoot at them, but they would kill their wives and children first and so took the castle . . . They are in a terrible fright at both places. There was nothing to do at Wakefield Market yesterday, but the great men were busy talking together, and were sending their best effects away and an abundance of people are for leaving the town.

Two days later he noted that it was thought that the Jacobites would enter Leeds that day, on 27 November he wrote 'they are in a terrible consternation in Huddersfield, Holmfirth . . . and all places hereabouts and are securing their best effects . . . they say there is a foreign invasion and that General Ligonier is recalled from towards Manchester'. The Duke of Newcastle's response to the Jacobite arrival in Lancaster was to fear their advance via Warrington to Lichfield 'to surprise the army there before they are all assembled'.[11]

Wade did not march south from Newcastle until 26 November, and then only slowly. While Cumberland was taking command of Ligonier's army in the west Midlands (he reached Lichfield on the 28th), there was no prospect of serious resistance to the Jacobite advance further north. The Earl of Cholmondeley, writing on 17 November that raising it would be 'impracticable as the rolls are lost and no arms to be found', felt unable to rely on the Chester militia. Instead

Locket containing likeness of Prince Charles Edward,
which according to tradition was given to a Miss Pedder
at a ball given at Preston on 27 November 1745

he raised a regiment under a commission issued by the government in October. However, on 23 November he wrote to Ligonier 'some of the men only having had their firelocks nine days. Therefore all depends on the regiments with you'. He was pessimistic about his chances of holding Chester and discovered that many of the cannon were defective and the ordnance stores inadequate.[12] On 20 November the Jacobites entered Preston and two days later their cavalry reached Manchester. A government agent forwarded a report from Stockport on 30 November on Jacobite conduct:

> They behave hitherto ('tis said) civilly and have all along since they came from Carlisle paid their quarters. I hear of no complaints of misbehaviour where they are; on the contrary the people (the mob I mean mostly) are so fond to see them, that upwards of 100 are said to have taken on with them ... they give out that 5,000 are in the western skirts of Yorkshire.

Local government and the local agents of the state were in disarray, 'our magistrates are withdrawn and the excise officers are fled'. Cholmondeley commented on the response to the Jacobite advance to Cumberland on 2 December:

> ... even small bodies of them have entered large towns, and collected the King's duties for their use; such is the panic of the common people, which they catch from others of higher rank; having observed that, ever since they left Scotland, that in the several counties they have passed through those who have called themselves the King's friends, have been the first to fly, and have by that means spread terror and apprehension in all parts.

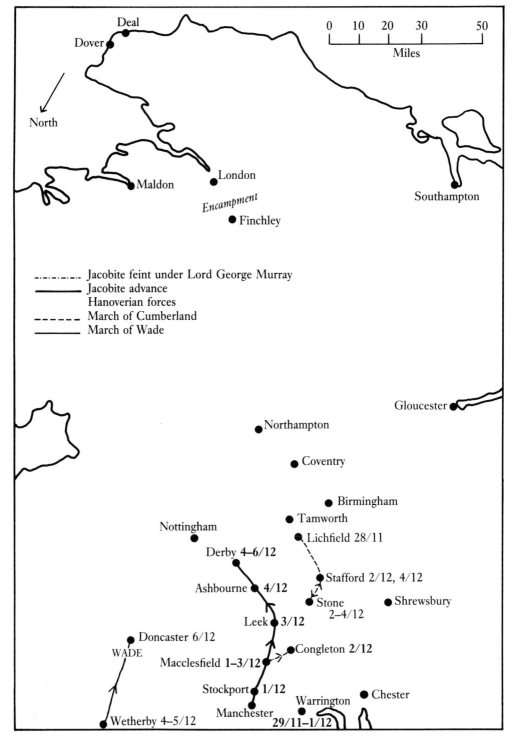

Deal

Dover

North

0 10 20 30 50
Miles

London

Maldon

Encampment

● Finchley

Southampton

.._.._.._... Jacobite feint under Lord George Murray
_____ Jacobite advance
Hanoverian forces
_ _ _ _ _ March of Cumberland
_____ March of Wade

Gloucester

●Northampton

● Coventry

● Birmingham

● Tamworth

● Lichfield 28/11

Nottingham
●

Derby **4–6/12**

●Stafford 2/12, 4/12

Ashbourne ● **4/12**

● Shrewsbury

● Stone
2–4/12

Leek ● **3/12**

Doncaster 6/12

WADE

Congleton **2/12**

Macclesfield **1–3/12**

Stockport ● **1/12**

● Chester

Warrington

Manchester
29/11–1/12

Wetherby **4–5/12**

Cumberland outmanoeuvred: the threat to London

He added of Lancashire a month later, 'long before the rebels entered that county I found that despair, fear and confusion had turned the minds of everyone so when the danger came nearer to them, not a justice was to be found or gentlemen of estate to do any one act for the safety or protection of it' and that the means of defence were worse than useless because the arms found in the county were used to arm the Jacobites. Lancashire had, not surprisingly, proved better recruiting country for the Jacobites than Dumbria, but the number of recruits was still disappointing. In addition, the speed of the Jacobite advance was simply taking them nearer Cumberland's army which, as Cumberland advanced to cover both Chester and Derby, they would either have to fight or outmanoeuvre. As a result, Richmond was relatively confident of the strategic situation on 30 November and chiefly fearful that the Jacobites would retreat into the Highlands. Cumberland and Ligonier were also optimistic.[13] Though there was no chance of a junction between the armies of Wade and Cumberland, the latter seemed strong enough to defeat the prince.

On the same day a Jacobite council at Manchester, impressed with the prince's news that the French would invade on 9 December, decided to march on for London. Convinced that the destruction of the roads ordered by the Duke of Devonshire, the Lord Lieutenant of Derbyshire, would block any advance through that county, a view Lord Chancellor Hardwicke did not share, Cumberland was impressed by deliberately circulated reports that the Jacobites intended to advance on Chester and north Wales. Attempts to block the Jacobite route to the south by destroying bridges failed. On 2 December a Jacobite detachment feinted towards Cumberland's army, which was accordingly drawn up for battle at Stone. The duke wrote that day to the Duke of Newcastle from Stafford, 'I went first to Stone to pitch on a field of battle, where there is a very good one, and then came back to Stafford to my quarters, dinner was but just over when we had news that the Rebels were advancing towards us and that they were within nine miles to Newcastle under Lyme . . . on this intelligence I have sent orders for the Infantry to retire directly to Stone'. The same day Sir Everard Fawkener, Cumberland's secretary, wrote to Newcastle:

> . . . if by staying at Lichfield His Royal Highness had resolved to provide against their reaching Derby, he must have left them at liberty to have got into Wales without any difficulty or opposition which it is hoped they cannot now do . . . our . . . intelligence, it is confounded by the multiplicity of it . . . If the motion westward was a feint, then indeed we shall by our advancing be less in reach of keeping them out of Derbyshire. What is most apt to perplex is, that often people who give intelligence, mistake a small part for the body.

This left the road to Derby clear. Wade was still far to the north: at Boroughbridge on the 3rd. Two days later he informed Fawkener from Wetherby that Cumberland 'may depend on my utmost diligence to come up as soon as possible towards him, but His Royal Highness very well knows, the Rebels can greatly out march us'. The Derbyshire Blues, the regiment raised by the Duke of Devonshire, retreated towards Nottingham on the 3rd, the Duke complaining of the Jacobites, 'I have no notion of an army being able to march at the rate these fellows have come'; while there was increasing concern in London. Ryder noted 'people in great pain for the City . . . Papists suspected of an intended rising as soon as the rebels are near London . . . preparations are making at Dunkirk for an embarkation to assist the rebels'. A discontented office-holder, commenting on panic in London and the cravenness in Yorkshire, wrote that the troubles would continue until Charles Edward was killed or captured and that 'the people of England if one may judge of them by the northern counties have not virtue or spirit enough to defend themselves against a bold invader so effectually has the late grand corruptor fitted us for slavery and arbitrary power' an analysis that exaggerated the extent of Whig zeal in pre-Walpolean England. Newcastle, fearing that Cumberland's dispositions were overly dominated by a supposed threat to north Wales, was convinced that the Jacobites were determined to march on London, possibly encouraged by a French invasion. He urged Richmond not to think this impossible or improbable, adding advice from the Earl of Derby that Charles Edward could 'very easily give you the slip'. Newcastle more phlegmatically noted late on the 5th 'The Duke of Devonshire says the rebels would very probably be last night at Nottingham', while the former MP Ralph Jenison wrote the same day that the Jacobites had slipped by Cumberland and were then at Nottingham.[14]

On the afternoon of the 4th the Jacobites had in fact entered Derby. They received a relatively favourable reception, but only gained three recruits. Swarkeston bridge, controlling the main road to London, was also captured, Cumberland's orders to destroy it arriving too late. Cumberland had been outmanoeuvred by the Jacobite feint on the 2nd. Richmond wrote to Newcastle painting a gloomy picture of Cumberland's ability to defeat or engage the Jacobites:

> . . . we are in a strange irregular way, and if the rebels had attacked us at Stone on Monday night [2nd], as we thought they would, we had been undone, and Ligonier said so himself. And it must be so, if they ever attack us in the night, if we are not encamped; and at Stone it was impossible for want of straw. It is necessary to hurry on our troops else they'll be in London before us, and yet these dreadful fatiguing marches, will make them incapable of fighting.

On 3 December Cumberland wrote from Stone to the Duke of Devonshire:

> . . . after the most fatiguing twenty-four hours for troops that can be imagined we are forced to retire back to Stafford and from thence I believe for Derbyshire. This is all occasioned by a countermarch of the rebels to Leake and as this night for Cheadle so that I fear they may be able to get there before me, no pains or trouble shall be spared but the weather is such that should we not have a halt this night the troops would be quite jaded . . . Should we come your way I hope that we shall find meat and bread for the soldiers.

The following day Cumberland wrote to Newcastle from Stafford:

> what I had some fear of has happened, for on my assembling all the troops on Tuesday last at Stone . . . where we all joined about four in the morning, with a view either to give the Rebels battle, or push on, to Newcastle [-under-Lyme] with our whole force should the Rebels have continued their route towards Wales, which seemed to be their point by all their movements. In this state the troops remained till nigh eleven of the clock in the morning, when such advices came as seemed to prove their going to Wales, and our Vanguard was already in

Ring given by Prince Charles Edward to Alderman Samuel Heathcoate of Derby, the leading local Jacobite. He was host at his home, 3 Full Street, to Lord George Murray, 4–6 December 1745

motion for Newcastle, which was but six miles further and where everything was prepared for the troops, but contrary and certain advices came that they had turned short and were gone for Leek and Ashburn which is the direct road to Derby. Had the troops been as able as they seem to be willing, I should have marched directly for Derby, but troops that had scarcely halted six hours these seven days, had been without victuals for twenty-four hours, and had been exposed to one of the coldest nights I have ever felt without any shelter, for the country produced not straw sufficient for two battalions; were not able to march without a halt and provisions, so we immediately came to a resolution of intercepting them at Northampton . . . . By this I flatter myself we cannot fail of intercepting them. However, I should humbly be of the opinion, that if without alarming the City, the Infantry that is about London could be assembled on Finchley Common, it would prevent any little part of them who might give me the slip, (for I am persuaded the greater part cannot) from giving any alarm there.[15]

Fatigue was important. The Jacobite army had been tired by its long march, but so had the royal troops, most of whom had also faced the disruptions and unpleasantness of a sea journey. Cumberland's men had been further tired by their marches in the west Midlands, as their larger army moved in response to what appeared to be possible Jacobite plans. On 2 December the duke excused the dispersion of his force, 'had I not cantooned half the battalions would have been in the Hospital'. Thus not only had both Cumberland and Wade been outmanoeuvred; their armies had also been exhausted. The need for new footwear bulked large in the campaign. On 18 September Charles Edward had ordered 6,000 pairs of shoes from the city authorities in Edinburgh. Several thousand fresh pairs were obtained in Preston and 6,000 were demanded in

Glasgow on the prince's retreat. By 4 December the shoes of Cumberland's men were in a terrible condition. He pressed George II successfully for fresh shoes and stockings for his men. Some were sent from Chester, although Cholmondeley was delayed by his fears that Jacobite parties would seize supplies. Margeret Bowes, aunt of George Bowes MP, expressed on 3 December her fear that marching in winter would cause problems for the royal army. Between 30 May and 3 July 1746 Robert Finlay of Glasgow supplied 3,058 pairs of shoes to Cumberland's army.[16] Soldiers marched on their feet, carrying their weapons and some of their supplies, a fatiguing business in which footwear and morale were crucial. Though, once he had been outmanoeuvred, Cumberland decided to intercept the Jacobite army at Northampton on what he presumed would be their march to London it is by no means clear that he could have done so and he might have exposed his army, strung out on the march, to attack. It would have been a formidable task to attack London. On 28 November Ligonier had tried to stiffen the morale of the pessimistic Cholmondeley by stressing the problems of attacking fortifications:

> ... suppose the rebels were hardy or foolish enough to think of attacking Chester; for God's sake how can they take it, is it possible for them to fly over the walls, and your Lordship knows that three pounders neither can make a breach in a thousand years, or make a garrison uneasy behind their walls, who on the contrary can slaughter everything that approaches from behind their sand bags, nor can the miserable three-pounders they have hardly hurt the tops of the houses.

However, the fate of Carlisle and Edinburgh, and Cholmondeley's comments on the state of Chester's defences suggests that the task was not impossible. The situation for the government was bleak. Cumberland hoped to be able to fight at Northampton, 'as it is an open country', but was more realistic when he assured Wade that he would be able to get to Finchley 'with the cavalry'. On the 4th Fawkener asked the JPs of Staffordshire and Warwickshire to assemble as many horses as possible at Lichfield the next day, two shillings being offered for each horse that could carry an infantry soldier. By this means 200 horses were collected in and around Wolverhampton. Henry Fox wrote to his brother from London that the Jacobites could 'march rapidly by Loughborough, Leicester etc. to get hither a day or two before the Duke could'. It was also reported that they might march via Cambridgeshire in order to secure a port on the Suffolk coast. The Earl of Halifax was told on the 5th that Jacobite cavalry was within five miles of Loughborough. Edward Coke MP wrote from London on the 10th that 'the consternation upon the Rebels slipping the Duke was here very great'. William Hewitt had earlier suggested to the Duke of Devonshire that little could 'be hoped for from the common people about London' who, he argued, would rather 'be disposed to join in plundering than defending the property of other people'.[17] The ministry was forced to try to assemble a new army at Finchley north of London, but this force of about 4,000 was far smaller than Cumberland's army, which contained most of the good units. Among those ordered to Finchley were some of the 43rd Highlanders or Black Watch, a unit whose reliability was questionable. Signs of pro-Hanoverian enthusiasm in London were of limited military value. The London weavers offered 1,000 men but the

Armada chest said to have been used by Prince Charles Edward during his stay at Exeter House, Derby. He is alleged to have kept the specie resulting from his forced loan and the seizure of the Derby Post Office here

experience of the campaign hitherto did not encourage the use of largely untrained volunteers and Cumberland was unimpressed by Bedford's regiment. The ministry suffered from having one centre of power. When the French and Bavarians had attacked the Habsburgs in 1741 Maria Theresa had been able to retire from Vienna to Pressburg (Bratislava), the capital of her kingdom of Hungary, while her enemies had had to choose whether to advance on Vienna, or Prague, the capital of the kingdom of Bohemia. They chose and took Prague, but Maria Theresa was able to continue fighting. During the War of the Spanish Succession (1701–14) Philip V had lost Madrid to the British-supported claimant 'Charles III', but he was able to fight on, supported by the troops and the proximity of his grandfather, Louis XIV. In Britain, however, there was little doubt that if George II lost London his regime would collapse. Some of his supporters would probably wish to fight on, especially in Ireland where there were both troops and concern about the maintenance of the Protestant ascendancy, and it is difficult to see Cumberland accepting Jacobite success without a battle, though Wade would probably have retreated to a fortress and negotiated. However, without London the logistical and financial infrastructure of the military establishment would have collapsed. Pay and supplies would become a problem for Cumberland, doubtless encouraging desertion among his soldiers and helping to dictate his strategy. It is probable that there would have been a measure of support from the English Jacobites once London had fallen, though, more significantly, it is difficult to imagine that it would not have affected the fleet, disrupting its supplies and influencing the determination of some officers. This might have helped the French, allowing them to send troops.

It was clear that government finances would have been hit by a march on London. On 1 October Weston had observed, 'The Association of the Merchants has saved the Bank for a time, but I doubt the first ill news will raise the same spirit again, which fomented by all the arts of the Popish party, may at once overset our bark in this present storm'. On 8 November Henry Pelham turned to this theme:

> ... we are plagued every day with new and different reports as to the progress of the rebels, they seem to act with some judgement, and great resolution, but as I am satisfied that the disaffection in this part of the kingdom is greatly decreased, and as we have now a great army in England, I can't doubt of our putting an end to this insolent and wicked attempt in time. We don't hear of any great embarkations, but our enemies are continually pouring in arms, officers, engineers and money, this gives spirit to the Pretender's friends, and enables them to keep together longer than they could otherways have done. Our great misfortune is the effect this has upon our credit, for though the stocks do not fall much, yet what ready money there is in the kingdom is pretty much hoarded up, and of consequence the raising our supplies difficult. A brush from Marshal Wade may possibly give new life.

Eighteen days later, Weston wrote 'we can't afford another *echec*'. It was with the experience of 1745 in mind that a memorandum 'Measures proposed to be taken with regard to the money in the Bank, in case of a French invasion' was drawn up in 1756 when invasion was threatened. The anonymous writer expressed the fear that if France invaded or was believed likely to invade there would be a run on the Bank of England and therefore a lack of ready money to pay the army and navy and proposed 'for the public safety to secure, before the alarm happens, a very large sum of money in some safe place, out of the Bank, where it may be in the power of His Majesty to dispose of . . . a million or more'. In December 1745 the Jacobite retreat helped government finances, Pelham writing on 20 December, 'a few days ago credit was sunk so low that I doubted whether we should be able to raise money enough to carry on the common business of this country'. Had the Jacobites advanced the situation would presumably have been worse.[18]

However, at the Jacobite council on 5 December the decision was taken to retreat. Lord George Murray argued that even if Cumberland did not catch up and the army at Finchley, whose strength he greatly exaggerated, was defeated the Jacobites would be defeated by the London militia; an unlikely eventuality. In the absence of English or French support, he pressed for return, despite Charles Edward's argument that a bold advance would undermine the regime. Under pressure, the prince was forced to admit that he had no promises of support from the English Jacobites, a consequence of the failure of particular attempts to communicate with them, the unexpected speed of the Jacobite advance and their understandable reluctance to commit themselves until success appeared likely. The unsanctioned nature of his enterprise and the speed of his advance explained why the prince was obliged to admit that he had no idea of when the French would invade, an unfortunate failure as the French had undertaken by the Treaty of Fontainebleau to support the Jacobite cause, and were in fact preparing an invasion and the ministry in London was concerned about it. The strategic situation appeared even more bleak when the council was informed by the English spy Dudley Bradstreet that another army of 9,000 blocked the way at Northampton, a deliberately misleading report. The weakness of Jacobite espionage and the difficulty of obtaining accurate intelli-

Exeter House, where the fateful decision was taken to turn back to Scotland. This view shows the rebuilt east front (c.1710) prior to its demolition

gence in the circumstances of the period, when communications were poor, rumour rife and agents untrustworthy, helped to undermine the prince's position at Derby, just as it had helped him earlier as he had been able to propagate encouraging falsehoods about English and French support.

The prince failed to win the support of the council and the decision was taken to retreat the following day, 'Black Friday'. The council meeting, rather than Culloden, really signalled the end of the '45 and the failure of Jacobitism. Clearly to march on would have posed problems and these seemed more immediate at Derby, than they had done at Carlisle, Preston and Manchester, when it had been possible to hope for English and French assistance. However, Lord George Murray and the other members of the council failed to consider adequately the problems facing any retreat, both to the Scottish frontier and subsequently. To retreat in the face of a hostile force was a difficult undertaking and it would be made doubly so by the threat from two royal armies. Cumberland's forces might be exhausted but they included cavalry and it only required a portion of his army to keep up with the Jacobites in order to disrupt their march. Wade's slowness might not make him appear a danger, but from Yorkshire he could threaten the Jacobite retreat through Lancashire, again if not by his entire force, by a more rapidly-moving portion of them. Far from their Scottish homes, the Jacobites were unlikely to desert, unlike the royal armies if they had been obliged to retreat. Nevertheless, compared to their advance, they would find supplies harder to obtain on their retreat, sympathizers among the local population less active and opponents more vigorous, and the weather would probably be harsher. Once the Jacobites had reached Scotland, desertion would be more of a problem and it was difficult to imagine that France would send assistance more readily or more clansmen rise than if they had been successful in England. Those who hoped to melt away into the hills, as after earlier risings, had not reckoned on the harshness and determination that was to characterize Cumberland's 'pacification' of the Highlands in desolation, blood and misery after Culloden.

On balance, it would have been wiser to press on. Ministers in London were confident that Charles Edward would be defeated in battle, but it was unclear whether he could be forced to fight. On 19 November Henry Pelham suggested to the Duke of Devonshire that if Wade could 'come to a fair field of battle, I should not despair of success'. The same day Henry Fox was not without his fears. On 21 November Newcastle wrote to Devonshire that Cumberland's army was 'so strong, that the enemy seem to be coming to certain destruction', but that was the force Charles Edward had outmanoeuvred. On 3 December an 'extremely anxious' Pelham consoled himself with the thought that 'a superiority of regular troops, which the Duke certainly has with him, must beat them out of the field'. However, pressing on was not really an option for the Jacobites not so much because of the military situation, however misrepresented at Derby, but because of the breakdown of confidence in the prince among his commanders. Lord George Murray had been only just in a minority at Edinburgh on 30 October. Charles Edward subsequently failed to retain his own supporters or to woo those of Murray. He lost support because of a breakdown of confidence arising from the failure of his promises over the English Jacobites and French. The Scots understandably considered themselves tricked, led into a more risky situation than they had envisaged and that a long way from home. It was not surprising that they wanted to return home, to the apparent security and greater predictability of Scotland. However, there is a need for caution in assessing the sources. So much comes from people like Lord Elcho, Lord George Murray and Murray of Broughton, who wrote after the event and who had a vested interest in blaming the prince, the French, the English Jacobites, anybody but themselves for the Jacobite failure and its dreadful aftermath. Charles Edward could behave like a spoilt child but his position at Derby can be defended and, as his Jacobite critics would not obey his orders at Derby or later, it was unreasonable for them to make him responsible for the outcome.

On 7 December Colonel Cuthbert Ellison wrote to his brother Henry:

I write you from Coventry where I was sent yesterday before our army then encamped between Coleshill and this place to mark out another camp in this neighbourhood, it being then supposed from the motions of the rebels and the long marches they made, that their intention was to slip between us and London. But the long and forced marches we made from Stafford to this town with our cavalry, and followed close by our infantry rendered that design of theirs abortive, but I question much whether that ever was their real intention. I am of the opinion that this principal attention is to avoid coming to any action either with this or Marshal Wade's army; and I am afraid from the badness of the roads and weather and the shortness of the days etc. that they may avoid both armies and reach Scotland before we can possibly get up to them. Though there is not a single man under his Royal Highness' command but what longs to engage them; were it only to put an end to the fatigues we must undergo till that happens . . . our troops are a good deal fatigued with constant marching and yet they are in very good spirits.[19]

Once the retreat from Derby had begun the crucial military and political question was whether the prince could be defeated before he reached Scotland and the year ended. Such a defeat would allow the mopping up of the Jacobite cause to be entrusted to loyal Scots and a portion of the British army, while the bulk of the army could be returned to Flanders before the start of the campaigning season. This would bolster the anti-French alliance and hopefully both discourage Britain's allies from heeding French approaches and provide protection for what was left of the Austrian Netherlands. The Jacobites, however, avoided defeat. This was due to a mixture of their own skills, Wade's movements and what appeared to be the second invasion of England that year, a French landing in Sussex in December. On 12 December Welbore Ellis, a pro-government MP, wrote to Lord Hartington, 'I must condole with you upon the general consideration of their retiring to Scotland which I fear will keep us in a long and destructive war'.

Wade with over 6,000 troops was at Wetherby when the Jacobites turned back. At Doncaster on the 8th he received a message from Cumberland, sent on the 6th, pressing him to block the Jacobite retreat in Lancashire. Wade had already decided to do so and planned to march via Halifax and Rochdale, but on the 8th he wrote, 'I fear the difficulties of providing bread, wood and straw will retard my march'. The same day Wade replied to the duke that he thought it would be difficult to cut the Jacobites off unless they wanted a battle adding that he would try to keep between them and Newcastle, 'as it is a place of the utmost importance to preserve', scarcely the aggressive note that the duke wanted to hear. On the 10th he had only reached Wakefield. A Council of War held there decided that it would be impossible to reach Manchester before the prince did, and that it was best to march the infantry to Newcastle in order to prevent any Jacobite attack, but that about 500 cavalry would be sent across the Pennines under Major-General James Oglethorpe MP. Oglethorpe (1696–1785), a member of a strongly Jacobite family, had resigned his commission during the '15, and visited 'James III' at Urbino three years later. Returning to England that year, he played a major role in the foundation of the colony of Georgia in the 1730s and, as an apparently loyal Whig, was given a commission in March 1744 to raise a regiment against a threatened French invasion.[20] A meteoric individual, with a varied military experience – he had served under Prince Eugene at the siege of Belgrade in 1717, attacked Spanish-held St Augustine in Florida unsuccessfully in 1740 and beat off a Spanish attack on Georgia two years later – Oglethorpe reached Preston on 13 December 1745, too late to impede the Jacobites who were already at Lancaster. His tired troops had been affected by bad weather, inadequate supplies, bad roads and hostile terrain. Oglethorpe was to be accused of lingering by Cumberland and court-martialled, though he was acquited. In the 1750s he reverted to Jacobitism.

Wade meanwhile was marching north, General Huske writing from Leeds on 12 December to Alderman Ridley of Newcastle:

> . . . we march tomorrow for Wetherby on our way to return to Newcastle where I hope we shall be in time enough to prevent any mischief that the rebels may do in your part of the world. How long we shall continue with you I can't at present say, but I believe no longer than while proper magazines can be provided for our marching into Scotland. We grow sickly . . . The Duke with his army is at Macclesfield. I question much if he will march farther north not knowing what landings there may be in the south.

Five days later Captain Richmond Webb wrote from Durham to Ridley requesting billets, 'having marched seven days successively without halting and fatigued to the greatest degree'. Wade himself had written to Lonsdale on the 13th from Grange near Wetherby, 'We are going forward to Newcastle, as fast as the bad roads and this rigorous season will admit of', lest the Jacobites attack Newcastle 'but I fear we shall reduce our army to nothing by long marches and encampments at this time of the year'. Two days later he wrote from Ripon to Cumberland of the 'frequent applications made to me by the general officers and colonels, from the extreme sufferings of the soldiers . . . the impossibility of our marching with greater expedition without entirely destroying the remains of our infantry', adding of the Jacobites, 'their motions are very expeditious'.[21]

Landings in the south were indeed to be important. In place of earlier indecisive manoeuvres in the west Midlands and in contrast to Wade, Cumberland seized the opportunity to pursue the Jacobites. Charles Edward reached Ashbourne on the 6th, Leek on the 7th, Macclesfield on the 8th and Manchester on the 9th. It was only on the last day that Cumberland, who had needed to rest his troops and acquire horses for a rapid pursuit, set off for Manchester with his cavalry and 1,000 infantry mounted on horses, writing to Newcastle, 'I fear our chase will be fruitless, for they march at such a rate that I cannot flatter myself with the hopes of overtaking them . . . impossible regular forces should move with that expedition rabble do, and who take by force whatever they want'. Having found some of the population of Manchester keen to harry them, now that they were retreating, the Jacobites reached Wigan on the 10th, while Cumberland rode to Macclesfield in harsh December weather. His aide-de-camp, Lieutenant-Colonel Joseph Yorke, wrote to his father Hardwicke that they had come 'through as difficult a country as ever cavalry went through, and the snow froze on the ground made it almost impossible to keep our legs'.[22] Informed that the Jacobites were still far ahead and influenced by governmental concern about a possible French invasion, Cumberland stayed three nights in Macclesfield. The Jacobites reached Preston on the 11th and next day their leaders debated proposals to remain there and thus both avoid the problems of retreating to Scotland and encourage the French to invade. The counter-arguments put forward by Lord George Murray of the vulnerability of Preston and the need to restore the army's strength in Scotland won the day but, in fact, though there was to be no stand in Preston to encourage the French, they were to help save the Jacobite retreat.

Prince Charles's targe. Like many of the Highland clansmen, Charles Edward was armed with the basket hilted sword and the targe. The most striking feature is the grotesque Medusa's head used as a central motif

French Invasion

In November 1745 the ministers in London, while concerned about French preparations, were more anxious about the Jacobite advance, and had made their military dispositions accordingly. On 9 November Newcastle wrote to Lonsdale:

> . . . we continue to receive daily advices of preparations carrying on at Dunkirk and other of the French ports for an embarkation; and it has been said that Lord John Drummond's regiment was actually embarked at Dunkirk. But as they have no men-of-war of great force in those parts, it is probable their view at present may be only to send small embarkations to Scotland or elsewhere, in order to support the rebels; and their design may be to get a great naval strength collected at Brest, where they have now several large ships and come with a large embarkation into the western part of this kingdom. I am assured our fleet will be in a good condition to oppose any such attempt.

On the same day Henry Pelham was inclined to doubt reports of a major expedition.

Five days later Ramsden wrote to Lonsdale that there were only 800 men embarked at Dunkirk and that the twelve warships fitting out at Brest were possibly being prepared for a lucrative, though not especially strategic, target; the British East India men. On 18 November, however, Stair warned Duncan Forbes that if Charles Edward did well it would encourage the Bourbons to 'send very considerable supplies of money, men and arms, to their friends in Britain and Ireland, both by diversion and otherwise'. The following day Pelham expressed his hope to the Duke of Devonshire that Charles Edward's invasion would be soon defeated, adding, 'for if it is not, all our accounts from abroad open a sad scene. It is pretty certain that France will support the Pretender openly, and I hear from good hands that the Duke of Richelieu and most of their favourite officers are destined for this service'.[23] In the summer, when the French had not intended to invade, the British ministry had greatly feared an attack, but in the autumn they underrated the danger until surprisingly late. On 3/14 October the French council decided to send 6,000 men to invade England as soon as seemed propitious. At the next council meeting, three days later, Louis XV determined that preparations should be made as if an invasion would be mounted. Although Louis XV's enthusiasm has been queried,[24] there seems little doubt of it. He pressed his doubting naval and war ministers, the Counts of Maurepas and Argenson, and ensured that at a time when France was fully-stretched by a war that had already lasted four and a half years a substantial force would be prepared. On 13/24 October by the Treaty of Fontainebleau the French promised assistance to the Jacobites. The British ministry relied on the navy to prevent any French action during this period, for as troops returned from Flanders they were sent to the Midlands or Newcastle, rather than to the south coast. The French continued their preparations, but the lack of coordination with Charles Edward's invasion of England was amply displayed by their later time-scale. On 5/16 November Maurepas ordered his protégé the Jacobite shipowner Antoine Walsh to assemble the ships for the crossing. Jacobite supporters were encouraged by Charles Edward's early successes. Des Varennes, the French chargé d'affaires in Madrid, wrote on 23 December 1745/3 January 1746, when news of the prince's unopposed arrival at Lancaster reached Madrid, that it was said to be 'only twenty-four leagues from London,[25] so that it is assumed he is near there at present, and that the 12,000 French troops which should have embarked on the 27th or 28th of December [16, 17th old style], if they arrive safely, will be able to settle the fate of the country'.[26]

The prince's decision to invade England too soon, with such a small force and without the support of the English Jacobites aroused disquiet in Paris, but preparations continued. On 2/13 December the Irish Brigade had began to move towards Dunkirk. The following day Newcastle sent Cumberlnd intelligence reports received the previous night that the French were gathering 'together a great quantity of small boats and vessels at Dunkirk, in order to transport a considerable number of troops into some part of England'. Voltaire drew up a manifesto for the invading force stressing that they were sent in response to requests from English patriots, who sought to dethrone the Hanoverians and not to harm the people and would leave as soon as the Stuarts were established. It was no more dishonest than William III's declarations in 1688, and arguably less so as the French did not intend to maintain an army in Britain. On 7/18 December the embarkation of cannon and supplies began at Dunkirk.[27] The following day the British cabinet cited 'the accounts received of the intended embarkation' as one of the reasons why they did not want Cumberland's army to advance further from London. The commander of the French invasion force the Duke of Richelieu left Paris on 12/23 December, a day after Charles Edward's younger brother Henry had set out for Dunkirk. Richelieu reached Dunkirk on 17/28 December to find insufficient artillery and a lack of officers. He subsequently declared that it was lack of artillery alone that prevented him from ordering an embarkation at Calais on that day, when the winds were favourable. They were not to be so again until 20/31 December, by which time news had arrived of the retreat from Derby.

It is reasonable to consider what would have happened had the French indeed embarked. Vernon, who was in command of the British squadron watching the French Channel ports, was well aware of French preparations, but uncertain as to their intentions, whether for Scotland or England. His force was not particularly large. On 18/29 November he had in the Downs only two 50-gunners, two 44-gunners, eight smaller ships and five Dutch warships whose reliability was dubious because of French pressure on the Dutch not to assist George II. On 3/14 December Vernon reported to the Admiralty that the French might be planning a landing from fishing boats at Orford Haven in Suffolk. A British spy informed Vernon that 15,000 men were to be embarked.[28] Vernon was involved in a dispute with the Admiralty over the strength of his force. On 13/24 December the Secretary of the Admiralty wrote to him:

> . . . you have seldom less than near twenty sail of ships or vessels of war under your command; that your force, including the two Dutch ships, had consisted of 1 of 60, 3 of 50, 4 of 44 guns, every one of which, not to mention the 20-gun ships and sloops, is superior to any strength of the enemy, that from your own intelligence, appears to have been in that part of the Channel.

Vernon, however, considered his force small and outnumbered, and feared that the French would be covered by a squadron from Brest or the Biscayan ports. His letter, sent from the Downs on 16/27 December, continued:

> . . . with a southerly wind it was very practicable for them to get by unobserved by our ships to the westward, and, if the others were ready to sail with them when they had slipped by, and they too strong for me, they might execute their descent before their Lordships could have time to provide a preventive remedy against it . . . My particular province . . . is to watch the coasts of Kent and Sussex, and therefore, if with a southerly wind we should put to sea, without certain advice of the enemy being at sea, and which way they were gone, if it comes to over blow for one night southerly we must be driven to the northward by it, and of course, leave the coasts of Sussex and Kent exposed to the enemy's attempts, which their constant spies the smugglers would not fail to give them advice of.

Vernon returned to the theme of the weakness of his force for its task two days later.[29] Had Richelieu's force embarked on the 17/28 they could probably have reached England. Had they done so they would not have met much initial resistance, though the speed of their subsequent advance might have been affected by a shortage of cavalry. In 1688 William III had seized horses locally. Amphibious operations in the eighteenth century were far from easy. The British expedition which landed on Belle Isle off the French coast in April 1761 was repulsed on the first attempt and lost half of its flat-bottomed landing boats as a result of bad weather. Transporting horses was a particular problem, as was landing them on a beach. John Maule MP noted that the Hessian troops that were transferred from the Low Countries to Britain were ordered 'to embark the foot without waiting for the horse, which otherwise would have been a great hindrance'. The Duke of Bedford was later to claim, 'I have never myself been much in apprehension of invasions of England, for as they cannot bring cavalry over with them in any number, I think our having always a body of cavalry in this kingdom would soon enable us to put an end to any attempt of this nature'. In 1745 the French hoped that it would be possible to transport horses once a port, Dover or Dungeness, had been seized.[30] Nevertheless, there was no doubt that the cavalry, whether mounted on transported horses, which would have to recover from the journey, or those acquired locally, would take a while to become operational. This would not prevent an advance, but would make it slower. Had 15,000 men landed they would have been able to defeat whatever irregular forces the local authorities had raised and they would have easily outnumbered the troops in and around London. The speed of the French advance would have depended on their route and the weather, for the roads through the Weald and the clay valleys would not be improved by rain, whereas the Downs would offer a better route; and on whether they decided to march straight on London or to seize local parts in order to open communications with France. As Dover, in particular, was fortified and there were a number of lesser strongholds, such as Deal, this might entail sieges. Sieges could be lengthy affairs or, as the French showed in the Austrian Netherlands, fairly rapid. The troops and artillery available to defend the south coast strongholds were inadequate. Clearly, if the French landed, the government would be obliged to concentrate as large a force as possible to defend London and this could only be Cumberland's army. From the French point of view the chance of such a concentration was lessened by Charles Edward's approach.

It was not surprising that the ministry was concerned about a French invasion. Pelham claimed on 10/21 December that, despite French preparations:

> . . . as our own seas are covered with ships of one sort or other, and as the enemy have certainly no fleets to convoy their transports, I am in hopes we shall not be visited from abroad in this part of the island, however too much precaution cannot be taken, where there is so large a stake . . . therefore orders will soon go to carry the Hessians directly to Scotland; in which case we may have the Duke and the greatest part of his army here. When this measure is determined, I shall think the country sufficiently taken care of. And we may hope to be once more masters of ourselves.

Such a course of action was hardly going to help defeat Charles Edward. Hardwicke's eldest son Philip Yorke MP wrote from London on the same day 'if 6 or at most 7,000 ruffians can cut us out so much work, judge what our situation would be if the French could throw over a like or larger number'. On 17/28 December Pelham informed the Duke of Devonshire that the ministry was increasingly certain that the French intended to invade despite not enjoying superiority at sea. He added that the infantry in Cumberland's army under Ligonier were:

> . . . making all the haste they can to London. We have at present a very small land force here and by our accounts it is in vain to think of these troops being of any service against the rebels in the north. This made us all come to the resolution of sending for them here, which in case this embarkation should take place, will be absolutely necessary for our defence. You have been much frightened in the north, we are a good deal so here now; the effects are terrible upon our credit. I pray for a speedy determination, for without that we are sure of a lingering death.[31]

Rumours of an imminent French invasion had circulated for a number of days,[32] and on 10/21 December it was reported in London that they had actually landed in Pevensey Bay. Though soon corrected, the alarm was raised even higher on 12/23 December when another landing on the Sussex coast was reported. Newcastle wrote to Richmond, then in pursuit of Charles Edward:

> We are under the greatest alarms of an immediate invasion from France. It was even reported that they were actually landed yesterday in Pevensey Bay. Admiral Vernon expects them every hour. For Gods sake hasten to us, for if they should come before Ligonier with his foot, we shall not have 6,000 men to oppose them . . . this day in Council . . . I was forced to differ even with my good and valuable friends the Chancellor and Lord Harrington. But the King decided for me, and it is now all agreed. The question was whether Ligonier or rather the Duke's whole army should come hither immediately or only six battalions . . . I was for all coming. London is the great object and must be preferred to all other considerations.[33]

Hardwicke wrote the same day to Joseph Yorke that the army was 'hardly sufficient' to cope with the Jacobites and the French.[34] The French were in no doubt that British forces on the south coast were inadequate. On 13/24 December the military commander at Dunkirk, Lieutenant-General Comte d'Aunay, reported that two spies had brought information that on the Kent coast there were only two or three militia battalions and one battalion of Scots who had said that they would not fight the prince, while off the Downs there were only five ships and it was said that Vernon was secretly for Charles Edward.[35] This claim was inaccurate, though there had been Jacobite supporters in the fleet the previous year and on 17/28 December 1745 Wolters reported that there were still sympathizers there.[36] French preparations and British weakness combined to produce concern and panic about an invasion for the rest of the month. A report that a party of smugglers that had landed near Beachy Head were in fact 12,000 French troops led Portsmouth to prepare for an attack. The ditch was flooded and the gates shut. On 25 December/5 January Stephen Weston wrote to his brother Edward from Exeter, throwing light both on the local response to the loyal subscription and on a sense of vulnerability that naval power did not ease:

> The Tories won't help us, and some of the Whigs who love their money better than themselves say this is only taxing the king's best friends, Lord Clinton has refused by telling us its unconstitutional . . . I doubt should any attempt be made from Brest or St Malo at this time we should fall a too easy prey since land forces we have none but the garrison at Plymouth, and that just now reduced by a draught for Bristol; part of our western squadron too being lately sailed to strengthen Vernon in the Downs, I think we are in a state to be pitied, and the utmost to be hoped for us is to run away with the money we are raising, leaving our estates and houses to the rage of the invaders. We must pray therefore for a north-east or north-west wind to shut up the western ports of France, since a south-east or south-west brings our enemies upon us, and at the same time denies us the assistance of our friends.[37]

One wonders how far the response of a loyal Exeter cleric would have differed in 1688.

Military weakness led the ministry to recall Cumberland. On 12/23 December Newcastle wrote to him:

His Majesty having received an account from Admiral Vernon, that a considerable number of vessels, besides small boats, are assembled at Dunkirk, and that there is the greatest reason to believe that an attempt will be immediately made to land a body of troops from hence on some part of the southern or eastern coast . . . your Royal Highness should immediately return to London, with the rest of the cavalry and foot, that are now with you.[38]

Richelieu was not, however, to be deterred from invading by Cumberland. It was Charles Edward's retreat, news of which arrived on 18/29 December, that discouraged him, though already there were serious problems with the preparations, including a shortage of transports. Richelieu was soon to suffer from the absence of a major port where the entire invasion force could prepare and concentrate. He intended to embark his troops at Boulogne, but on 18–20/29–31 December, while supplies were being moved between Boulogne, Calais and Dunkirk, British warships and privateers inflicted serious damage, leading to the loss of over thirty ships. Vernon was reinforced by Admiral Martin who had been watching Brest from the western approaches.

In England it was assumed that Charles Edward's retreat would lead to the cancellation of the invasion. John Tucker wrote from London on 14/25 December:

. . . our alarms continue about the French landing though I hope it is without foundation, for as the rebels are flying towards Scotland, and all our troops ordered from Flanders, I cannot see why the French should put themselves to the hazard of an invasion at this time of the year which must be attended with much danger and difficulty especially as the person in whose favour it is supposed to be made is leaving the country with the utmost precipitation – on this day seven nights ago this good City was in the utmost consternation . . . so easily are people inclined now to give into this contrary extreme and to speak slightingly of the men whom a week past were looked upon as invincibles.[39]

Stephen Weston was more confident by 28 December/8 January, though still worried about the Tories:

. . . for their whole view is arming the country, that if hereafter an Excise Scheme or anything else they are pleased to damn should be set on foot by ministers, they may be able with effect, to sound the trumpet; but to give their money towards supporting or encouraging a standing army, let the circumstances be what they will, they will never come into, for I am strongly of the opinion that the world is turned upside down and most of the Tories are become republicans . . . The rebels being drove back into Scotland to starve gives the French no encouragement to go on with the invasion, and especially as they must by this time be convinced of the little chance they can have of ever returning, when the nation and every man in it is ready to cut their throats; so that I hope matters will soon mend.[40]

By quoting either half of the letter a misleading impression can be created of Weston's view of English opinion about resistance to the Jacobites. The truth appears complex and fractured, while reading entire correspondences provides a sense of shifting assessments, a point bought out forcefully in Tucker's letter.

Horatio Walpole subsequently linked the effect of the prince's retreat to ministerial divisions in France over the wisdom of supporting him:

He said Cardinal Tencin was violent for France, supporting the Pretender's son here in

1745. The other ministers were not fond of him. They advised him against hazarding a number of men till at least they saw prospect of success. And when he came into England and found nobody join him here, they used that answer against the French intermeddling considerably.[41]

In fact the prince's retreat did not lead the French to cancel their invasion plans and the government in London was therefore arguably foolish to countermand the orders to Cumberland to march south, especially since the mobility of the royal troops, and therefore the flexibility of their possible response, was lessened by their insufficient cavalry, as was pointed out on 10/21 December:

> The methods which . . . have been taken to suppress this rebellion . . . have seemed . . . to be too slowly carried into execution and I am sorry to say the neglecting so long to send for the regiments of horse and dragoons which are still in Flanders is but too strong an instance of it since everybody have from the beginning agreed that even a greater number of horse than we have now on foot were absolutely necessary to extinguish this rebellion.[42]

Demoralization, problems with supplies, delayed preparations and poor relations between Richelieu and Henry Stuart were responsible for the failure to take advantage of the favourable winds between 31 December and 3 January, though the build up of British naval strength – Martin's first ships reached the Downs on 31 December – made success increasingly problematic. As in 1744, and more generally in the War of the Polish Succession, schemes for or ideas about invasion depended upon seizing a window of opportunity presented by initial surprise, before the British had time to assemble sufficient naval forces to block the plan, but the difficulty of combining land and sea preparations and of embarking a large enough force made this far from easy.

Nevertheless, the French government remained determined to press on. On 20/31 December the Count of Argenson, the war minister, wrote to Richelieu, replying to a letter of his of two days earlier. Argenson accepted that it was bad that the supplies and artillery had not been embarked fast enough to allow Richelieu to benefit from favourable sailing weather, but his remedy for deficiencies, such as artillery horses, was to find them in England. Encouraging news of the engagement between Cumberland's vanguard and the Jacobites on 18/29 December was forwarded by Richelieu three days later, indicating the speed at which messages could travel. The Marquis of Argenson, brother to the count and foreign minister, agreed with Richelieu that the favourable account required confirmation, and pressed him on 24 December/4 January to continue with his preparations. Four days later Maurepas wrote 'les retardements ne pouvoient plus venir que des circonstances insurmontables, comme celles de la mer, des vents et des batiments enemis en forces superieures', while the Marquis of Argenson informed Richelieu that he was certain that he would seize all the opportunities that presented themselves to execute a project of which he knew the importance better than anyone. Louis XV was certain he would sail as soon as possible, and Charles Edward's difficulties made it more important to help him. It was accepted that delay led to a loss of secrecy and provided the British with opportunities to prepare their resistance, and Richelieu was given permission to embark where he thought best. Argenson was, however, unsure whether the force would sail and on 31 December/11 January he wrote to the envoy in Madrid that it was prevented from doing so by the British fleet which he claimed consisted of thirty warships.

In Boulogne a council of war on 25 December/5 January revealed that plans to sail two days later would be affected by the tides, so that insufficient ships would be able to put to sea, and it was feared that this would expose them to the British navy. Richelieu postponed a decision until the weather improved, but Louis XV left no doubt of his determination that an attempt should be made. Orders were issued to prepare a cavalry force at Calais for the invasion. Richelieu made plans to sail on 29 December/9 January, but this was thwarted by a strong north-east wind. Following the arrival on 2/13 January of fresh orders from Louis to invade at once, Richelieu ordered the Irish Brigade to embark and sail for Rye, but this was cancelled, as were preparations for an embarkation at Calais, in response to reports of British warships in the Channel. From then on the impetus for an invasion was lost. Concerned about supplies and health, Richelieu began on the 8/19th to disperse his troops to nearby posts. The plans now discussed were for a smaller invasion force, sailing either to Maldon in Essex or to Scotland. Richelieu proposed on 15/26 January the dispatch of 4,300 men to Scotland from Dunkirk and Ostend. John Maule MP, a protégé of the Duke of Argyll, whose Jacobite background – his father and uncle had taken part in the '15 – led to unwarranted suspicions of his loyalty, wrote from London on 4/15 January, 'it is generally believed the intended invasion from France upon England is over' and that instead the French troops would be sent to Scotland.

Maurepas was determined that the Brest fleet should be sent to recover Louisbourg on Cape Breton Island, the base covering the approach to the St Lawrence that was regarded as the essential first prize in any British conquest of Canada, and which had been captured by them the previous year. This was, in fact, to happen though the French fleet, affected by storms and disease, was unsuccessful and badly battered.[43] Had the Brest fleet been used in support of Richelieu it might have diverted the British warships outside Ostend which made the expedition to Scotland impossible. Troops were embarked at Ostend and Dunkirk on 26–28 January/6–8 February, but disembarked in the face of superior British naval power. A disillusioned Richelieu sought his recall, which was granted, and on 1/12 February he left Dunkirk for Paris. The news of the victory at Falkirk did not revive French interest and the troops released from Richelieu's force were added to Saxe's army in the Austrian Netherlands. Though Louis XV remained determined to assist Charles Edward and insisted that the Irish Brigade be kept at the Channel ports, and plans continued for moving small forces to Scotland, the opportunity for a major French invasion had passed. On 9/20 January Robert Trevor had written 'their *armada* keeps hovering over our coast' and eleven days later a London newspaper had reported an alarm at Hastings when British ships were mistaken for French vessels,[44] but fears were already abating. It was reported from Hurdwick in Devon on 19/30 January, 'We have been under great apprehensions here for some time past of a French invasion but I hope now it is all over, and that we have nothing to do but to drive the rebels out of Scotland'.[45] Wolters informed the Admiralty on 14/25 January that the French embarkation had been suspended, adding three days later that by letters from Paris of the 13/24th 'the scheme of an invasion was looked upon at Paris if not as utterly impracticable at least as very dangerous and difficult: everything relating to the troops and shipping was however kept in a readiness'. By 28 January Newcastle was concerned not about the prospect of an invasion, but rather that more French troops would be sent to Scotland.[46]

The Retreat to Scotland

The understandable failure to coordinate Jacobite and French operations helped to defeat both. By turning back at Derby the Jacobites removed the vital impetus of apparent success and immediacy that the French required to overcome the obstacles they faced and set sail. By not invading, the French left the Jacobites to fight alone. Charles Edward had hoped that his successes would encourage the French to act. He was correct in his assumptions that his advance would motivate them and it certainly left foreign commentators, both friendly and hostile, convinced of the weakness of the Hanoverian regime. Charles Bentinck wrote from The Hague on 20/31 December 1745, 'is there so little spirit left in England, that 6 or 7,000 Scotch can frighten the whole nation out of their senses?', and reported that it was said there that the rural population supported Charles Edward. On 13/24 January 1746 the Marquis of Argenson commented to Richelieu that it was clear that the British nation had no zeal for their actual master and that they did not really oppose Charles Edward.[47] The prince failed to weigh adequately the logistical problems that mounting an expedition posed and the difficulties of both communicating and coordinating operations. Nevertheless, the prospect of a French invasion helped him get his army back to Scotland.

On 13/24 December pursuing troops engaged the Jacobites for the first time. Oglethorpe's cavalry skirmished with their rearguard between Lancaster and Garstang. Charles Edward reached Lancaster that day, but he was increasingly disinclined to flee before Cumberland and he insisted on spending a day in the town and thus risking battle. However, on the 14th Murray persuaded the prince to continue the retreat, arguing that the Highlanders would be overwhelmed by weight of numbers. On the 15th they left Lancaster and Oglethorpe entered the town, but his pursuit was called off on receipt of Newcastle's instructions to deal with the French landing. Cumberland was very disappointed, writing that day to Newcastle, 'I am very sorry that Mr Vernon's frights should have saved the Rebel army now at Lancaster whither we had drove them, and where I hoped to have kept them at bay, till I could have had the assistance of Marshal Wade's army utterly to have destroyed them', while his aide-de-camp, Joseph Yorke, wrote:

> I am really quite sick at my stomach and heart with the misfortune. The rebels have fled before us in the utmost consternation thus far, and I am convinced in my own mind twenty-four hours more would have decided this affair. Their horses are so fatigued that they

can do no more, our men in high spirits, and the country all up ready to join us and assist us against the rebels, now they saw themselves supported by the king's troops. What the consequences of our returning may be, God only knows. The spirits of the soldiery and the poor country must be depressed. They may wait quietly at Carlisle for their reinforcements, refresh their people, put new life into 'em, ruin the bordering countries, and in a little while advance with fresh vigour and fury into the bowels of the land, in spite of all that Marshal Wade's army can do against 'em: whereas, had we pushed on our advantages, and put an end to this body, the French would never have returned into the island; or if they did, we should have had more than sufficient force to withstand 'em . . . We have lost our opportunity, and I dread only to think of the consequences.

Richmond also saw the recall as an opportunity lost and he further argued that if an invasion did take place, Cumberland's cavalry would reach the south too late to be of any assistance,[48] a dubious point in the light of the likelihood that any French invading force would have few cavalry. It would have been more accurate to claim that the cavalry would have been very exhausted, though by this stage the conflict was increasingly taking on the dimension of moves by debilitated players and the French would probably have fallen into the same category after the pleasures of crossing the Channel in December and wading ashore.

Heavy rains helped to delay the Jacobites on 16 December, so that they only got as far as Shap. Cumberland, having received new orders to pursue the Jacobites rather than march on London, reached Lancaster, but on the following day his troops were hampered by the rain, snow, wind and bad roads that were also hindering their intended victims. The duke reported from Lancaster, 'I much fear the twenty-four hours given them by our halt at Preston will render our pursuit fruitless, unless they should attempt to make a stand at Carlisle . . . it will be impossible for me to pursue them further than Carlisle for want of provision for both man and horse'. On the 18th a successful Highland charge at Clifton led to the repulse of troops that were pressing the Jacobite rearguard and allowed it to disengage successfully. The Jacobites under Murray revealed in the engagement an ability to take advantage of the terrain and the fire-power of Bland's dragoons proved unable to protect them from the claymores of the MacPhersons, who had only 150 yards to run and that covered by a dark and cloudy night. The dragoons were also unable to face hand-to-hand fighting and they retreated after about two minutes. Welbore Ellis had indeed suggested that it would be difficult for Cumberland's force to defeat the retreating Jacobites, 'I can scarce doubt that the Duke with his horse and one thousand volunteers will reach them before they get to Carlisle, but if he should, if the country be so inclosed as I have heard it described, he can do nothing with his horse, but may be destroyed if they know how to avail themselves of the hedges'. In fact it was the fire-power of the duke's men, rather than their ability to charge, that was at stake at Clifton, though the Jacobites were indeed assisted by the terrain. The Jacobite success was wildly exaggerated on the Continent. Varennes reported from Madrid on 13/24 January that, after the defeat, Cumberland had been recalled to London and some of the royal family were preparing to flee the country.[49]

The engagement at Clifton, the last battle fought on English soil, led Cumberland to decide to wait until all his troops had come up and on the 19th

Preston Decr yr 18th

I have Just time Yr Hor. to tell you where I am in pursuit of yr rascally rebels but despair much of getting up with them our only hopes was part of Wades Army stopping them but suck is the Inactivity of that army that I have no hopes, the Duke is forty miles before us with a body of horse this is yr sixth days march without halt with a thousand voluntiers from yr Army & Blighs Regt our men much fatigued but in great Spirits how farr we shall persue I know not but see them out of England I dare say wee have pickt up a few. the pretender flys before yr Army I mean of Rascals. I am ever yours

Col: Cornwall

'In pursuit of the rascally rebels': a letter from Lt.-Col. Edward Cornwallis in Preston to Horace Walpole on 18 December 1745

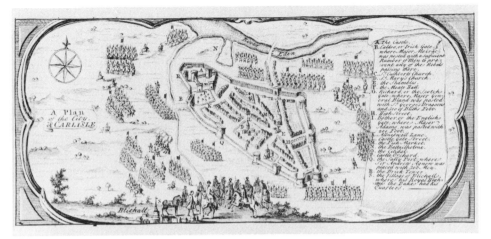

Carlisle, 1745 showing the position of the Duke of Cumberland's army on 21 December

The Duke of Cumberland refusing to treat with rebels outside Carlisle

the Jacobites were able to enter Carlisle. Joseph Yorke was hopeful that they would be kept there by the problems of crossing rain-swollen rivers but, in fact, on the 20th Charles Edward and his army forded the Esk. A garrison of 350 men was left in Carlisle Castle in order to show that the prince was determined to return to England and to avoid the necessity of his besieging the town on his return. It was hoped that such a force would delay Cumberland's pursuit. The castle became Cumberland's target for his cautious advance, after Clifton made it impossible to keep up with the Jacobites, while Cumberland had already determined that due to supply problems he would be unable to pursue them beyond Carlisle. The defenders, under the Lancashire Jacobite Colonel Francis Towneley, had only ten cannon. They sought to strengthen the defences with ramparts and iron spikes and burnt down houses that might cover the attackers. On 21 December Cumberland reached Carlisle and described the castle as 'an old hen-coop, which he would speedily bring down about their ears, when he should have got artillery'.[50] He summoned guns from Whitehaven, had batteries constructed for them and blockaded the defenders, cutting off their water supply. The siege was not without its problems, 'the wetness of the season, which makes it difficult to raise the earth, the badness of the ways for conveying the artillery, the want of engineers, ammunition etc'.[51] On 27 December the cannon arrived and their superior firepower doomed the defenders:

> A battery of six eighteen-pounders was perfected the 27th at night, and on Saturday was fixed with good success, but the shot failed a little so that the fire was slacker on Sunday, however this little loss of time was of no consequence as a supply is received which will be continued as fast as there is occasion; and the battery was augmented that night. Overtures for a surrender were made Saturday night and again on Sunday night, but his R.H. would not hearken to anything.[52]

Execution of rebels at Carlisle

Cumberland set the match to the first gun himself and his guns reputedly fired over 1,100 shots on the 28th. The outgunned defenders saw their fortifications battered and the walls breached in two places. They surrendered on the 30th, unable to obtain any terms other than the promise that they should not be put to the sword, but be reserved for the royal pleasure. Only those who had been captured at Prestonpans and then joined the Jacobites were hung at once; though thirty-one prisoners, brought from Scotland and from the English prisons to which those who had surrendered at Carlisle had been moved, were hung for treason the following autumn at Carlisle, Brampton and Penrith. Cumberland had initially opposed giving any quarter to the defenders of Carlisle. He wrote to Newcastle 'I wish I could have blooded the soldiers with these villians but it would have cost us many a brave man, and it comes to the same end, as they have no sort of claim to the king's mercy, and I sincerely hope will meet with none'. It is not necessary to turn to the claims that the Jacobites at Clifton had refused quarter, which Cumberland reported to Newcastle, to explain the duke's attitude. He was a hard man, accustomed to employ savage discipline, and in his response to the Jacobites, four of whom he had hung outside the castle during the siege, he revealed both the fear and hatred that they had aroused in the Hanoverian regime and his own preference for uncompromising action. Guy Dickens, an officer-diplomat, had written about Scotland on 25 October, 'the least clemency shown this time, would be cruelty to present and future ages'.[53] Cruelty was to be used as a policy. Most atrocities in continental warfare were committed at the expense of the soldiers and civilians of other combatants. In Britain, however, the cruelty used by Cumberland was at the expense of subjects of the Crown. The contrast with the Jacobites is instructive. Charles Edward intervened frequently in the cases of both his own soldiers, in trouble for indiscipline or other faults, and of those of civilians suspected or known to have committed hostile actions. His interventions were merciful, reflecting not only his own personality, especially when things were going well, but also an effort to win the hearts and minds of the population. However, the prince had to counter a tradition of regarding Catholics as quintessentially cruel. The *Penny London Post* of 8 January 1746 carried a fairly typical report:

> There is advice . . . that 200 Protestants in the Languedoc in France, having assembled in the fields, to serve God in that peaceable religion, in which they were bred, they were suddenly surrounded by a large body of dragoons, who massacred thirty of them on the spot, and made the rest prisoners, seventy of whom have since been sent to the galleys, and the rest hourly expect the same fate – This black exploit is agreeable to the religion and slavery which is at present attempted to be forced on the free-born Protestants of England by our dangerous and inveterate enemies the French.[54]

In practice Jacobite conduct in England was not characterized by cruelty. During the retreat the army was harassed, especially in Cumbria, though the significance of this is open to debate. Speck wrote of the men of Penrith, 'Although they prudently laid low when the rebel army marched through their town on the way south', they adopted a different attitude subsequently,[55] though it could be argued that it was their passive position on the march south that was crucial. Neither side appear to have enjoyed the enthusiastic support of the bulk of the population, certainly to the extent of armed action. The absence of mass recruitment to the Jacobite army is obvious, but equally they encountered little serious resistance, other than at Carlisle, and that collapsed as soon as it became clear that Wade's force of regulars would not bring relief. The '45 in England was a struggle between armies that did not meet in battle, apart from a partial encounter at Clifton, rather than a conflict between these armies and civilians, whether sympathetic or opposed to the Jacobite cause. Joseph Yorke had observed in July 1744 that 'actions now-a-days are rarely decisive',[56] but a major engagement in '45 would probably have been so, certainly in the case of a Jacobite defeat, but also probably in that of a victory over one of the three forces confronting them in early December. Such a victory would have demoralized the other forces and induced some of the generals, officers and men to consider their own future. Had it been accompanied by action on the part of the French it might well have been militarily decisive and possibly politically also as, in so far as the English Jacobites were ever going to rise, the combination of a victorious Charles Edward and the French should have ensured the event. Such speculation may be dismissed as pointless hypotheses or the 'revisionist obscurantism' and nostalgia that interest in Jacobitism has been held to display, but these arguments are of value only if the options facing individuals in the past are ignored and it is assumed not only that the path of history is pre-ordained and obvious, but that the past belongs to the victors. Such views are not those of humane thinkers and readers. They are also inaccurate.

7 From the Return into Scotland to Culloden

If the rebels should join and in consequence retire to Perth, to wait a new supply from France, my opinion would be, to have embarked six battalions from hence, to have landed at Aberdeen, to have acted in conjunction with your Lordship, by which means, the rebels would have been deprived, of the subsistence, which they might otherwise draw, from Aberdeenshire, Banffshire and Murray and of the facility of recruiting their army.

Earl of Stair (London) to Loudoun, 9 January 1746[1]

I'm afraid the troubles are far from being over, though I hope all the danger to the government is past . . . I don't think they'll meet the Duke fairly . . . the slowness of the motions of so heavy a body as our army gives them opportunities of assembling, separating upon expeditions, and assembling again when they please. Hardy people who can sleep sound on the ground, and wet through without catching cold; who can live upon a little oatmeal made into a cake upon a flat stone before a fire in the open air, or mixed with hot water; whose officers can bear the same fatigues . . . must have a great advantage over regular forces who must live as well in the field as at home, and whose officers are many of them of delicate constitutions . . . if the nature of our troops would allow of their being as expeditious as the rebels, they had been scattered long ago.

Lord Glenorchy (Taymouth) 16 March 1746[2]

Britons, behold the Royal Youth, 'tis he
Who fights your Battles, sets your Country free,
The Rebels hear, and tremble at his Name,
And Ch—s with Envy, eyes his rising Fame.
See there the Highlanders, in fearful plight,
On Carrion Horses make a hasty Flight.
Satan has caught 'em in his Net, and see
He drags 'em onward to the triple Tree.

Verses at foot of caricature – *The Highlanders Medley* or *The Duke Triumphant*[3]

Charles Edward's return altered the military situation in Scotland. This had improved for the government following his advance into England. Edinburgh had been reoccupied, while in the north the Earl of Loudoun and Duncan Forbes had built up their forces based on Inverness, reinforced Fort Augustus on 3 December and eight days later captured the equivocating, but secretly Jacobite Simon Fraser, Lord Lovat. However, Lovat escaped and raised his clan, while an attempt by forces under Norman MacLeod and Grant of Grant to relieve Aberdeen was defeated on 23 December at Inverurie by Lord Lewis Gordon, who had raised a new Jacobite army in the north-east. Over 1,000 men from the Irish Brigade under Lord John Drummond had arrived in the north-east from Dunkirk in late November, Drummond himself escaping British naval pursuit to land at Montrose on 26 November/7 December. As French troops, Drummond's force was able to press that the Dutch, who had promised not to act against France, should be withdrawn and they were accordingly replaced by 6,000 Hessians under the command of the future Frederick II of Hesse-Cassel, who had married George II's daughter Mary in 1740. Ironically, Frederick was to encounter major problems as a result of his subsequent conversion to Catholicism. Thus Jacobite forces in Scotland had increased in size and much of the north-east had been occupied, but the geographical balance of power still left the government with many of the strategic sites, including Edinburgh, Stirling and the forts in the Great Glen.

Charles Edward's return threatened to alter this situation. On 22 December Andrew Fletcher, the Lord Justice Clerk, expressed his fear that the prince would march on Edinburgh, where there were only 1,250 regulars. Worried that

John Campbell, 4th Earl of Loudoun by Allan Ramsay

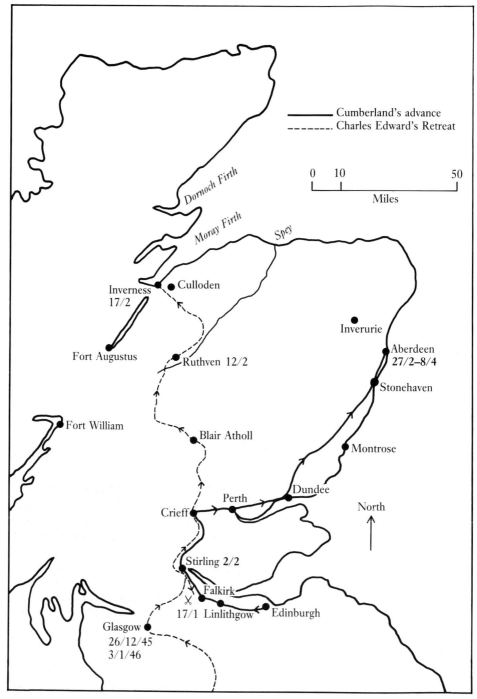

Scottish operations, January–February 1746

Cumberland would stop at Carlisle, he sought relief from Wade.[4] In fact, the prince chose to march not on Edinburgh but on Glasgow, an understandable choice given the wealth and vulnerability of the city and his past problems with Edinburgh Castle. Glasgow was entered on 26 December and money and supplies demanded. This enabled the government in London to send re-inforcements to Edinburgh. The command of the army to be sent to Scotland had first been offered to Wade, a senior officer and a loyal MP whatever his other faults, but he declined it on the grounds of age and ill-health. The prospect that he would have to face an unpredictable enemy in battle could hardly have encouraged him. The post was given to Lieutenant-General Henry Hawley (*c.* 1679–1759), who had served in the War of the Spanish Succession, at Dettingen and Fontenoy and been wounded while at the head of his regiment at Dunblane in 1715. A notorious disciplinarian, Hawley was more energetic (and confident) than Wade, writing on 31 December that he would march on Edinburgh 'where they seem to have renewed their panic, but I think without grounds. For the scrub remains the Duke has drove before him, are not capable of undertaking anything'. Hawley was concerned about a shortage of money, gunners, forage and supplies and about the presence of Highlanders in his army, but Newcastle was determined to provide him with a large force and wrote to Cumberland about the rebellion on 28 December:

> ... it is of the utmost importance that a speedy end should be put to it; that the public credit may soon revive, and the peace of the country be restored, which, during the continuance of the rebellion, does, and must, so necessarily suffer; for this reason His Majesty destined for that purpose, as great a force, as could be collected, from the troops now in the North; leaving always sufficient garrisons for Berwick, and Carlisle, and for the security of the town of Newcastle. And as the Rebels may possibly form two parties; the one of the Highlanders returned from England; the other of those now assembling at Perth under Lord John Drummond; it is very possible, Mr. Hawley may be obliged to divide his force, and to have two armies also; which makes it necessary to have a number sufficient to enable him to do so, if there should be occasion.

Newcastle felt that it was necessary not only to send troops to help Edinburgh and Stirling, but also that Carlisle be made 'as strong as possible' in case Charles Edward attempted to invade England again. A substantial force advanced from Newcastle to Edinburgh. On 2 January 1746 Fletcher wrote from Edinburgh:

> ... the first division of the troops viz a battalion of the Royal and Battereau's regiment arrived here this evening from Dunbar twenty long miles in one day, but were carried all that way on our country horses and entertained at the expense of the country . . . . They were received into Edinburgh betwixt five and six this night with huzzas, illuminations etc to the great mortification of the Jacobites, and now I have the pleasure to tell you that this place is in no apprehension from the rebels and we hope to send them soon back to starve in the mountains, they threaten to besiege Stirling Castle.[5]

Hawley himself left Newcastle on that day, reaching Edinburgh on the 6th, where a sizeable force was soon built up, though he complained about their quality and the lack of artillery in particular. Hawley had advanced in order to defend Edinburgh. His subsequent agenda was set by Charles Edward who

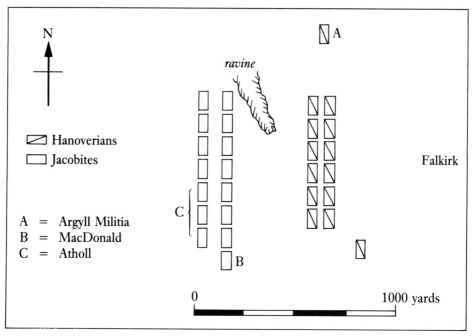

Plan of the battle of Falkirk

decided to besiege Stirling Castle. It had been suggested to him that he should march on Edinburgh, but he apparently preferred not to attack Hawley. By keeping his options open the prince could benefit best from whatever the French might do and in the meantime he could improve his position in Scotland by seizing Stirling. On 3 January 1746 Charles Edward left Glasgow. The town of Stirling surrendered to the besieging Jacobites on the 8th. The castle was held by its Lieutenant-Governor, Major-General William Blakeney, who was subsequently to conduct a gallant, though unsuccessful, defence of Minorca in 1756 when Richelieu commanded one of the most successful French amphibious operations of the century. It was well fortified and the Jacobites were obliged to bring up their siege artillery. Hawley mounted an unsuccessful attempt to seize the artillery at Alloa and then set off to march to the relief of Stirling, confident that the Jacobites would retreat before him. On 16 January his vanguard under Major-General John Huske reached Falkirk. On the 15th and 16th the Jacobites had been drawn up in battle formation east of Bannockburn, but on the 17th they advanced to seize a commanding position on Falkirk Moor, a plateau above Falkirk to the west. Hawley's army was encamped between Falkirk and the moor and when, to his negligent surprise, he was informed that the Jacobites were advancing across the moor and would seize the top of the ascent to it from his encampment, he ordered his troops to advance. They did so in the face of driving rain. Hawley had about 8,500 men, as he had been reinforced by 1,500 Argyllshire militia, while, having left 1,200 men to continue the siege of Stirling, the prince had about 8,000 men, the largest force he was to command in battle during the '45. The previous month a government official had warned 'if they get to Scotland, the French and the other rebels there joined with them will I fear make a formidable army'. Lord George Murray left an account of the engagement in which he commented on 'the infinite advantages' the Jacobites:

> . . . had from their position – the nearness of the attack, the descent of a hill, the strong wind and rain which was in their back, and directly in the enemy's face; and that they had some mossy ground upon their right, which prevented the enemy's horse from being able to flank them; and that by reason of the badness of the road, and steepness of the hill, their cannon were of no use to them; in a word, the Highland army had all the advantages that nature or art could give them.

Murray stressed the discipline of the Highlanders and described the battle as beginning with the uphill charge of the royal cavalry:

> They came at last at the full trot, in very good order, within pistol shot of the first line. Then Lord George Murray gave orders to fire, which was done with such execution, that it entirely broke them; but after that there was no possibility of making the MacDonalds keep their ranks; many of the first line of the right, pursued the horse, and fell in with some of the enemy's militia. In about five minutes after this first fire, the left . . . were charged by the enemy's foot, and also a body of horse; upon these they spent a good part of their fire, so that when they attacked the foot, they had scarce any of theirs left, but went in with great bravery, sword in hand. What did them most damage was these three regiments of the enemy's foot who flanked them; and the second line of the Highlanders' left, instead of moving farther to the left, or keeping their line till they should receive orders, crowded in with the first line . . . the rest of the second line fell into confusion . . . . Those who had attacked, seeing the three regiments of the enemy that were upon their left, entire and nothing to oppose them, retired back to the ground they had at first been drawn up upon.

Murray was clear about the faults of the Highlanders:

> . . . without a body of regular troops, the Highlanders, by themselves, have many disadvantages, by their not being disciplined, and especially their not rallying quick after an attack . . . . Had the MacDonalds on the right, either not broke their ranks, or rallied soon after, they, with the Atholl men, would have cut the whole enemy's foot to pieces, for they were close at them, and must have drove them down the hill before them; and by speed of foot, not a man of them could have got off from them. Had there been any officer on the left, to have ordered two or three battalions from the second line, or reserve, to have faced those of the enemy that outflanked them, they would have had a complete victory.

Murray criticized poor generalship on the Jacobite side, especially with respect to the command of the reserves, but he also found fault with Hawley. He argued, correctly, that had the royal troops marched straight up the hill as soon as the Highlanders approached, they would have gained the crest first. Alternatively had they defended their camp and Falkirk, the Jacobites would have faced a difficult task. Murray concluded with a bleak view of the military value of the Jacobite army:

> . . . the best of the Highland officers, whilst they remained at Falkirk after the battle, talking of the affair, were absolutely convinced, that, except they could attack the enemy at very considerable advantage, either by surprise or by some strong situation of ground, or a narrow pass, they could not expect any great success, especially if their numbers were no ways equal,

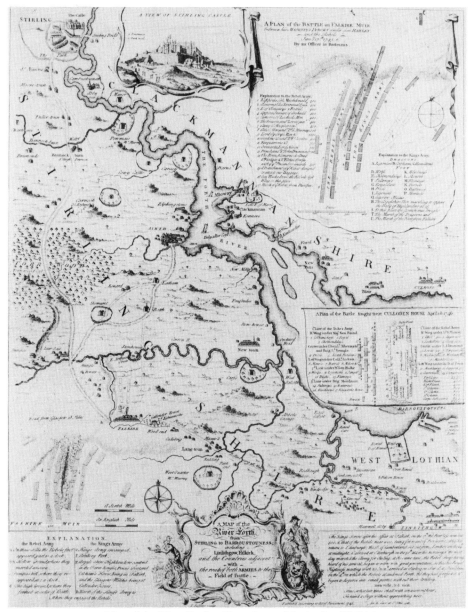

Map of the River Forth with an inset of the battle of Falkirk

and that a body of regular troops was absolutely necessary to support them, when they should at any time go in, sword in hand; for they were sensible, that without more leisure and time than they could expect to have to discipline their own men, it would not be possible to make them keep their ranks, or rally soon enough upon any sudden emergency, so that any small number of the enemy, either keeping in a body when they were in confusion, or rallying, would deprive them of a victory, even after they had done their best.[6]

Doubtless frustrated by the failure to exploit the advantages presented by the terrain, Murray was possibly over critical of his own men. The force that had broken most at Falkirk was the regular one. Loss of control during a rapid advance was a common problem in the warfare of the period, understandably so, given the primitive nature of communications and the fact that infantry units were essentially trained for firing in line, not charging forward. The difficulties facing the royal force are revealed in a letter from Brigadier-General James Cholmondeley. He described the rout of the main body, making it clear that a lack of fighting spirit had been decisive:

> . . . they [the cavalry] began the attack with spirit which did not last long, nevertheless they broke a considerable body of the Highlanders, but another body coming upon our left flank, our foot gave a feint [sic] fire, and then faced to the right about, as regularly as if they had had the word of command, and could not be rallied, 'till they got a considerable distance, altho' I do not think they were pursued by two hundred men.

Cholmondeley's account of how he and other officers successfully led two regiments on the right is briefly cited by W.A. Speck, who continued by writing that Cholmondeley 'even managed to get some of the dragoons to come to their aid'. Cholmondeley made clear, however, that they fought with little enthusiasm:

> I went to the Dragoons and rallied about one hundred of them, and told them, that I had repulsed the enemy with two weak battalions, and that if they would march up, I would head them, and that I would order the two battalions to march up briskly at the same time, and give them their fire, and that they should fall in, sword in hand, these were greatly pleased with this, and with many oaths, and Irish exclamations, swore they would follow me, I marched them up, to the two battalions but when we were to advance, they kept at least one hundred yards behind me; with some difficulty, I got them to the top of the hill, where I saw the Highlanders formed behind some houses and a barn (I was forced to fire a pistol amongst them, before I could get them to do this), I then returned to the two battalions to march them up, here General Huske joined me, and I told him, that if we could get some more battalions, to join us, we might drive them, but as night was drawing on he ordered me to retire.

Cholmondeley was in no doubt that Falkirk was a 'scandalous affair',[7] and his testimony written on the 21st should be set aside more optimistic accounts from officers in the royal army, such as that of Captain Richmond Webb, who wrote to Matthew Ridley on the 24th:

> I don't doubt but you have had sad accounts of our army, but I'll assure you we have sustained so inconsiderable a loss that it's hardly worth mentioning – except poor Sir Robert Munro and three or four more good officers – many circumstances concurred to make the thing unlucky, but after all we find that 2,000 men that will behave well is sufficient to beat them, and if that terrible wet night had not come on so soon we must have defeated them. We are preparing to attack them as soon as possible. They have suffered much in the action by desertion and from the fire of Stirling Castle.[8]

Webb was correct to point to the success of the right wing, but it is clear from Cholmondeley's account that they had required firm leadership, which was absent on the matching Jacobite left, while their front was protected in part by a ravine. Another account from the royal army, which throws light on why Hawley advanced from his strong camp and sent his cavalry into the attack first, was provided on 25 January 1746 by James Stuart Mackenzie, second son of the 2nd Earl of Bute and nephew of the Duke of Argyll, in whose interest he sat as an MP for Argyllshire. Hitherto his claim to fame had been that he had fallen in love with the famous opera dancer Barberina, but had been prevented from marrying her at Venice when Argyll persuaded his friend and fellow Scottish peer the Earl of Hyndford to have her arrested at Venice and brought to Berlin to fulfil a contract to dance there, while the pursuing Mackenzie was expelled from the country when he arrived:

> . . . as I acted in the capacity of Aide-de-Camp to the General I had occasion to be in every part of the line, during the action . . . . We lay there till midday . . . when there was an alarm given that the rebels were in full march towards us, upon which the whole army was drawn up in the front of our camp, which was a very strong one by the natural situation of the place; advice was brought us that the rebels were not advancing directly towards our camp, but were marching up on some high grounds which were to our left, and about $1\frac{1}{2}$ miles from us, so the general who was reconnoitring those high grounds sent me to order the cavalry to move that way immediately, and the infantry and artillery to follow them as fast as possible, he being afraid the rebels might get by us on the left, and perhaps cut off our communication with Edinburgh, or, at least, get away from us, which was the thing we were most afraid of. As soon as the troops could come up we were formed into two lines, with all our cavalry (which consisted of six squadrons) on our left on the summit of the hill; as the general imagined the enemy was more afraid of horse than foot, he ordered the dragoons to begin the attack, which they did very briskly, but the Highlanders making all their efforts against them, and giving them a sharp fire, Hamilton's dragoons most scandalously gave way, which soon put the other squadrons into confusion. They again coming in upon the foot, broke them, this caused a general panic, many of them threw down their arms and ran away, whole platoons on the left of the first line went off, and by that means broke the second line; what hindered the rebels from pursuing our left, God knows! if they had, they must have cut almost the whole left wing to pieces. Two or three battalions on our right kept their ground, and even obliged the left of the rebels to retreat, so that we were a matter of half an hour on the field of battle after all firing ceased, but night coming on, and there having been during the whole time of the action a violent storm of hail rain and wind, our ammunition was so wet, that not one in twenty muskets would go off, upon which it was judged proper to retire to our camp, where we drew up expecting the Highlanders would come down upon us. By this time numbers of our foot rallied, and some of the dragoons; so when we had remained about half an hour under arms and found the rebels did not care to attack us a second time, we were ordered to burn the tents, and march to Lithgow directly, but the tents were too wet to burn, so most of them fell into the enemy's hands, who came to Falkirk about an hour after we had left the camp . . . our ammunition was entirely spoilt with the rain, so that it would have been impossible for us to have remained in our camp that night. We were obliged to leave seven pieces of cannon on the field of battle, for some of our runaways had carried off the horses belonging to the train . . . our artillery did not come up time enough to do us any service, which was a great disadvantage to us, especially as we had to do with the Highlanders, who don't at all love cannon . . . this unfortunate affair which does us very little honour, for they were inferior to us in numbers, had no artillery, and made but very little use of their broadswords, which is the weapon they rely most upon, and yet notwithstanding all this, if the victory was to be given to either side, it certainly was theirs . . . we have long expected the Hessians with great impatience, their hussars would be of great service to us at present, as well as their regular troops to animate our men, who seem to have lost all spirit, and sense of honour.

Archibald Cunningham, a captain in the Royal Regiment of Artillery who was in command of ten cannon, explained the failure of the artillery. Cunningham was told that:

... he must march the artillery up an adjacent hill in the rear of the first line of the army. The roads were here so very bad and intricate that it was not only out of his power to keep up with the first line, but the rear line also passed by the train, and were both forming, before he could possibly bring up the artillery. Then two of his largest guns in the front stuck in a bog, which he could not disengage by any endeavours he could at that time use, neither could he bring forwards any of the guns that were behind except two 4-pounders and one 1½-pounder. He had gone but a little farther with these, when meeting a bad piece of ground, which he was endeavouring to avoid, he heard a discharge of small arms ...

and saw the infantry fleeing. This led his own men to flee and Cunningham consequently ordered the three guns to withdraw. Thomas Ashe Lee, an officer in Wolfe's regiment, attributed the defeat to poor generalship and the failure to move up the artillery earlier. Cumberland urged harsh measures, 'As to the behaviour of the Irish dragoons, I am not surprised .... For God's sake purge the foot; for they did not use to run away'.[9]

The battle revealed that the royal troops could stand firm, but it was a Jacobite victory. Hawley's men had mostly been driven from the field, the second line of foot without firing a shot and the cavalry had failed to cope with the Highlanders. Clearly the heavy rain and the growing darkness of a late winter afternoon reduced the effectiveness of the infantry, making it harder to aim accurately and wetting their powder so that it would not ignite. Equally the terrain was against the royal troops. Nevertheless, a more mobile opponent, such as the Jacobite army, was likely to have the advantage of terrain and to avoid being obliged to fight on ground of its opponent's choosing. Falkirk was scarcely propitious for the Hanoverian cause. As Hawley fell back to Edinburgh the strategic purpose of the Falkirk campaign was clearly achieved by the Jacobites, rather than their rivals. Stirling Castle had not been relieved. Instead, Edinburgh feared attack. On 23 January Samson Gideon noted the effect of Falkirk in London, 'The fatal bad news we received yesterday from the north of which the papers abounds has stopped the rise of our funds and sunk peoples spirits considerably'. Charles Edward's brother Henry used the news of the victory to redouble pressure on the French to send assistance.[10] It was felt necessary to replace Hawley as commander by Cumberland, who left London on 25 January, arriving in Edinburgh on the morning of the 30th.

Falkirk was an opportunity lost. Charles Edward was urged on 18 January to reoccupy Edinburgh and the situation was certainly propitious for an advance. Though the Hanoverians had only had about 420 men killed (to the Jacobite 50), their losses were greater once wounded, prisoners and fled are considered and the morale of most of Hawley's force was poor. Thus, though his army was larger than Cope's at Prestonpans, it was unlikely that it would be more successful, and the Jacobite force was far larger than it had been at the earlier engagement. Hawley could have sought to defend Edinburgh, a better prospect than a winter retreat to Berwick and Newcastle, and that would have been a more formidable challenge than a force arrayed on a battlefield. Charles Edward had few cannon and they could not have been moved from Stirling speedily, especially as he did not have command of the sea. To storm city walls without covering artillery fire was a formidable task, though better-defended places, such as Prague and Bergen-op-Zoom, fell to storm during the War of the

Austrian Succession and a force of motivated irregulars was arguably best suited for such a task.

Whatever the military possibilities of an advance on Edinburgh, it is clear, from what happened, that the alternative was disastrous. The aftermath of Falkirk witnessed stress-related ill-health on the part of Charles Edward, who found it preferable to go to stay at Bannockburn House with his lover Clementina Walkinshaw rather than deal with recriminations among the Jacobite leaders over the failure to obtain a complete victory. The siege of Stirling Castle continued, but the Jacobites were hindered by the strength of the defence and the incompetence of their own siege engineers. On 18 January the castle rejected a summons to surrender. The besiegers had little to counter the castle's artillery. An unsympathetic townsman recorded on 26 January, 'great firing from the trenches upon the castle with small arms, from nine in the morning till six at night, without any execution'. On the 28th the Jacobites finished their battery, but when the following morning they began to fire their three cannon at the castle, the defenders replied with thirteen guns which 'dismounted their guns, beating their mouth, broke their carriages and levelled their trenches in a sad manner, and a great numbers of them killed'.[11]

Not surprisingly Jacobite morale, which, as at Carlisle, had fallen during the siege, fell even further when it became clear that the castle would not capitulate. The prince paid only one visit to the trenches, a foolish oversight that was to cost him dear. His army had suffered serious desertion since Falkirk, a problem that could probably have been avoided had they advanced on Edinburgh and that was exacerbated by their opponents' awareness of it. News of Cumberland's journey north led Charles Edward to send Lord George Murray orders to prepare to fight Cumberland west of Edinburgh at Linlithgow or Falkirk. Given this decision, it seems clear that the failure to march on Edinburgh after Falkirk was mistaken, not least because the force there was also to be reinforced by three regiments. However, there was to be no battle. On the evening of the 29th Murray sent the prince a document he and six clan chiefs had signed pressing for a retreat to the Highlands in view of the military situation. Particular attention was devoted to desertion, Murray noting that 'some of their battalions were a third weaker than they were before the battle'.[12] Because of this any Jacobite force would be outnumbered by Cumberland. In fact Murray exaggerated the desertion rate. It was proposed that the Jacobites drive Loudoun from Inverness, consolidate their position in the Highlands and thus strengthen their army, rather than continuing to besiege Stirling.

The prince was horrified by this advice, pointing out that a retreat would damage morale, would not prevent Cumberland from pursuit and would wreck chances of Bourbon assistance. Failing to persuade the clan chiefs, he was obliged to accept a retreat which began disastrously on 1 February. News of the decision led many clansmen to set off towards their homes, while on the 1st confusion and poor staffwork led to the abandonment of artillery, prisoners and wounded. The retreat deprived Cumberland of a battle. He both wanted one and had been advised by Blakeney that, because of a shortage of supplies, he could only hold Stirling Castle for another ten days. On 30 January Webb informed Ridley that the army would set out for Stirling the following morning,

Falkirk 29th January 1746

We think it our Duty in this Critical Juncture to lay our opinions in the most respectful manner before your Royal Highness. —

We are certain that a vast number of the Soldiers of your Royal Highness's Army are gone home since the Battle of Falkirk, and notwithstanding all the endeavours of the Commanders of the different Corps, they find that this evil is increasing hourly, and not in their power to prevent and as we are afraid Stirling Castle cannot be taken so soon as was expected if the enemy should march before it fall into Your R.H's hands, we can foresee nothing but utter destruction to the few that will remain; considering the inequality of our numbers to that of the enemy — For these Reasons we are humbly of opinion that there is no way left to extricate Your R.H. and those who remain with you, out of the most imminent danger, but by retiring immediately to the Highlands where we can be usefully employed the remainder of the Winter by taking and mastering the Forts in the North, and we are morally sure we can keep as many men together as will answer that end, & hinder the enemy from following us in the mountains at this Season of the year, and in spring we doubt not but an Army of Ten thousand effective Highlanders can be brought together and follow your R.H. wherever you think proper; this will certainly disconcert your enemies and cannot but be approved of by Your R.H's friends both at home and abroad, if a landing should happen in the mean time, the Highlanders would immediately rise either to Join them, or to make a powerful diversion elsewhere. —

The hard Marches which your Army have undergone

Address by the clan chiefs at Falkirk, requesting Charles to retire to the Highlands, 29 January 1746

'I hope to God our men will stand. I think we have all the reason in the world to expect they will'. Cumberland was more optimistic, writing to Newcastle that day that he would take enough troops 'to drive them off the face of the earth, if they will do their duty, which we must expect'. He also drew up a new order of battle, reflecting the experience of Falkirk, 'I put all the cavalry on the third line, because the rebels by all accounts don't fear them as they do our fire, and on that I depend'. Cumberland left Edinburgh on the 31st singing an old Scots melody 'Will you play me fair, Highland Laddie, Highland Laddie?'.[13]

Retreating across the Forth the Jacobites held a council meeting at Crieff, where alongside bitter recriminations and accusations of treachery Murray pressed for a retreat to Inverness via the Tay and the Highlands. Hopeful of a French landing and fearing desertion in the Highlands, Charles Edward wanted to go via the coast. It was finally decided that the prince would lead the Highlanders through the mountains, while Murray, the Lowlanders and the cavalry took the coast road. The retreat was described in an anonymous letter of 6 February:

> As soon as the rebels passed the Forth, the men deserted fast, so that they were not above 3,000 when they went through Crieff; they marched in a great hurry to Perth, but did not enter it with their main body, only detached 1,000 who spiked up twenty pieces of cannon which were left there, and threw all the ammunition into the river. The inhabitants of Perth as soon as the Highlanders were gone rung the bells, and took up arms, and seized about twenty men that had loitered behind.

The writer disagreed with 'the general opinion, that they are so dispersed as puts an end to any further enterprises' but wrote 'the Highlanders cannot be pursued by reason of the great fall of snow last week in the Highlands'.

There was relief in Edinburgh at the Jacobite retreat, Andrew Fletcher being carried away by the occasion on the 5th, 'The glorious turn his R.H. has given to the King's affairs, in so short a time surpasses everything in history . . . the rebels continue to fly'.[14] However, the situation was not propitious for a pursuit. Cumberland reached Stirling on 2 February and Crieff on the 5th, Joseph Yorke writing from the latter, 'the only difficulty will be subsistence, which is bare already, but when beyond Perth will be much worse, for they have destroyed all they could in their flight . . . . Every step we take here grows worse and worse, and ever since we left Stirling we have gone up hill, and I see nothing but snowy mountains above us'.

Cumberland was convinced that 'the rebellion is now crushed, and nothing left but the punishment due to their crimes', and on the next day, the 6th, he reached Perth. Joseph Yorke wrote thence on the 8th, making it clear that Cumberland's circle was determined to extirpate rebellion in Scotland:

> The want of several necessaries has obliged us to stop here . . . but I hope soon we shall be able to move forward and extirpate the race if we are not stopt by lenity, as has been the case on former occasions . . . I hope we may not be deprived of the power to revenge the nation on the beggarly wretches . . . the thing must be put an end to so effectually now, that it will never be able to break out again; otherwise you may depend on having it again in a very short time . . . I don't doubt soon but we shall have shut 'em up within the Lochs, where it will be at least a summer's work to clear those parts of 'em and to destroy their *clannism*, but it must be gone thro' with.

An expedition towards Blair Atholl led Yorke to return to this theme.[15]

Yorke was, however, overly optimistic, when he suggested that Loudoun and Forbes would be able to defeat any Jacobite attack. Though in retreat, Charles Edward was not without strength. His men captured the barracks at Ruthven and on 16 February the prince spent the night at Moy Hall. An attempt by Loudoun to surprise him there that night led to the 'Rout of Moy' when the advancing column of 1,500 men was intimidated in the dark by the shouts of five Jacobites into thinking that they were facing the entire Jacobite army. They retreated in panic and confusion. Loudoun's force was then affected by serious desertion and on 17 February a Council of War decided that it would be impossible to defend Inverness. As the Jacobites advanced on the town that day, Loudoun retreated into Sutherland. He left some men in the castle, but it surrendered, and Loudoun was criticized for deciding to leave a force there, but failing to leave an adequate one.

When subsequently defending himself, Loudoun complained that he had only received money and arms on 9 February after waiting for four months for them and that they arrived 'at a time when the troops were ready to disband for want of pay, and when the arms could be of very little use, as it was then impossible to assemble people, as that very day the rebels took the barracks of Ruthven'. He defended his advance on Moy. Although the prince's army was larger he determined to attack it at daybreak, 'what encouraged me to this, was that they lay scattered at five miles distance, and the principal people of them assembled in the nearest house to me', a marked contrast to Cumberland's camp the night before Culloden when Charles Edward planned a dawn attack after a night march. Loudoun complained that when he fell back on Inverness his force was affected badly by desertion, that the town itself was defenceless, that he had left Fort George there well supplied, and that his retreat across the river at Inverness had been rendered dangerous by Jacobite knowledge of his retreat and the speed of their advance.[16]

The fall of Inverness shook Cumberland's confidence and was regarded as 'very bad news' in London. Far from taking part in a clearing-up operation, much of which could be conducted by loyal Scots, it was now clear that the Jacobites were still a formidable military force who would not collapse on their own. The problem this posed was exacerbated by the general military situation, specifically the French advance in the Austrian Netherlands. Thomas Orby Hunter MP, the Deputy Paymaster of the Forces in the Austrian Netherlands, had warned Henry Pelham on 3/14 October 1745 of his fears about the recall of troops to Britain, adding 'I don't see where there can be a possibility of preserving the remains of our army here'.[17] Diplomats had commented that this recall had served France's purpose. Giovanni Giacomo Zamboni, an Italian in London who for many years had acted as a diplomatic agent for a number of second-rank rulers, including the Elector of Saxony, the Landgrave of Hesse-Darmstadt and the Duke of Modena, as well as being a procurer of young women, reported on 10/21 September 1745 that Charles Edward would be lucky to safely leave the 'labyrinthe in which he had had the courage to enter in order to support the ambitious projects of France, but in the meantime France had obtained her end by obliging the ministry to recall forces from Flanders'.[18]

Silver plaid buckle said to have been given to Prince Charles Edward by Finlay Macrae. It is inscribed 'Tearlach Stuart. Righ non Gael 1745'

This was underlined in the winter of 1745–6 when, having already recalled the British forces from the Austrian Netherlands, the ministry in London was obliged to send British-paid Hessians to Scotland to replace the 6,000 Dutch troops, whose value had been destroyed by French diplomatic pressure. On 20/31 December 1745 Trevor noted Dutch fears concerning the transfer of troops to Britain and wrote 'the point now is to keep things here, and in Brabant in *statu quo*, till England recovers her activity'. He was concerned about the possibility of a Franco–Dutch peace. On 21 January/1 February he commented on the French advance on Brussels, 'our Hessians are useless; having one leg in and the other out of their transports'. On 14/25 February, four days after the fall of Brussels to Saxe, Trevor attributed this blow primarily to Charles Edward, 'is justly to be imputed to the cursed rebellion at home'. The situation was to deteriorate further.

In December 1745 John, Earl of Dunmore, a British general, had warned that the garrison of Antwerp was under strength, arguing 'without such a number, in case of any attempt of the enemy's Antwerp is in no state of defence whatever'. Trenches were opened before Antwerp on 24 May, the garrison surrendering after a week. Mons fell on 10 July after a month's siege, Charleroi was stormed on 2 August and the citadel of Namur capitulated on 1 October. The campaign of 1746 had therefore delivered most of the Austrian Netherlands to France. This was a serious loss, Trevor viewing it as one not only for Britain and the Dutch, but also for Austria 'at once is its own dominions, the theatre of the common cause, the barrier of its two most natural and serviceable allies, and indeed the cement of their intimate union with the House of Austria'.[19] The situation was made more serious by the possibility that the alliance would disintegrate. The Dutch were known to be discussing peace with France, the Count de Wassenaer-Twickel arriving in Paris on 9/20 February, while the French were also putting out peace-feelers to Austria. Circumstances appeared favourable for a general peace: the French had clearly failed to overthrow Austria, Bavaria and France had settled their differences and Carteret's anti-French alliance had not made conquests at the expense of France. John Tucker noted on 24 December 1745 'many people think this a favourable conjuncture on which we may found solid hopes of a general pacification', but he doubted it on the grounds that 'France will not easily part with the conquests she has with so much facility gained in Flanders'.[20] On 14/25 December the Treaty of Dresden brought peace between Austria and Prussia. Chesterfield was convinced that this would be followed by a general peace, as it ended Maria Theresa's hopes of regaining Silesia from Frederick the Great, while he claimed 'The Dutch neither can nor will carry on the war any longer; France is willing enough to get out of, that is, advantageously, and we must pay for our folly, the sooner we pay it, the less we shall pay. I therefore conclude that all these jarring atoms, will somehow or other, soon jumble into some peace or other'.[21]

Dutch anger about the recall of troops from the Austrian Netherlands, especially the Hessians, was accompanied by threats to Britain that they would alter their attitude towards France. On 20 October 1745 Lord Hartington wrote to his father, the Duke of Devonshire, 'the Duke of Newcastle desired me to tell you, that the letters from abroad are not very agreeable, the Dutch are in a hurry to make a peace and want to include us in it and desire that we will consent to restore Cape Breton immediately'.[22] This situation was exacerbated by Franco-Dutch negotiations in December 1745 and January 1746 in which the French hoped to split the Dutch from Britain. They offered to restore the Austrian Netherlands and thus re-establish the Dutch buffer zone, if the British returned Cape Breton to France, which they were known not to want to do, while the issue of who should be recognized as King of Britain was employed as an excuse to treat with the Dutch separately.[23] At the beginning of 1746 there was talk of Dutch neutrality, while Trevor encountered difficulties in his negotiations for settling a plan for the forthcoming campaign.[24] The progress of operations against the Jacobites was brought up in his conferences, as he reported to Pelham on 14/25 February:

> . . . our measures for crushing the rebellion are taxed here with having been disproportionate and ill-placed: our dread of a French invasion to have been by some even affected, but by all to have been over hasty, and unsupported by any rational, and certain intelligence: the promises which I made by order upon every notification of the recall of our national troops, of their being to return as soon as possible, are now reclaimed; and the total silence now observed on that head in my last notification is attributed in great measure to a want of zeal and a disgust in our military gentry themselves to their own trade . . . I was told in so many words by the First Deputy 'that, if every time France pleased to send over a single battalion to Scotland she could operate a diversion of 30,000 men in England's quota to the combined army, England was not an ally for the Republic.'

Trevor warned of a danger that the Dutch would negotiate a peace unilaterally 'unless our present administration gives some immediate and public proof of its ascendant at home, and of its zeal abroad, illustrated by some real and speedy succour in the Low Countries (which can consist in no other than in British or Hanoverian troops) . . .'[25]

The fall of Brussels had increased the tension that was already serious after the movement of the Hessians. In Vienna at least one senior Austrian minister argued that the British had withdrawn the Hessians in order to lose Antwerp and thus increase the chance of a compromise peace based on the exchange of Flanders for Cape Breton.[26] There was thus a crisis of confidence over British intentions and capabilities within the anti-French alliance. A few British politicians could sympathize with these fears, Chesterfield arguing that the Dutch were being offered insufficient assistance. Edward Southwell, an opposition Whig MP from Bristol, explained his decision to support the ministry in the Commons, 'it is our interest to keep the Dutch from any neutrality or separate treaty with France and therefore it is our interest, by an address agreeable to the King's speech to show our immediate inclination to support them as far as our circumstances will admit'.[27] Many were unsympathetic but all too aware of the consequences. Arthur Villettes, envoy in Turin, was reduced to hoping that 'Providence has some means in store for us by which we may extricate ourselves and our friends out of so many difficulties', while Horatio Walpole responded by turning away, albeit temporarily, 'the prospect of the continuance, or conclusion of this war is to me so dismal that I am resolved to think of it as little as I can'.[28]

Thus, alongside the crisis of early December 1745, the possible collapse of the Hanoverian regime, must be placed that of early 1746, the all too likely splintering of the anti-French alliance. It was not only that the Jacobites prevented the British government from fulfilling its commitments to defending the Austrian Netherlands or, as the President of the French Council of Marine noted on 13/24 January, that the British were not in a position to mount an expedition against Canada,[29] and thus to follow up the success at Cape Breton. Far more threatening was the danger that the Dutch and Austrians would accept a peace or armistice during which the French could concentrate their efforts against Britain. The Dutch had already been accused of neglect and treachery for the deficiencies in their defence of the Austrian Netherlands. Recalling their ships from Vernon's squadron off the Downs exacerbated this practice.[30] The British argued that it was necessary to deal with the Jacobites before they turned to the Continent, Horatio Walpole writing 'that the nearest way for the Duke of Cumberland to go to command in Flanders was thro' Scotland'.[31] However, they could not be surprised that their allies failed to share this view, and this helps to account both for the concern and anger in ministerial circles about missed opportunities and for the determination to crush what were believed to be the seeds of future rebellion. The Jacobite retreat might look encouraging, but Falkirk, the failure to engage during Cumberland's march to relieve Stirling and Inverness were all setbacks and were seen by many as such. The crucial military decision in this respect was that the Hessians were not returned to the Austrian Netherlands as Cumberland, convinced he had enough men and concerned about supplies, had initially thought of doing when they arrived at

Leith on 8 February. He ordered the Earl of Crawford to have the ships that had brought the Hessians prepared and revictualled so that they could take them back. They would have been most welcome, both militarily and politically, in the Low Countries, but instead they were retained. The views of Cumberland's circle thus became more realistic, though Jacobite strength was still underestimated. On 19 February Fawkener informed Fletcher that, unlike Fletcher, the duke 'does not seem to apprehend the rebels are in a condition to form any enterprises . . . the clans are reduced to a very small number, and the others are not considerable, their own accounts do not make them three thousand men, and we don't take them to be much above two'. The following day Fletcher wrote of this concern to hear 'that the rebels still continue great bodies in arms'. Cumberland decided to send back the Dutch, but keep the Hessians, whom he ordered to advance to Stirling and Perth. James Cholmondeley wrote to his brother from Edinburgh on 21 February expressing his concern about the possibility of reversing French gains in the Low Countries, and added:

> I can by no means look upon this rebellion as over. Should the Duke leave the army our rascals would lose their spirit and should the rebels gain any advantage over any of our advanced parties it would intimidate us, it would give great spirit to their men and may set all afloat again. Were we to send ten or twelve thousand men to Flanders you would leave very few here who had seen any service.[32]

The Earl of Glenorchy wrote from Taymouth on 16 February 1746, 'The rebels are assembling very fast in the north, and those who went home from them are joining them again. They give out they'll attack Inverness, Fort Augustus and Fort William and demolish them before our army can come up to them'. He also noted one consequence of the rebellion, socio-economic disruption and a weakening in what could be regarded as deference or as economic bonds. Explaining to his daughter a fall in rents on his Argyllshire estates he noted 'the people are unwilling to pay in these turbulent times'.[33] Four days later General Huske wrote from Perth to Thomas Hill, friend and former tutor of Richmond, 'this rebellion may soon be over, but I promise you that if some speedy method is not soon fallen upon, and soon executed, you will have another rebellion before its long'. Hill himself informed Richmond on 3 March, 'an account came yesterday that they had made themselves masters of Inverness, and that some troops were landed from France, which had made the duke countermand the orders that have been given for the return of the Hessians, and they are now commanded to march northwards. In my humble opinion though the fire does not flame so violently as it did, it is very far from being extinguished'. Newcastle wrote to Richmond three days later:

> Our accounts from Scotland are very bad. The rebels are certainly reassembling; and it was thought, they will have more real Highlanders, than ever. The rebels have got Inverness, and the castle. Lord Loudoun is retreated further north. The Duke complains extremely of the country, and I am afraid with the greatest reason. H.R.H. is afraid the rebels will also get Fort Augustus. But he has taken care to secure, I hope, Fort William. H.R.H. deserves his statue in gold for having stopped the Hessians.[34]

Maule wrote to Fletcher from London on 1 March, 'the news of Loudoun's retiring, the taking of Inverness, and the blockade of the castle, with the arrival of the two ships from France, very bad. I hope our great people here won't fancy the rebellion yet over. This is the sixth or seventh time that we have had here the whole of this rebellion at an end, but always breaking out again with fresh vigour'. He supported the retention of the Hessians and on 4 March wrote from London:

> The folks here who some days ago believed the rebellion was over are again begun to have their fears, and its no wonder for I am of the opinion it looks worse than ever; these rebels are now quite desperate, they are near their own homes, which will make them fight better than they would do anywhere else and they'll get more to join them than ever they had before. Join to this the difficulty of subsisting the king's troops in the country.

On 1 April Maule was very upset by talk of the return of troops to Flanders, 'I think its madness to have the least notion . . . as long as this cursed rebellion subsists', a view he repeated on 8 April with reference to the dispatch of troops to reinforce Cape Breton. John Tucker came to a pessimistic conclusion on 18 March, 'affairs in Scotland look worse and worse the rebels are triumphant, and the French sending them constant succours, whilst the Duke seems to have too small a force to encounter them'.[35]

The international situation, the demands of British foreign policy and the consolidation of Jacobite strength in the Highlands therefore required speedy action by Cumberland, but he faced serious problems, principally supplies and the weather. Fawkener wrote from Perth on 8 February, 'His Royal Highness has been here since the 6th refreshing the troops, and getting together some store of provisions and forage, for as we may advance further, we are not to depend on the country for anything, this work is pretty forward'.[36] The duke was, however, obliged to return to Edinburgh to sort out problems with the supply of money and bread. He arranged an important change in that of money, which had posed serious problems for Hawley. Tax revenue held by collectors in the north of England was to be sent directly to Edinburgh, instead of going via the Treasury in London. This at once increased the funds at the disposal of Cumberland's army and improved its credit. Supplies of bread were harder to arrange. The principal contractor in Edinburgh was, like many European army contractors, a Jew, Gomes Serra. He faced a difficult situation as grain was in short supply and Cumberland's demands rose with the arrival of the Hessians. Nevertheless he was able to provide two weeks supply of flour, thanks to which the duke was able to move from Perth to Aberdeen, where he arrived on 27 February, having left garrisons behind at Blair Castle and Castle Menzies to prevent the Jacobites from advancing into the Lowlands. It was necessary to move along the coast in order to ensure the supply of provisions. Supplies had been sent by sea from Newcastle to Edinburgh. Fawkener wrote to Fletcher from Perth on 10 February asking him to send coal for the army by ship to Montrose 'and so along the coast to Aberdeen'. He complained that the army was forced to remain at Perth by a shortage of bread. After Cumberland occupied Aberdeen troops and provisions were sent thither from Edinburgh by sea. The north-eastern coast appeared to be the logistical key to the Highlands, for the occupation of the ports of Montrose, Stonehaven and Aberdeen would also make it harder for the French to send reinforcements and supplies. Webb wrote from Aberdeen on 8 March:

> As to the rebels, I believe they had some thoughts of dispersing till they had information of an embarkation of troops made by France in their favour – upon which they have had the impudence to assemble again near Inverness in a large body of Highlanders . . . give out they will meet our army and oppose our crossing the River Spey . . . we shall have fifteen battalions of foot and six squadrons of cavalry if they can but get food to live on . . . our stay here has been but eight days yet, which has been employed in sending out partys securing posts cutting off the rebels provisions and refreshing our own troops.[37]

The following day, Joseph Yorke, also in Aberdeen, explained why Cumberland was not able to move with the speed he thought necessary, but offered a generally optimistic account. He drew attention to the 'poverty of the country', and therefore the need to provide supplies, and to ways blocked by snow, and admitted that 'delay in this case hurts all Europe'. Yorke was wrong to claim both that Loudoun would be too strong for the Jacobites and that Fort Augustus would hold out, but he predicted correctly that when Cumberland advanced the River Spey would not be held against him:

> With all these detachments out, they would fain persuade us that they will dispute the passage of the Spey. Whether they imagine we are fools and will believe this or are really fools themselves and will attempt it, I can't tell; but to convince the world that there is a good deal of difference between regular and irregular troops on these occasions, I must confess I would fain flatter myself it is their intention. These people have no tents nor can they, by their own confession, encamp if they had. Firing cross a river would not suit with their constitutions, since they pretend to nothing further than a *coup de main*; and lastly, within the space of ten miles there are upwards of forty fords . . . it does not seem probable to me they will be so civil as to play the ball thus into our hands.

Yorke drew attention to the advantage of resting the troops in Aberdeen, where the health of exhausted men could recover and reinforcements could arrive, but could not avoid the threatening international situation, 'every hour produces some new cause to curse the vile authors of all our misfortunes. I don't see that we shall quit this country in time enough to go anywhere else'.[38]

Fawkener explained the continued stay at Aberdeen on 4 April by referring to 'the climate, the season of the year, and the necessity of having magazines of provisions' but he was convinced it was beneficial, 'our troops are in exceedingly good condition, their fruitless marches under Marshal Wade, in the dead of winter and always encamped, had quite worn them down, but they have recovered strength as well as spirit by the rest they have had here, and since the Duke's departure from Edinburgh, at least a thousand recovered men are joined the army from the hospitals'. In late February Cumberland had ordered blankets to be sent to the army. On 1 March Fletcher had expressed his hope that the weather would improve 'and thereby disappoint the rebels' expectations of destroying our army by long marches in bad weather and without cover'. Four weeks later Fawkener informed Fletcher that he expected the rebels to disperse

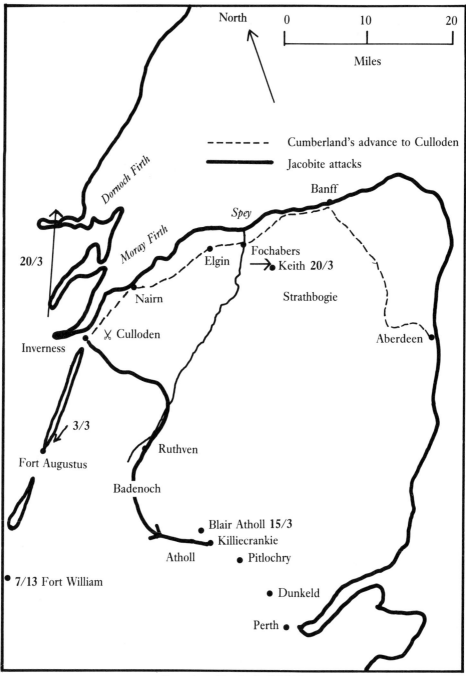

Operations, March–April 1746

as Cumberland advanced, that the duke felt that he had sufficient troops and had not asked for the reinforcements then arriving and that the army was to move on 2 April.[39]

The soldiers at Aberdeen were trained to deal with the most fearsome aspect of fighting the Highlanders, hand-to-hand combat with men wielding broadswords. This essentially required a refinement in bayonet tactics. The bayonet was a comparatively recent innovation, introduced to European armies in the closing decades of the seventeenth century and at the beginning of the eighteenth. Initially plug bayonets were used, but these knife blades inserted into gun muzzles prevented the guns from being fired, as happened to the detriment of the forces fighting the Jacobites at Killiecrankie in 1689. They were replaced by socket bayonets, blades fixed permanently to collars screwed around the outside of muzzles.[40] The bayonet tremendously increased infantry fire-power by leading to the end of the pikemen and thus ensuring that all infantrymen were both able to discharge offensive and defensive tasks. However, the bayonet did not have the same defensive capability as the pike and Prestonpans and Falkirk had revealed its limitations. The infantry at Aberdeen were trained to deal with the Highlanders' weapons of broadsword and targe (shield) by pointing their bayonets not at the opponent immediately to their front but at the man to his left, whose right side would be vulnerable, particularly if his broadsword was raised to deliver a blow. These new tactics were to be employed at Culloden, though that battle was decided by fire-power. However, it could be suggested that this fire-power was helped by greater confidence in the ability of units to resist the Highland charge.

Cumberland's army remained at Aberdeen until 8 April, by which time the Spey was low enough to be fordable. This period was not one of inaction. Indeed both the Jacobites and their opponents manoeuvred extensively to gain advantages. Neither side realized that they would soon be facing a major battle that would settle the matter and both therefore hoped that their operations in the difficult days of early 1746 would enable them both to gain control of areas that might yield supplies and improve their defensive position, and more crucially to campaign more effectively in what promised to be a long summer of activity once the weather improved. There were operations in the Great Glen, Perthshire, the north-east and to the north of Inverness. They are easy to overlook if Culloden is presented as an inevitable development or if attention is concentrated on Cumberland's soon-to-be victorious army, but they are of considerable importance, not least if it is appreciated that Charles Edward no more had to fight the duke at Culloden than he had earlier had to fight him in order to cover the siege of Stirling. If a major encounter had been postponed and Cumberland had been allowed to proceed unattacked to his objective, Inverness, as he had earlier been allowed an uncontested crossing of the Spey, then subsequent operations would have been greatly affected by developments in February and March, as indeed had been the Jacobite plan. Lord George Murray was convinced that the Jacobites could remain undefeated for several years and eventually force the Hanoverian regime to terms. He sought to prevent Cumberland from using Aberdeen as a base to overrun the north-east, while Jacobite forces consolidated their position in the Highlands by seizing the forts in the Great Glen, defeating

Prince Charles Edward's seal

Loudoun and driving back their opponents in Perthshire. By going onto the offensive they would gain ports through which French supplies could be received, encourage such French action, raise morale among the Jacobites, discourage their opponents and harry anti-Jacobite clans, while forcing Cumberland both to disperse his troops in defensive operations and to respond to their initiatives.

Fort Augustus fell rapidly, surrendering on 5 March after a siege of only two days and the explosion of the defenders' magazine. On 7 March the fast-moving Highlanders appeared outside Fort William. Capture of this would have added a valuable new port for receiving French aid that was better placed than Inverness, but Grant, the siege engineer who had been so successful at Fort Augustus, was killed by a cannon-ball and his French replacement Mirabel proved as incompetent as he had been at Stirling. The defence was helped by supplies and a determined commander, Captain Caroline Scott, who had been sent by Cumberland. The fortress was also stronger than Fort Augustus, which was why Lord George Murray had opposed the siege. On 31 March a sally by the garrison destroyed the Jacobite batteries, leading the Jacobites to abandon the siege on 3 April.

Operations against Loudoun were more successful. The earl had retreated from Inverness to the Black Isle and planned a rendezvous with Cumberland at

Banff for 10 March, reflecting the duke's initial determination to press on rapidly from Aberdeen. Loudoun had increased his mobility by seizing all the boats on the Cromarty and Dornoch Firths, but he found that much of his force, which had been enlarged with men provided by William, Earl of Sutherland, was unwilling to leave the region, while the delay in Cumberland's advance lessened the need for a rendezvous. Loudoun was able to defy the boatless Jacobites under George Mackenzie, Earl of Cromarty. Cromarty was superseded by James Drummond, Duke of Perth, who gathered together a fishing fleet at Findhorn and, in a thick fog that provided cover from the war ships in the Moray Firth blockading Inverness, the Jacobites, 3,000 strong according to Loudoun, landed on the north side of the Dornoch Firth on 20 March. In an operation made very confused by the thick fog, 200 of Loudoun's men surrendered, while Loudoun, Forbes and Sutherland retreated, eventually to Skye. Cumberland was thus deprived of the Highlanders with whom he had hoped to rendezvous. However, Jacobite strength was still diverted to achieve objectives to the north of the Great Glen, Cromarty being sent to recapture money dispatched by the French that had been seized by pro-Hanoverian Scots.

The Jacobites had also advanced into the Atholl country in northern Perthshire, threatening to fulfil Fletcher's fear of late February that they would advance on Perth. The Jacobites themselves feared a pincer movement from there and Aberdeen, Lord George Murray writing:

> There was about three hundred of the Argyleshire Highlanders at several posts in that country, and it was apprehended their numbers would increase, and it was given out that General Campbell was coming from Argyleshire with one thousand more; and then the Hessians were to march from Perth, and join them, as also the garrisons of Blair and Castle Menzies, and to march together towards Badenoch: and, by choosing a strong camp, they might harass us much on that side, especially their Highlanders. At the same time, the Duke of Cumberland was to march from Aberdeen.[41]

Such a combination would indeed be threatening because from Badenoch the besiegers of Fort William could be attacked, any force attempting to deny Cumberland the passage of the Spey could be taken in the flank and it would be possible to advance on Inverness from the south-east. On 15 March, Murray set off from Inverness with 700 Atholl men. Marching over thirty miles in twenty-four hours, they seized the thirty posts occupied by the Highlanders, as well as two with regular troops and the pass of Killiecrankie, without any casualties. On 17 March Murray then began to besiege Blair Castle. As he only had two 4-pounders, one of which was inaccurate, and nobody trained in undermining fortifications, the seven-foot thick walls were impregnable, but Murray decided to starve the defenders into surrender. Murray's advance led to a failure of nerve at Perth where Frederick of Hesse and John, Earl of Crawford decided to fall back to Stirling, until overruled by Cumberland. Such a retreat would have cut land communications between Cumberland's army and Edinburgh and forced it to become entirely dependant on supplies transported by sea. Frederick and Crawford, who had served in the Austrian army in 1735, with the Russians in 1738 and the Austrians in 1739 against the Turks, and at Dettingen and Fontenoy, then advanced towards Pitlochry, the Jacobites falling

Highland broadswords at Blair Castle

back to there from Dunkeld. However, Frederick showed no desire to force Pitlochry and the pass of Killiecrankie. The situation appeared ripe for a major engagement, but Frederick was reluctant to attack without the prisoner cartel (agreement to exchange) that Cumberland refused to allow him to negotiate and did not wish to expose his troops to ambush at Killiecrankie. Andrew Fletcher wrote of the Hessians on 1 April, 'I am afraid by their slow motions, and the attention they give to carry all their baggage along with them, that the castle of Blair for want of provisions may be in some danger, I do not believe that the Rebels are in condition to face the Hessians there'. Cumberland was unimpressed by what he saw as an absence of fighting spirit on the part of Frederick.[42] The ill Charles Edward refused to send Murray the 1,200 reinforcements he sought to achieve victory, claiming that he did not have such a force with him in Inverness. Murray finally returned to Inverness, without an engagement, in response to reports that Cumberland was about to advance. Blair Castle was thus relieved, though the strategic dilemma Murray had feared was avoided and there were no Hessians at Culloden.

While the Jacobites were taking the initiative in the Great Glen, the Atholl country and to the north of Inverness, Cumberland was not inactive at Aberdeen. He had sent forces forward to cover the approaches to both routes to

Strathspey, via Meldrum and Cullen, and through Kintore, Inverurie and Strathbogie. The Jacobites responded by moving forward. On 16 March Major-General Humphrey Bland advanced on Strathbogie to surprise the smaller Jacobite force. The next day the Earl of Albemarle, a veteran of Dettingen and Fontenoy, wrote to the Duke of Newcastle from Aberdeen:

> You, happy Londoners may be surprised at our long stay here, but the deep snow, bad weather, and consequently bad roads, and above all these difficulties contrary winds keeping our provisions and necessarys coming from Leith has obliged His Royal Highness, against his will, to it, but now that the aspect of the sky seems more favourably inclined I believe we shall march soon, Bland with four battalions, Kingston's horse and Cobban's Dragoons moved from hence last Wednesday to Inverary, Old Meldrum, and places adjacent, this day Mordaunt with four more battalions and cannon, marched from hence to those quarters, and Bland from thence to Strathbogie in order to attack a large detachment of the Rebels commanded by Roy Stewart, if they keep their post, and he thinks himself much inferior to them, he will encamp and send for Mordaunt to join him and attack them with their whole force, in which case we shall hear of our success by tommorrow evening, for I don't doubt wherever they stand of beating of them, These Highlanders (notwithstanding the way of thinking of some) are sad cowardly rascals.

However, surprise was lost and the Jacobites were able to retire to Fochabers without loss. The Jacobites counter-attacked on 20 March by a night raid on Keith which surprised a body of Campbell militia, leading to their surrender. Bland withdrew from Keith to Strathbogie. A subsequent move on Keith was repulsed by the Jacobites.

A rough front line had thus been defined, but Cumberland had failed to put military pressure on the Jacobites and to counteract their advances elsewhere. It was not surprising that ministers in London were worried. On 5 April Lord Chancellor Hardwicke wrote, 'the long continuance of this execrable rebellion, notwithstanding the vigilance and activity of H.R.H., the barefaced and open assistance daily given to it, and the sly, underhand supports and encouragement it meets with, gives me the utmost anxiety. Besides the public calamity to the Kingdom, it hangs upon the wheels of all business and infects and clogs every measure'. He turned for consolation to the start of the conventional campaigning season, 'when the season will permit the Duke to move, I doubt not that all will be retrieved'.[43] The previous day Cumberland had excused his failure to advance 'I have met with so many difficulties, as have hitherto prevented me. But, the three last days of dry south wind have brought up our firing and provisions and have I hope rendered the Spey fordable'.[44]

The Jacobites were indeed in severe difficulties. Shortage of funds forced them to pay their soldiers in kind and encouraged desertion. The sickly Charles Edward contributed nothing either to strategic planning or to the financial situation beyond reiterated statements that the French would send assistance. They had, in fact, sent 396,000 écus in three ships. *L'Emeraude* reached Aberdeen just before Cumberland's army and had to leave the port without landing her cargo. The squadron returned safely to Dunkirk, with the exception of *L'Aventurier* which landed some supplies at Peterhead on 25 February/8 March before being forced to run aground by three British warships. The ship was burned, though the crew escaped and Charles Edward was provided with a small sum of money, useful but no substitute for the 1,000 troops the squadron had carried. The *Prince Charles* sent later in the month carried 252,000 livres (about £15,250), over 1,000 pistols and broadswords and 13 barrels of powder. The ship was fast and small, but it could not evade interception in the Pentland Firth on 25 March/4 April. The boat sought to escape by sailing into shallow water near Tongue, but the *Sheerness* was able to seriously damage it with cannon fire. The crew landed, only to be captured, with the money, by Lord Reay, one of Loudoun's supporters. Charles Edward sent Cromarty to recapture the money but he failed both in this and in seeking to elicit support from Sutherland and Caithness and his force was defeated by pro-Hanoverian Sutherlanders the day before Culloden.

On 20/31 March the French agent d'Eguilles reported that the prince had only sufficient money left for two weeks. The loss of the cargo of the *Prince Charles* made it impossible to see any hope of paying the troops and impelled the Jacobites to abandon their diverse operations of March and to seek the battle that Cumberland wanted. Murray's operations in Atholl would, if successful in battle, have led to a march on Perth and the consequent dislocation of the military structure of the Hanoverian forces in Scotland, Cumberland running the risk of being left in Aberdeen rather as Wade had been at Newcastle, an undefeated strategic irrelevance. The prince, who in his paranoid style distrusted Murray's attempt to negotiate a cartel with Frederick of Hesse, had refused to send Murray the forces he deemed necessary, but he had little alternative to offer bar fighting Cumberland in the very area in which he wished to engage. Cumberland proposed to advance to Inverness, after which he had no fixed plans, intending to act in accordance with 'what Rebels may do, on our moving forward'. The duke's forces were not to be exhausted or divided or strung out by having to reply to Jacobite initiatives. Charles Edward had initially intended to advance on Cumberland, but the general malaise in which lack of funds played a major role made this impossible.

Instead it was to be Cumberland who took the initiative, marching from Aberdeen on 8 April via Old Meldrum, Banff and Cullen, which he reached on the 11th, to cross the Spey between Fochabers and the mouth of the Spey at noon on the 12th. The water came up to the 'middles' of the infantry, but the sole losses were one dragoon and four women drowned. The 2,000 Jacobites on the opposite bank retreated without fighting. The river was a formidable obstacle, Cumberland writing, 'it is a very lucky thing we had to deal with such an enemy, for it would be a most difficult undertaking to pass the river before an enemy who should know how to take all advantages of the situation'. Joseph Yorke sent an account to his father in which he dwelt on the strength of the position and the respective morale of the two forces:

If the rebels had defended this river, we should have found some difficulty to have passed so cheap; for I never saw a stronger post in my life by nature, and a very little art would have rendered it very strong and tenable. The rebels here, who were chiefly the Lowlanders, complain bitterly of the Pretender and the clans for not coming down to them which, joined to the entire want of money, renders them mutinous and fearful. The greater part of the Macintoshes left them some days ago and the men desert in droves . . . . Our men are in high spirits and showed the utmost alacrity in fording the river, though up to their waists.[45]

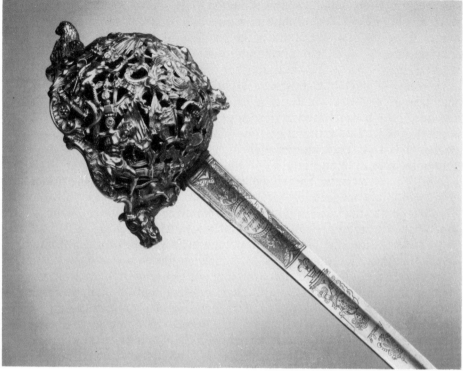

Prince Charles Edward's basket-hilted sword, possibly presented to him with the targe as part of the accoutrements of Highland dress by the Duke of Perth. Tradition has it that the sword was taken from Charles Edward's baggage waggon by the Duke of Cumberland

The Spey crossing was, without doubt, a lost opportunity. Fawkener was reinforced in his opinion that the Jacobites would not fight by their failure to contest the crossing of the river 'for the Spey was worth more than any two clans they have'. Albemarle argued that they could have contested the passage of the Spey, Findhorn and Nairn 'with ease and no danger to themselves'.[46] Had the Jacobites been present in larger numbers and supported by artillery they would have been better placed to contest the crossing, though it would have been far from easy to supply such an army for any length of time and the strategic initiative would still have rested with Cumberland. Given the unequal terms on which the Jacobites were to fight at Culloden and on terrain that was not to their advantage, it is surprising that more of an effort was not made to take advantage of the Spey, the last major natural obstacle before Inverness, even if the force had been no larger than the 2,000 men deployed under Lord John Drummond. Such a contingent was, of course, outnumbered, but Cumberland would have been able to deploy only a section of his army, and neither his cavalry nor his infantry's fire-power or new bayonet tactics would have been of much value had his men been attacked while leaving the water. In addition, the effectiveness of the duke's artillery would have been limited in what would probably have been a subsequent mêlée. The Jacobite response can be blamed on the dispersal of forces in operations that owed much to clan concerns, the failure of Lord George Murray to retain a central position over the previous month, the reluctance of Charles Edward when in his black moods to consider matters in a prudent and balanced fashion and a degree of lack of concern over Cumberland's moves. The Jacobite failure to concentrate their dispersed forces was one of the reasons cited by Fawkener on 15 April for his conviction that they would not fight. Lee wrote, 'some few of their clans which had not joined them occasioned that infatuation among them, which suffered us to pass the Spey and Findhorn without opposition, where thousands must have fallen'.

The prince now faced the prospect of a major battle or the loss of Inverness. The latter might not seem too serious as he had held it for less than two months, but Inverness in the hands of Cumberland would be very different to the town in the hands of Loudoun. From it Cumberland would be able to strike south-east to Badenoch, down the Great Glen, over to the west coast and north into Ross and Sutherland. Considering how to act if the prince avoided battle, Glenorchy suggested to the duke that the rebellion would last until the Jacobites were '. . . shut up behind Loch Ness, and a chain which might be easily made there'. Charles Edward could have retired and avoided an engagement as in early February at Stirling, but the situation was now very different. In early February the prince's retreat was protected by the effects of the weather on terrain and communications, while Cumberland's advance was hindered by supply difficulties. Now the snows were melting, the rivers dropping and the winds abating, while the duke's men were well paid and fed and their morale was high. Cumberland reported on 13 April, 'we have had the finest weather that could be wished, for our first encampment, and have hitherto found plenty of straw and forage'. Two days later he added 'tolerable plenty of everything for our incampments. The only hindrances we had on our march, were several broad waters, which the men were forced to wade'. Fawkener wrote from Nairn on 15 April 'we have been most fortunate in our setting out, dry weather, no want of anything even of straw or fuel, and fair winds to bring along our little fleet with us'.[47]

The retreat from Stirling had badly damaged the morale of the prince's army and led to many desertions. Another retreat would be more damaging, especially as it would follow the repulse at Fort William and the retreat from Atholl. It was already proving difficult to keep the army together. Murray noted, 'many of our people, as it was seed time, had slipped home; and as they had no pay for a month past, it was not an easy matter to keep them together'. This was not a problem that affected the Jacobites solely. On 10 April Glenorchy wrote to Joseph Yorke, seeking to excuse the desertion of his own men:

This is the time of year for sowing their grounds by which their families are to be supported, which makes country farmers very earnest to go home after being six months absent . . . I believe this restlessness is in the nature of the Highlanders, for it is the same thing with those in the rebellion. Their chiefs can never keep them long together; they are every now and then running home, and their masters are forced to fetch them out again.[48]

Not only would retreat encourage desertion in an army whose food supply had collapsed thanks to a breakdown in administrative arrangements, it would also make it harder to gather together the scattered units of the army.

To give these units time to arrive, the Jacobites sought to delay Cumberland's advance as they marched forward close to the sea, where a squadron provided artillery cover and intelligence and, more significantly, supply. On 13 April the duke advanced via Elgin to Alves. The following day he pressed on to Nairn, despite an effort to cut off his advance guard, which Cumberland thwarted with cavalry action, under Bland. Bland pursued the Jacobites beyond Nairn.[49] Their delaying action had failed, unsurprisingly so in light of the disparity in numbers. Charles Edward had his army drawn up for battle outside Culloden House on 15 April, but Cumberland chose not to advance that day, his twenty-fifth birthday, preferring to rest his army at Nairn. Instead, the prince chose to regain the advantage by launching a dawn attack on Cumberland's camp, hoping through surprise both to offset the disadvantage in numbers and to employ the hand-to-hand combat that would nullify the duke's superior fire-power. Charles Edward also claimed that in night fighting secret sympathizers in Cumberland's army would be able to assist him, a statement that revealed his capacity for self-deception.

The night march was not successful. Instead of moving, as planned, in three separate columns and keeping to the pace of the Highlanders, only one route was followed while on the difficult moorland and in a dense fog the Irish troops from France were unable to keep up with the Highlanders. Unexpected obstacles included a bottle-neck created by a stone wall and dykes on the wet moor. Murray, who led the van, wrote 'before we got six miles, the road had been so bad, and I was stopped so often, by aide-de-camps sent to me to give time for the line to follow, that it was near two in the morning; and having still four long miles, it was found impracticable to be near the enemy till it was within an hour of day-light, and as our only hope was surprising them, and attacking them before day, we were forced to give it up'.[50] The situation was somewhat more complex. The van would probably have enjoyed surprise had it attacked, but the delays affecting the rest of the force ensured that only 1,200 men would have been available, against 8,000 in Cumberland's force. The Jacobites had set off too late, because of an unsuccessful attempt to recall men who had left to search for food in Inverness, the time required for the march had been underestimated and the force as a whole had lacked the cutting edge required for the operation. The men were hungry and tired, the officers divided over the merits of the march and the plan was not adequately conceived. It was also based in part on the expectation that their enemies would be drunk from celebrating Cumberland's birthday. In fact they had had relatively little to drink and the duke's camp, far from slumbering after an evening of bacchanalia, was prepared for action.

No longer needing to maintain secrecy, the Jacobite army returned across the moor faster than they had set out. Most of them had returned to Culloden by about 6 a.m. It was not the best of preparations for a major engagement, though had the battle been fought outside Nairn, and an element of surprise gained or Cumberland's fire-power been otherwise limited, the situation would have been different. As it was, military activity between the evening of the 15th and the following afternoon was divided into two: the night march and the battle. The failure of the first did not make the result of the second inevitable, but the prince's stubborn insistence on fighting near Culloden, despite being warned of the disadvantages of the site, can in part be attributed to the exhaustion and wilfulness that he experienced after a retreat that he had sought without success to prevent. On 5 March Albemarle had written to Newcastle expressing the hope that the Jacobites would contest the passage of the Spey, 'for as I make no doubt of beating of them, a brush would put an end to this cursed and unnatural rebellion, and without such a thing this affair may be tedious and lasting, for these villains will lead us a dance from one bad country to a worse, and through the worse people I ever knew'.[51] Charles Edward was about to provide the engagement for which Albemarle had been hoping.

8 Culloden and its Aftermath

It is not an easy task to describe a battle. Springs and motions escape the eye, and most officers are necessarily taken up with what is immediately near themselves; so that it is next to impossible for one to observe the whole: add to this, the confusion, the noise, the concern that the people are in, whilst in the heat of action.

Lord George Murray on Falkirk[1]

They have not had such a thrashing since the days of Old Noll [Cromwell], and whatever the Jacobites may insinuate to lessen their losses; believe them not, for the country is covered with their dead bodies and arms and the gaols are full of their prisoners; what pity it is that so much resolution and bravery as our troops had that day, could not be united in the confederate armies and fall upon the grand enemy of the liberties of Europe but I hope the time is coming when we shall speak with him . . . I hope we shall soon finish this rebellion and bring their nobles in chains and their chiefs in fetters of iron.

Major Webb, 21 April 1746[2]

Your Royal Highness has been fully informed how deeply we are engaged in Scotch Reformation, which your indefatigable labours and glorious success on the day, which makes the date of this labour, has given the opportunity for.

Hardwicke to Cumberland, 16 April 1747[3]

Culloden was a battle decided by fire-power. Its result reflected the strength of the defence, undisturbed by early exchanges of musket fire and not subject to artillery bombardment, when it was able to deploy well-disciplined fire-power against a clearly visible target. The battle was indeed a killing-field and several battle-hardened soldiers commented on the slaughter. Lieutenant-Colonel

George Stanhope, who had been wounded at Fontenoy and served at Falkirk, informed his elder brother Philip, 2nd Earl Stanhope five days later:

> . . . our regiment being next to Wolfe's that was on the left of the second line, and both regiments outflanking Barrell's of the front line had the finest opportunity imaginable which we did not let slip of giving the column of the rebels that was not forty yards distance from our regiment's right the most infernal flanking fire that ever was given and saved Barrell's by it and contributed greatly to turn the whole for the rebels were soon after put to flight, and when we marched on to pursue them I never saw such dreadful slaughter we had made lying as thick as if they grounded their arms and our men gave no quarter to them; I reckon two thousand of them killed in the field besides full a thousand killed in the pursuit by the horse and dragoons with a great many of their chiefs.[4]

Much of the blame for these losses can be attributed to Charles Edward for he insisted on fighting on what he was warned would be a disadvantageous battle

Culloden Moor, site of the battle, 16 April 1746

field. Charles Edward was determined to fight on Drummossie Moor south of Culloden House. Two other sites were proposed to him if he insisted on fighting east of Inverness. Lord George Murray, who thought Drummossie Moor 'not proper for Highlanders',[5] suggested some rough ground close to Dalcross Castle. In addition, on the 15th Murray suggested that Brigadier Walter Stapleton and Colonel Ker of Graden should examine the ground on the south side of the River Nairn. They found it hilly and boggy, and thus unsuitable for Cumberland's cavalry and cannon, but Murray's advocacy of this battle field was overruled on the grounds that it might allow Cumberland to march to Inverness. Relations between Charles Edward and Murray were so poor that his support for an idea invited the opposition of the prince who did not anyway wish to appear to fall back before Cumberland. A number of leaders, including Murray, only agreed to support the uncertain night attack on Cumberland's camp because it appeared to be the sole alternative to fighting on Drummossie Moor.

When on the morning of the 16th the Jacobites returned to the moor Murray suggested three alternatives to Charles Edward: retiring to Inverness, dispersing into the hills to subsequently reform and fighting south of the Nairn. The prince rejected the ideas, arguing that Cumberland would be at an advantage at Inverness, that, short of food, the clansmen could not afford to retreat to the Highlands and that to fight south of the Nairn would be to expose Inverness. Charles Edward was correct to doubt the value of retiring behind the walls of Inverness. Cumberland, reinforced by sea, would have battered them with artillery. Once dispersed, it is difficult to see the clansmen reforming in a substantial force: they would either have been too busy protecting themselves from punitive raids by the duke's troops and Highland allies or would have negotiated their submission. The battle field south of the Nairn was definitely better than Drummossie Moor and it has been argued that 'Cumberland could have been defeated on the 17th [sic] on Lord George Murray's chosen field'.[6] Certainly Cumberland would not have been able to use his cavalry, the Jacobites would have enjoyed a steep slope for their Highland charge and the effect of crossing the river would have been to disrupt the duke's formation. Against that, Culloden was not a cavalry battle. The duke's dragoons offered mobile fire-power and could fight dismounted. The morale of his men was such that they were unlikely to break provided they could inflict sufficient damage on their opponents with their fire-power. Had the battle been fought south of the Nairn it is difficult to see Cumberland's force suffering more than a repulse. More likely there would have been a confused engagement in which the fire-power of the duke's forces was less than at Culloden, more Jacobites would have reached their opponents than on Drummossie Moor, some of Cumberland's units broke but most did not, and the prince's army would have been able to retire without being harried by pursuing cavalry. Had such an engagement left an unbroken Jacobite force then the campaign could have continued, though it is difficult to see how Cumberland could have been prevented from capturing Inverness and employing his consequent strategic advantage to seize other Jacobite strongholds, such as Fort Augustus. The rising might have ended in a series of agreements between hungry clans and a government anxious to move troops back to the Low Countries and uncertain whether the duke could subdue the

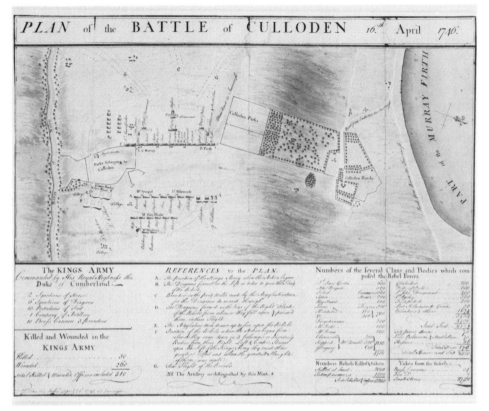

Plan of the battle of Culloden

Highlands. Glenorchy wrote of the Jacobites on 15 April, 'I rather think they will march from place to place and harrass the troops'.[7] This scenario would have satisfied neither Cumberland, a man not given to conciliation who craved both total victory and believed it necessary, nor Charles Edward and his Irish advisers who wanted the total victory that could bring a crown and distrusted the Scots.

Having rejected Murray's advice, the prince also ignored that of the Marquis d'Eguilles, who, pointing out the smallness of his force and their hunger, urged fighting south of the Nairn or retreat. The Jacobites were therefore still on the moor when Cumberland's force advanced onto it. The duke had about 9,000 men, while the prince's force, weakened both by the absence of men who had turned to find food or sleep after the night march and by the fact that several of the units that had taken part in distant operations in March had still not rejoined the main army, was about 5,000 strong. Their strength was reckoned greater by their adversaries, the Jacobite order of battle, including 176 cavalry but excluding Lord Kilmarnock's unit, being given as 6,626 and 12 pieces of artillery. Jacobite chances were diminished by a number of poor decisions. The prince refused Murray's request to throw down those walls of the Culloden Park enclosures that might affect the charge of his Atholl men. The Jacobite front line was not drawn up parallel to that of Cumberland's but at an angle that left the MacDonalds on the Jacobite left, angry at not being granted their customary place of honour on the right, and further from the duke's forces than the Atholl men on the right. The prince's cannon began an artillery duel at about 1 p.m. at a range of about 500 yards, but his inexperienced gunners lacked the training of Cumberland's and did little damage. In contrast, the duke's ten 3-pounders, sited in gaps between the regiments at the front of his three lines, inflicted considerable casualties, especially when they switched to grape-shot and fired on the front line of the Jacobites who were also suffering from hail and rain in their faces. The prince, unaware of the damage being done, did not give the order to charge until pressed to do so by Murray, but the MacDonalds refused to obey. Cumberland's dispositions had meanwhile altered to take advantage of the Culloden enclosure and to provide support for his front line on its left. James Wolfe's regiment of foot was ordered to march so that it was at right angles to Barrell's regiment on the left of the front line. The Argyll men and the dragoons were ordered to occupy the enclosure and to make holes in the walls through which the dragoons could advance.

The charge began after an artillery bombardment whose length is variously described. The slant of the Jacobite line, the nature of the terrain, which was partly waterlogged, the difficulty of seeing what was happening in the smoke produced by the guns and the independent nature of each unit's advance led to a certain amount of confusion and bunching but the left of Cumberland's front line was reached. The duke described the fighting two days later:

> They began firing their cannon, which was extremely ill-served and ill-pointed. Ours immediately answered them which began their confusion. They then came running on in their wild manner, and upon the right where I had placed myself imagining the greatest push would be there, they came down there several times within a hundred yards of our men, firing their pistols and brandishing their swords, but the Royals and Pulteney's hardly took their fire-locks from their shoulders,[8] so that after those feint attempts they made off; and the little squadrons on our right were sent to pursue them. General Hawley had by the help of our Highlanders beat down two little stone walls, and came in upon the right flank of their second line.
>
> As their whole first line came down to attack at once, their right somewhat outflanked Barrell's regiment, which was our left, and the greatest part of the little loss we had was there, but Bligh's and Sempill's giving a fire upon those who had outflanked Barrell's soon repulsed them, and Barrell's regiment and the left of Monroe's fairly beat them with their bayonets; and I dare say there was neither soldiers nor officer of Barrell's and that part of Monroe's which engaged, who did not kill their one or two men with their bayonets and spontoons, and they so fairly drove them back, that in their rage that they could not make any impression upon the battalions, they threw stones at them for at least a minute or two, before their total rout began.

A very similar account, clearly drawn up by Cumberland's staff, describing the action on the left of the duke's line, added that the soldiers 'having given their fire followed it so well with their bayonets that the Rebels soon gave ground in spite of their Broad-swords which they now found were not so terrible as they had flattered themselves'.[9]

Cumberland's account was complemented by that of Joseph Yorke, who was on the left, though he may have underestimated the duration of the artillery bombardment and he appears to have exaggerated the degree to which the Jacobite advance conformed to a plan:

> When our cannon had fired about two rounds, I could plainly perceive that the rebels fluctuated extremely, and could not remain long in the position they were then in without running away or coming down upon us; and according as I thought, in two or three minutes they broke from the centre in three large bodies, like wedges, and moved forward. At first they made a feint, as if they would come down upon our right, but seeing that wing so well covered, and imagining that they might surround the left because they saw no cavalry to cover it, two of these wedges bore down immediately upon Barrell's and Monroe's regiments, which formed the left of the first line; and after firing very irregularly at a considerable distance, they rushed furiously in upon them, thinking to carry down all before them, as they had down on former occasions. However, they found themselves grossly mistaken; for though by the violence of the shock Barrell's regiment was a little staggered, yet Major General Huske (who commanded the second line), perceiving where the weight was felt, rode up to the regiment, and bidding the men push home with their bayonets, was so well obeyed by these brave fellows, that hundreds perished on their points. At the same instant, the rebels who came round the left of Barrell's and in the pell-mell broke through the line, met their fate from the fire of Wolfe's and Ligonier's[10] on the left of the second line. The broad-swords succeeding so ill, the rebels turned their backs, and in flying were so well received by the cavalry under Hawley and Bland, who had broke down two dry stone walls, and unperceived had gained their rear, that a general rout and slaughter ensured among them . . . In the meantime, that wedge which was designed to fall on our right, after making three feints, as if they were coming down upon us, in order to draw away our fire, seeing that the right kept shouldered with the greatest coolness, and the three squadrons were moving towards their flank, followed the example of their right wing and fled for it. Immediately the horse were in amongst 'em, and the lines of foot advanced with shouts of victory and with the regularity of well disciplined troops.

Fawkener sent an account to Fletcher on 19 April:

> The action began by the fire of their canon which ours soon answered, which brought down their first line consisting altogether of their clans in a great hurry to attack us, their right wing a little out fronted our left where they fell in a little, and there was our principal —— [word missing], but our men fairly beat them back with their bayonets and made a great slaughter of them. They made the same movement on their left, but the regiments on our right where His Royal Highness was did not take their fire-locks from their shoulders, though the rebels came down firing their pistols and brandishing their swords, three times within less than an hundred yards, so they dared not attack but went off without attempting anything.

Fawkener continued by describing the action of the duke's dragoons and cavalry and the casualties and stated that the battle lasted less than half an hour.[11] Lee stressed that although Barrell's regiment was in difficulties, nobody fled. He emphasized the role of fire-power, adding 'that their boasted broad-swords were of no significance to well fixed bayonets in determined hands'. The determination and skill with which Cumberland's men used their bayonets were clearly important, though Edward Weston was wrong to write from Whitehall, 'The dead were almost all killed with bayonets, and are their best men. Barrell's regiments had not one but what was bent and bloody'. He added, 'The cry of the battalions immediately after the action was "Now, Billy, for Flanders"'.[12] However, fire-power had so thinned the numbers of the advancing clansmen

A Jacobite Incident: Culloden *by D. Morier. Jacobite prisoners from the '45 were used to pose for the painting*

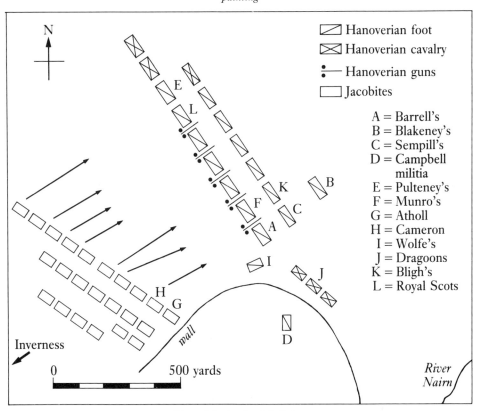

Plan of the battle of Culloden

that their chance of defeating their more numerous opponents was limited. Eighteenth-century musketry faced a number of problems; difficulty of aiming, the heaviness of the gun, the deterioration of weapons with use and the eccentricity of the ball. A recent consideration argues that the effectiveness of the musket should not be exaggerated as it 'ultimately remained a single-shot weapon with a complicated loading drill'. As a result 'the key to the musket's proper employment was to bring as many barrels as close to the target as possible', while high casualty figures 'were from closely controlled fire, at the beginning of an action, and at point-blank range'. Good morale was also important, in that the soldiers should have confidence in their commanders.[13] These were precisely the conditions under which Cumberland's men fought at Culloden; the number of barrels increased by the flanking position of the units forward from the left of the front line, while the general rate of fire was increased by the absence of any disruptive fire from the Jacobites who did not, as they charged, use their guns before discarding them in favour of their broadswords. In general, infantry rates of fire appear to have fallen during the course of battles, but Culloden was a short engagement unlike, for example, Dettingen where the 'engagement with the cannonading lasted from a little after nine in the morning till after four in the evening';[14] Fontenoy, which lasted from 6 a.m. until 1 p.m., though the British infantry did not advance until 10.30 a.m.; Roucoux (1746) which lasted several hours; and Laffeldt (1747) where the hard fighting for the village lasted four hours.

Indeed one of the features that distinguished Culloden from the battles in the Empire and the Low Countries was the speed with which the engagement was finished and its completeness. Usually battles were not clear victories and, when they were, it was unusual for the defeated army to disintegrate. An example of an engagement where this happened was Narva, where in 1700 Charles XII of Sweden defeated a vastly superior Russian force. The Russian entrenchments were stormed and they were unable to maintain any coherent line of battle. In addition, the Russians were not able to employ any concentrated fire-power on their attackers. In 1697 the Austrians under Prince Eugene similarly defeated another far larger army, that of the Turks, at Zenta, causing possibly 30,000 casualties. The Turks were hampered by having their backs to a river, over which most of their artillery had already crossed. Both at Narva and Zenta the defeated army was a force whose training and discipline did not match the standards that were to be reached in the western European armies of the 1740s with their stress on a consistently high rate of fire-power.

It is easier to understand the fate of the Jacobites at Culloden if it is appreciated that the 'military revolution' customarily dated to the period 1560–1660,[15] should rather be applied to the following century. Crucial to this latter period was the increase in the size of armies, their improved training and discipline and the greater fire-power that came with the introduction of the flintlock and the bayonet. The infantry became a more powerful killing machine.[16] As this was common to all the major powers, with the exception of the Turks, this greater effectiveness was seen in higher casualty rates in battles between conventionally armed forces whose results were often inconclusive, such as Malplaquet (1709), and in decisive victories when, as rarely happened,

A watercolour depicting the traditional account of the rescue of the clan colour of the Stewarts of Appin. After the battle Donald Livingstone saw the colour lying on the ground. Tearing it from its staff he wrapped it around himself and escaped with it. It was handed over to Stewart of Ballachulish and so escaped the fate of twelve other Jacobite clan colours which were burnt at Mercat Common, Edinburgh

fire-power could be applied against less well-armed forces, as at Culloden. The defeat of the larger armies of non-European powers by smaller well-trained forces, for example Clive's victory over the Nawab of Bengal at Plassey in 1757, was another example of the same process.

The results were certainly seen in the casualty figures at Culloden, although these were variously reported. Captain Thomas Davis wrote from Inverness on 18 April:

> . . . of the complete and cheap victory His Royal Highness the Duke has gained over the rebels the 16th instant. Thank God the loss of our side was very inconsiderable (viz.) Lt.-Col. Rich has lost a hand and received a wound in his head, poor Lord Robert Carr is killed and about ten officers more are killed and wounded with about 200 private men most of Barrell's and Monroe's regiment they being the two left battalions of the first line where the heat of the action was. His Royal Highness is extremely well pleased with the behaviour of his troops and returned the army thanks for their brave and gallant behaviour. There is not the least thing to be said against any one man that was in the action, which I hope will clear us from the scandal of Falkirk.
>
> The action with cannonading and all did not last above half an hour in which about 1,500 of the rebels were killed and 700 taken prisoners . . . It is very certain that the proportion of their officers killed is great. We likewise took ten pieces of their cannon which they had with them in the field beside eight more that were taken in town, and in the neighbourhood. Above 3,000 stand of arms with eleven stands of colours the Pretenders and all their baggage belonging to their army was likewise taken, all the French picquets with their ambassador surrendered themselves after the action. The Pretender is gone in the hills, with some of the rebels. This is very certain that of the 9,000 rebels there is not 1,000 of them left together, parties are out after him, and others, I pray God they may have success, in hopes of having revenge for the unnatural orders he gave out in the morning before the action not to give a man of us quarter, which writen orders have been found upon them.[17]

These orders, whose veracity has been questioned,[18] were used to excuse the slaughter of the fleeing Jacobites. Partly outflanked, pursued by more mobile cavalry and both exhausted and hungry, it is not surprising that so many Jacobites were unable to escape. They were not trained to make a fighting and firing retreat, had no large, fresh rearguard to cover their flight, and lacked the necessary flexible leadership, though circumstances were hardly propitious for skilful generalship. Individual units, such as Stapleton's Irishmen and the Jacobite cavalry, a small and poorly-mounted force, were able to cover the retreat of part of the army, but they were soon bypassed, broken or pushed back. Joseph Yorke estimated that 2,000 Jacobites were killed on the field and that there were 1,000 prisoners, with only 44 men in Cumberland's army killed and about 250 wounded. Cumberland suggested 2,000 men killed on the field and in the pursuit and 548 prisoners. He gave his own casualties as 'above 300'. Stanhope claimed over 1,000 prisoners and under 300 casualties in the duke's army, of which over 100 were in Barrell's regiment. The variation was clearly greatest in the case of Jacobite casualties, not surprisingly since their army was not composed of regular units whose losses could be counted exactly, there was no body-count on the battle field and many of the Jacobites fled, if they could, to their homes after the battle. Fawkener noted that the Jacobite claims of the number of their men killed were greater than Cumberland's estimates, but argued that they included all of their missing. There were soon to be reports in

Original Orders under
Lord George Murray's own
Hand, from April 14 to 15.
1746.

Orders from the 14th to the 15th Aprl
1746

Vie James (in English King James)

It is His Royall Highness positive Orders that
Every person atatch themselves to some Corps of the Armie
& To remain with that Corps night & day till the
Battle & persute be finally over; This regards the
foot as well as the Horse

The Order of Battle is to be given to every
Generall officer & every Commander of Regiments
or Squadrons.

It is required & expected that each individuall
in the Armie as well officer as Souldier keep
their posts that shall be alotted to them, & if
any man turn his back to Runaway the next
behind such man is to shoot him.

No body on pain of Death to Strip the
Slain or Plunder till the Batle be over

The Highlanders all to be in Kilts & no body to throw
away their Guns; by H.R.H. Command George Murray

Original orders attributed to Lord George Murray

A nineteenth-century representation of the atrocities by the Duke of Cumberland's men after Culloden

the press that the duke's army had murdered innocent spectators and the wounded. The French hastened to surrender after the battle.[19]

The victory was widely celebrated. Bells were rung, bonfires lit. The news reached London on the 23rd. That day Maule 'had a bottle of the oldest wine in the cellar . . . to his Royal Highness' health' and wrote on the 24th, 'I never saw anybody in such glee as the King was this day at the Levee which was much crowded; he complimented the Duke of Argyll upon the behaviour of the Argyllshire men'. An effigy of Charles Edward dressed in a plaid and with a Scottish bonnet on his head was burnt in Manchester, in Kirkburton a picture of the prince was shot at and a frying pan rung, and at York the Pope, Charles Edward and 'a child in a warming pan' featured in the celebrations. In Northumberland Lancelot Allgood drew up an address for the High Sheriff, gentlemen, clergy and freeholders to George II, congratulating him on Culloden and adding that they were sure that with God's blessing his troops would defeat the wicked attempts of all his enemies. The address, which was sent to the Lord Lieutenant for presentation to George, added that no invasions or domestic traitors would ever deter the signatories from defending George's title against the Pretender and his adherents. The pro-Jacobite *National Journal* complained about popular zeal in London where it alleged unilluminated windows were broken and money extorted. In Weymouth guns were fired, healths drunk and windows illuminated.[20]

In Scotland the situation was less happy. In his speech of 14 January 1746 opening the parliamentary session George II had distinguished between the situation in the two kingdoms:

> The daring attempt, which the rebels have since made upon this part of my kingdom has been happily disappointed; and, as their precipitate flight, before a small number of my troops, must greatly dispirit their followers; so, that inviolable duty, and loyalty, which have been so universally, and steadily shown by my faithful subjects, and shall never be forgotten by me, must convince them, how vain, and ill-grounded their hopes were of any addition of strength from such an enterprise.

The unwillingness of many of the English to assist against the invasion could be overlooked in the light of its failure, the small number of those who had risen for Charles Edward and the profuse demonstrations of loyalty after the Jacobite retreat began. An indeterminate number of English rebels went home after Derby and got away with it unless they were denounced. More English joined than the Scots claimed. In Northumberland over a dozen tenants of the Duke of Somerset joined the rebels including a number of prominent individuals. Lochiel and an English gentleman named Clifton claimed that the Jacobite army could have had a lot of recruits had they had arms to give them. The big psychological barrier, besides lack of arms, was the fear that the Scots would return to Scotland, leaving the English in the lurch. The Jacobite leaders were in London and the south of England, expecting a French landing with troops to protect them and arms to give them. The English Jacobites had not acted in any fashion that required political changes from the ministry or made them possible. Mid-century pressure for an improved militia owed little to its poor showing in the '45. In Scotland, in contrast, the Hanoverian regime had been overthrown and the British army humiliated. The government was determined to ensure that there was no recurrence of the '45. This affected military policy after Culloden and subsequent political changes. Fawkener had already written from Aberdeen on 28 February, 'were I a director in this government I would turn things over and over and never leave them quiet till I had put them upon such a foot that in a country where there are a million of men able to bear arms, people should not be struck with a panic whenever France is pleased to talk of landing eight or ten thousand'.

The military aftermath of Culloden was harsh. The Highlanders were regarded as barbarians, compared unfavourably with the Gauls by Lee who sought an historical comparison to the campaign by reading Caesar. Cumberland had already allowed his soldiers to plunder Jacobite property on the march from Stirling to Perth, though it is worth pointing out that in early 1716, in a fruitless attempt to delay Argyll's march, the Jacobites had burnt down settlements in this region, such as Crieff. The actions of the duke's men were criticized prior to Culloden, especially in loyal Scottish circles. Maule wrote from London on 4 March:

> There are many here who much disapprove of the plundering that has been but too much practised by the Duke's army, no good can result from it, and the rebels will certainly make reprisals a hundred fold, so that the whole country will be a scene of blood and rapine and many a man that has merit with the government undone. In the meantime it is not lawful for any man to complain lest he be taxed with disaffection.

The duke regarded such action as effective. On 4 April he wrote to Newcastle:

> The orders which were sent to the Governor and Commandant of Fort William, before it was threatened with a siege, to seize all the cattle and demolish the habitations of those in Lochaber, who were actually out in rebellion, has had a very good effect, as all the rebels of that country have deserted, to go home to their own habitations, it obliged them to undertake this siege, which will only discourage the men and add to their present distraction.

He added that by disarming the local clans he trusted he had 'quieted all behind us'. However, Cumberland, did not resort to systematic violence on a massive scale until after Culloden when he could spare the troops for punitive expeditions and it was safe to do so. These expeditions were ordered to kill the Jacobites and destroy their property. In theory rebels who made an effort to surrender their arms were to be allowed to return home, with the exception of their leaders, but this practice was not always observed, and though some Scottish officers, such as Loudoun, behaved honourably, some of the harshest treatment was meted out by lowland Scots. Fawkener wrote from Fort Augustus on 5 June, 'persons sheltering or concealing rebels should no doubt be treated as such'; and, after noting that Lord George Sackville, Colonel of the 20th Foot, a veteran of Fontenoy who had been praised by Cumberland and was to acquire notoriety as the 'coward of Minden' and as the rigorous Secretary of State for the Colonies during the War of American Independence, had been sent into Lochaber, added 'these hills will now have been thoroughly rummaged, and the inhabitants will have learned that they have placed a vain trust in them. Those who have submitted have been spared, the others have born the reward of their own wickedness and obstinacy'. Some of the expeditions, especially those sent into remoter sections of the western Highlands, were especially cruel, characterized by killings, rapes and systematic devastation that did not exempt loyal Highlanders. Those who complained, such as Duncan Forbes, were not heeded by the duke, and were often abused. Lee had no sympathy, writing from Fort Augustus on 31 May about the troops:

> . . . dispersed through the several parts of this heathenish country, converting them to Christianity, and propagating a new light among them. Some few of them bring in their arms, others skulk in the woods and mountains, but we take care to leave them no sustenance, unless they can browse like their goats.

The situation was probably exacerbated by the extent to which much of the army disliked having to operate in Scotland. Albemarle, Cumberland's successor as commander there, wrote from Edinburgh in October 1746, 'to be ordered to remain in Scotland and to have no douceurs is intolerable and what no flesh and blood can bear. I have applied and shall again . . . to attend His Royal Highness abroad next spring'.[21]

Militarily there was no need for such activity. About 4,000 men assembled at Ruthven after the battle, but Charles Edward, convinced that continued trust in the Scots was pointless and that he should go to France in order to return with an army, refused to join them and ordered the Jacobites to look to their own

The inside front cover and title page of The Lyon in Mourning. *Pasted to the inside front cover is a portion of the prince's blue Garter ribbon and a piece of the dress he used as a disguise*

safety. It is unclear whether the 4,000 could have waged guerilla warfare to any purpose, especially as they lacked sufficient food supplies and had no money. Fortresses could not have been taken without artillery and resistance to the raiding parties would simply have invited more systematic devastation. The men at Ruthven dispersed and Cumberland was able to exploit his capture of Inverness to retake Fort Augustus and establish himself there in what was a good base for scouring the Highlands. In early May a Jacobite rendezvous was called at Muirlaggan on Loch Arkaig in the hope that another rising could be organized, but lack of support led to its abandonment, which was hardly surprising in light of the experience of the '45 and the promise that was now held out of combining with a force that Charles Edward was to bring from France. The prince himself was fleeing through the heather, evading the frenetic pursuit of Cumberland's men, until on the morning of 20 September 1746 he sailed for

France. He posed no military threat and devoted his energies to a successful escape rather than to raising support for another rising. Despite the energy and ferocity expended on the hunt for him, it was possibly as well for the government that he was not captured. McLynn has claimed that he would probably have been executed but the only 'leading Whig luminary' he can cite in support of this view is Horace Mann, the envoy in Tuscany, while the claim that the government had virtually suspended due legal process in Scotland,[22] must be qualified, not least by a consideration of the trials that did take place. In 1744 Parliament made it high treason to hold correspondence with the sons of the Pretender and attainted them of high treason in case they should land or attempt to land in Great Britain. This would have meant an automatic death penalty for the prince, but any trial would have attracted international pressure. It would have been less contentious and more useful to hold him prisoner until he could be deported to Italy as a valuable concession in a peace in which France otherwise would have held most of the trumps. Louis XV's honour was engaged in the prince's cause. An amnesty for the Jacobites and a clause guaranteeing Charles Edward's safety formed part of the plan for a general peace drawn up by the French in May 1746, though the French were willing to renew their guarantee of the Hanoverian Succession. The Marquis d'Argenson also wrote a letter pressing clemency on the British for all Jacobites and suggesting that otherwise France would employ reprisals. This suggestion aroused outrage in Britain where it was considered totally unacceptable to have domestic matters dictated by a foreign power, an attitude that was common in relations between major powers.[23]

After Culloden the ministry was still concerned about the possibility of a Jacobite revival in Scotland. When Charles Edward left Paris to seek Spanish assistance in January 1747, Newcastle wrote 'We are alarmed with the departure of the Pretender's son, and with the preparations at Brest', though he added that that would not prevent the dispatch of British troops to the Low Countries. There was an important, though overlooked, panic in late 1747. In August Hardwicke replied to a report from the Earl of Findlater:

> It surprises me that any of the sensible Jacobites, who know the world, can still, after all the experience they have had, really be persuaded that France means anything more than to make them the engines and dupes of her own politics, without being much in earnest to push the point they have in view. I don't believe that France has any immediate design of this nature; but I entirely concur in your Lordship's doctrine, and have preached it all this year, that it is absolutely necessary to keep a sufficient body of troops in the northern parts to crush every tentative towards a rising.

The following month Ossorio, the experienced and well-connected envoy of Britain's ally Charles Emmanuel III of Sardinia, noted ministerial fears of French action in support of the Stuart cause which appeared to have numerous supporters in Britain, especially Scotland. Cumberland was less inclined to panic, 'I allow that . . . the spirit of Jacobitism that has showed itself in England is very disagreeable, and that Scotland is as willing to rebel as ever though I should believe rather too weak in numbers to dare to do it without a powerful assistance from France'. However, Chesterfield, by then Secretary of State for

(5)

TRUE

COPIES, &c.

A true Copy of the Paper, *which was read by* Arthur Lord Balmerino, *upon the* Scaffold, *at* Tower-Hill, *and delivered by him to the* Sheriffs *of* London, *just before his* Execution, *on* Monday, Auguſt *the* 18*th* 1746.

I Was brought up in *True, Loyal,* ANTI-RE-VOLUTION *Principles;* and I hope the World is convinced that they ſtick to me.

I muſt acknowledge I did a very *inconſiderate* Thing, for which I am heartily ſorry, in accepting of a Company of Foot from the *Princeſs* ANNE, who I knew had no more Right to the *Crown* than her Predeceſſor the PRINCE OF ORANGE, whom I always looked upon as a *vile*, unnatural Uſurper.

To make Amends for what I had done, I joined the KING when he was in *Scotland*; and when all was over, I made my Eſcape, and lived Abroad till the Year 1734.

In the Beginning of that Year, I got a Letter from my *Father*, which very much ſurprized me: It was to let me know he had the Promiſe of a *Remiſſion* for me. I did not know what to do; I was then, I think, in the *Canton* of *Bern*, and had no Body to adviſe with: But next Morning I wrote a Letter to the KING, who was then at *Rome*, to acquaint

The first page from a collection of the last words of those listed for execution

the Northern Department, wrote to the duke on 20 October 1747, 'As the symptoms of rebellion appear now very strong not only in Scotland the usual seat of it, but in many parts of England, where the Jacobites publicly and riotously assemble, avowing and publishing by their dress, their words, and actions, their infamous principles; His Majesty thinks it would be very expedient, if not absolutely necessary' to recall six battalions, 'as well to discourage and check this rebellious spirit at home, as to damp the hopes which it might give to our enemies abroad to attempt an invasion of these kingdoms, if we had no more than our present small force to defend them'. Cumberland wrote to the Duke of Newcastle the same day, throwing interesting light on his views about the 'pacification' of Scotland:

> . . . such alarms in England occasioned by the French troops sent to Calais and Dunkirk, as well as for the impertinencies and insolencies the Scotch Jacobites are every day committing . . . I always declared my opinion, that affairs in Scotland never would go right, in the manner they were then and are still administered, and though I think it of great importance to keep the Duke of Argyll and the Campbells in good humour and even so far as to put the Duke of Argyll at the head of His Majesty's Scotch affairs, yet I can never think it adviseable to have him sole and absolute disposer of all the king's favours in the kingdom. From what I am able to see at present I am not much alarmed for this winter in that part, as I know the number of Highlanders has been very much thinned, as well by what they lost in the rebellion, as by the number of men drawn out of the country for the kings and the States General [Dutch] service and as I am of opinion they will not let themselves be deluded by French promises of assistance and little corps that France might contrive to send them, for which reasons I think our security in that country depends entirely upon the diligence of our fleet in preventing any considerable embarkation of troops from landing in a body in Scotland . . . . The only real danger which I can foresee, which we might be liable to this winter, would be the French assembling a number of small vessels at Calais and Dunkirk and risking an embarkation which they might push over with a fair wind and land either in Kent, Sussex, or Essex.

Cumberland argued that the best way to prevent this would be to move troops from the United Provinces to England, and indeed three days later five battalions were recalled, one for Newcastle and four for Kent and Sussex.[24]

Late 1747 marked the apex of ministerial fears about Jacobitism following Culloden during what was left of the War of the Austrian Succession. This reflected concern about Jacobite activity in England and Scotland and French success in the campaigning season of that year. In 1748 fears abated as peace negotiations progressed, Hardwicke writing to Findlater in October, 'If the prospect of peace has damped the Jacobite spirit, I hope the news of its conclusion will operate more strongly'.[25] Cumberland had been proved correct in his assessment of Jacobite chances. There was no real prospect of another rising, while Charles Edward failed to obtain Bourbon support. McLynn attributes this in part to Louis XV, 'this neurasthenic ditherer had allowed himself to be overruled by his ministers' and argues fairly that the French were reluctant to make a winter campaign. He does, however, exaggerate the importance of Jacobite proposals angering the French, when he places greater weight on Charles Edward's demands for assistance towards an attack on England, rather than Scotland,[26] than on the fact that French interests might have been better served by obtaining a favourable peace. Although Louis XV was willing in the winter of 1746–7 to provide 6,000 men for another Highland expedition, there was a lack of determination to support the prince which clearly contrasts with the situation both in early 1744 and in the winter of 1745–6. This owed something to experience of the difficulties of dealing with Charles Edward and the failure of the '45, but diplomatic and naval considerations were more important. Optimistic hopes of overthrowing the Hanoverian regime had been replaced by a desire for peace which led in late 1746 to the opening of Anglo-French-Dutch negotiations at Breda, which lasted until March 1747. The French were aware that support for the Jacobites would compromise them with Protestant powers, especially the Dutch, and Frederick the Great, who appeared a possible intermediary in negotiations, as in early 1746. The French indicated to both that their support for the Stuart cause was negotiable. Eleven days before Culloden the Marquis d'Argenson wrote to the French envoy in Berlin concerning Frederick's negotiations and claimed that the best policy for George II was to abandon Maria Theresa if France agreed not to back the Jacobites. The previous month the Prussian foreign minister had felt able to tell the British envoy that France supported the Stuart cause in order to obtain peace.[27] In October 1746 Puysieulx, the French plenipotentiary at Breda, wrote to d'Argenson, whom he was soon to succeed as foreign minister, to discuss the possibility of dividing the hostile alliance.[28] Generally crucial to successful peace negotiations, that course would not be eased by support for the Jacobites.

Negotiations did not prevent invasions in order to apply pressure. On 30 November 1746 Austrian troops crossed the Var to invade Provence in an attack that had been encouraged by the British and was supported by their navy. Superficially there were some parallels with recent events in Britain. The French feared that the Protestants in the south might support the invasion, both sides encountered supply problems in the winter campaign, the invading forces were distracted by a rising in their rear in Genoa and the invasion was mounted in order to divert French efforts from the Low Countries. The Earl of Sandwich, British plenipotentiary at Breda, hoped that success in Provence would lead to military superiority in the Low Countries, while George II told Ossorio that it would enable the dictation of peace terms to France. He did not mention improving the position of the French Protestants. On 21 January 1747 the French successfully counter-attacked and by 3 February the invaders had recrossed the Var. However, the British consoled themselves with the thought that 'the common enemy must still feel the weight of this diversion, whether Count Brown be on that, or this side that river, as they will not be at liberty to make detachments from their army to other places, with such a force in front still ready to penetrate, upon the first occasion, into Provence again'.[29]

The parallel with events in Britain cannot be pressed far, not least because there was no Protestant rising, as there had been in the Cévennes during the War of the Spanish Succession. Militarily, the obvious contrast was that the ability of the French to intervene in Britain was limited by the British navy. There were rumours of Bourbon naval action in support of the Jacobites in the aftermath of Culloden and for the rest of the war. They helped to cause a fall in the price of stock on 22 April 1746. There were fears of an invasion of Ireland in June 1746 when the Brest fleet sailed. However, such worries became less convincing as the balance of naval power swung increasingly towards Britain. In 1746 D'Enville's fleet failed in its objective of regaining Cape Breton and returned to France, victims of disease and shipwreck.

In May 1747 Anson defeated a smaller fleet under La Jonquière off Cape Finisterre and on 14 October 1747 Hawke won the most brilliant action of the war, the Second Battle of Cape Finisterre. The British decision to retain most of the fleet in home waters, from where they mounted an unsuccessful attack on L'Orient in September and October 1746, rather than following up the fall of Louisbourg by invading Canada, further reduced the chances of French naval action. However, irrespective of the naval situation, it was clear that the French had no need to assist the Jacobites to the point of mounting an invasion of Britain. The campaign of 1746 had in effect restored France to the position she had enjoyed in late 1741. She had acquired both an important area, the Austrian Netherlands, and a position from which pressure could be applied on Britain. Whereas in 1741 France could intimidate Hanover, by 1746 she had made gains from which the Dutch could be invaded and, as her closest ally, their plight was also that of Britain's. It was to be the realization that the Dutch could neither protect themselves nor fight on that led the British ministry to accept the need for peace in early 1748. In his pro-government London newspaper the *True Patriot* Henry Fielding claimed on 6 May 1746 that the Jacobite rising had given 'Marshal Saxe the important capital of Brussels . . . it is not at all improbable that the battle of Culloden Moor may save Mons, and prove a means of recovering Brabant', but he was wrong on both counts. Having made gains in the Low Countries in 1746, France improved her position the following year. Her armies under Saxe overran Dutch Flanders, outmanoeuvred Cumberland when he sought to regain Antwerp and defeated him at Laffeldt, and stormed the great Dutch fortress of Bergen-op-Zoom, giving the town over to massacre, rape and pillage. When the French could intimidate their opponents by preparing for the next campaign, 'there are vast convoys of bombs and other the like stores continually coming to Antwerp' noted Thomas Orby Hunter in October 1747,[30] there was no need to assemble forces near the Channel ports that would be less credible as a threat because of the difficulties of large-scale amphibious operations and the strength of the British navy. Overthrowing the Hanoverian regime might have been of more value to the French, even if the French had not benefitted to the extent suggested in the *True Patriot* of 7 January 1746, when Fielding offered a dream of what would have happened had the Jacobites been successful, that included, twenty-five days after the proclamation of the Stuart king, 'This day the *Gazette* informs us, that Portsmouth, Berwick and Plymouth were delivered into the Hands of French Commissaries, as Cautionary Towns; and also twenty Ships of the Line, with their Guns and Rigging, pursuant to Treaty'.

Arguably a Stuart Britain would have been less able and willing to challenge France both in European diplomacy, as the Hanoverian regime did actively in the post-war years of 1748–55 and, more seriously, in the struggle for control of North America that led to the outbreak of hostilities in 1754 and to the Seven Years War of 1756–63. This obviously cannot be proved, though it is a reasonable assumption. Nevertheless, in the period from mid-1746 until early

Allegorical design by Lt. Wilhelm Schilling which contains small pictures depicting the French attempt on Louisbourg and other scenes from the Wars of the Austrian Succession, plus the battle of Culloden

1748 it was not really practical for France to provide substantial assistance to the Jacobites and it was more sensible for her to concentrate on the major sphere of operations that already existed in the Low Countries. The French were also willing to bargain away their support for the Jacobites for gains elsewhere, demanding acknowledgement of their right to fortify Dunkirk as an equivalent in September 1747. There was no prospect of assistance from Spain for action on behalf of the Stuarts, not least because Ferdinand VI, who succeeded Philip V in July 1746, negotiated actively with Britain in an attempt to secure his objective of an end to Spanish participation in the war.[31]

Therefore, though there was little prospect of an immediate revival either of Jacobite activity or of foreign assistance for the Stuart cause, it was nevertheless not surprising that the British government should feel less than secure on these points, especially in light of the speed with which Charles Edward had gained control of much of Scotland in 1745. Furthermore, they felt it necessary to ensure that there should be no resumption of Jacobite activity and no prospect of foreign intervention or an invasion winning domestic support on a future occasion. A harsher note was to be struck than in the aftermath of the '15 and the '19, and a more comprehensive attempt was to be made to alter the political and security situation in Scotland, one that was linked to a far-reaching reversal of the Highland governmental system. The pro-Jacobite *National Journal* suggested ironically in its issue of 12 June 1746 that the government should resort to genocide. A letter from 'A true modern Whig' urged the need to wipe out all Scots, defended the killing of the wounded at Culloden and urged the slaughter of all Jacobite women of childbearing age:

> ... because there is no doubt but many of them will breed Jacobites as chidren generally suck in the principles of their mothers and nurses, which can never be eradicated but by great posts and pensions, and this, you know, is often a great disappointment as well as loss to us honest people. I am also of the opinion, that all the corn in Scotland, designed for seed, as well as all the cattle, ought to have been seized, and all implements of husbandry destroyed, except what belongs to the few that are known to be well affected, which would infallibly starve all those rebellious wretches in a year or two. This would effectually extirpate them, and save us the expense of transporting them to our colonies, where they may do great mischief by infecting the people with their principles.

That was not, of course, to be government policy, though reading descriptions of the conduct of Cumberland's troops it is easy to appreciate why such articles were written. In September 1746 Albemarle wrote to Newcastle:

> I am one of those, that notwithstanding the hopes entertained by most that this kingdom was restored to peace and quietness, always feared from the bad inclination of the people in most of the northern counties and from their stubborn, inveterate disposition of mind, nothing could effect it but laying the whole country waste and in ashes, and removing all the inhabitants (excepting a few) out of the kingdom.

Far from eighteenth-century Britain appearing as a 'polite and commercial society', as indeed the country that is most commonly presented to modern audiences, one of aristocratic ease and elegance, urban bustle and balance, a land of stately homes and urban squares where the vigorous if not seamy side of life was Hogarthian, rather than etched in the starker dimensions of the charnel-house, any account of the aftermath of Culloden reveals both the blood-lust that led to the slaughter of the wounded and the refusal of quarter immediately after the battle and subsequent planned savagery. The argument that the slaughter after the battle reflected the actions of troops that were out of control should not be pushed too far. Quarter was granted to the French soldiers who surrendered, and to Jacobites in French service. The subsequent punitive campaigns spread devastation far and wide and even if Highlanders could flee the approach of troops and warships the destruction of their homes and farm implements and the seizure of their cattle were for many, especially the weak, equivalent to sentences of death or at least severe hardship and malnutrition. Reports of Jacobite atrocities[32] had lessened whatever reluctance there might have been to punish the Highlanders, who were commonly presented as subhuman, though the cruelty that was inflicted varied in its intensity and some honourable men applied their instructions in a favourable manner, thus earning criticism from Cumberland and his acolytes.

The savageries in the Highlands were not unique. Central and eastern European wars were especially brutal, ethnic and religious differences separating civilians from troops, and the search for supplies presenting a considerable problem. The Ukrainian administrator Samiilo Velychko wrote of the Ukraine and Galicia in the 1700s, 'I saw many towns and castles empty and deserted, and the walls, once constructed by men to resemble hills, now serving as the homes and refuge for wild beasts'. In 1742 an officer with the Austrian army reported of the Prussians and Saxons, 'we all see the barbarous and inhumane effects of their visit in Moravia, and never was the like seen or heard of, and it is really scandalous beyond all measure that first towns and villages should be strongly taxed under contribution on arrival, and on departure pillaged and burned to the ground; this one may call the cluster or rabble of piratical incendiaries and not the generous valiant behaviour of a Christian army'. Attacks upon civilians were more common further east, particularly in the Balkans, where little distinction was observed between soldiers and civilians. The Muslim population of Montenegro was massacred by the Serbs. When Prince Cantemir of Moldavia rebelled against the Turks in 1711, he called the entire adult male population to military service, and when the rebellion was suppressed many fled to Russia. Guerilla warfare was a marked feature of the Balkans. The attempt by the Russians to instigate Greek risings during their 1768–74 war with Turkey led to Turkish atrocities.[33]

Western European operations were by no means free from savage fighting or atrocities. Henry St John complained that English conduct during the unsuccessful attack on Cadiz in 1702 had jeopardized their chances of winning support in Spain, 'Huns, Goths or vandals never proved themselves such barbarians as we have done. Neither saint, nun, church, or convent were spared'. A British commentator wrote of the French in Germany in 1743, 'we hear of sacrileges, murders, rapes, and all the acts of people exasperated by despair'. The looting of Cherbourg by drunken British troops in 1758 did little for their reputation. People fled from war zones, as from the Rhineland to neutral Denmark in 1761, scarcely suggestive of any confidence in the limited nature of warfare. The effects of war were long lasting in combat zones. Thomas Jones, travelling through Savoy, found 'many ruins of villages destroyed at some time by the French'. John Moore wrote in 1779 of the pillaging of the Palatinate ninety years earlier, 'the particulars of that dismal scene have been transmitted from father to son, and are still spoke of with horror by the peasantry of this country, among whom the French nation is held in detestation to this day'.[34]

The situation in the Highlands was more comparable in the level of punitive action to eastern than to western Europe, unsurprisingly so in light of the strength of hatred, the fear engendered by the near-success of the '45 and the difficulty of distinguishing between soldiers and civilians. To ravage the lands of a clan was to weaken its military potential. Scotland was not the sole region in western Europe in the eighteenth century where rebels were treated harshly. The rising of French Protestants in the Cévennes region in 1702–10 was suppressed with gruesome punishments.[35] To make such comparisons is not to extenuate the cruelty displayed and enjoyed by some in the Highlands.

The treatment of the Jacobite clans is, however, yet another qualification of the notion of the British uniqueness in the eighteenth century. This notion, which owes much to the Whig myth of the triumphal progress of liberty in which Britain was decisively separated from the path of continental autocracy and Catholicism by the Glorious Revolution, essentially relates to a specific vision of English history. It is increasingly seen as inappropriate, a consequence of revisionist perspectives on English history and new work on that of Europe.[36] It is certainly inaccurate if the sphere examined is that of Britain, rather than England.[37] The problems of a multiple kingdom in which coercion had recently played a part in maintaining cohesion and enforcing a new political order were not unique to Britain and if, as seems obvious from the perspective of an account of the '45, these problems are not ignored, then it is harder to present the customary cliché of British history in this period – one of peace and stability, liberty and property, politeness and tolerance. This image has been qualified by recent work on English society and public order; from the Highlands in 1746 it simply looks ridiculous: the culture of an oppressive foreign elite, the mask of repression.

Cumberland had closed his account of Culloden by writing to Newcastle, 'It will be absolutely necessary, that new forts be erected here [Inverness], and where Fort Augustus stood, and whoever his Majesty may think proper to order to inspect their construction, should be sent down immediately as the season is now come for works of that kind'. Albemarle was also convinced of the need to base control of the Highlands on sound fortifications, writing to Newcastle in October 1746:

> Fort George, Fort Augustus and Fort William should be made strong, defensible, and capable of containing considerable garrisons; the barrack of Inversnaid at the head of Loch Lomond should be made defensible ... It would be highly requisite that the officers quartered in those forts and barracks proposed to be erected should be empowered to put the laws in execution that relate to the disarming of the Highlands, the change of their habit, etc.; this would effectually answer all the ends of the Act of Parliament.[38]

The eighteenth-century British state was not one given to expensive programmes of fortress construction, at least in Britain, though the situation was different in overseas possessions, such as Gibraltar and Minorca. In 1746, however, William Skinner was sent to Scotland to build, as chief engineer of North Britain, defensive works that could control the Highlands. He proposed restorations and additions to Fort Augustus and a major new fort near Inverness at Arderseer Point. This Fort George was not begun until 1749 and it took about a decade to construct and man, costing over £100,000. A 'state-of-the-art' bastioned fortification, it remains to this day an impressive work and a trip to it is a worthy complement to a visit to nearby Culloden. Work was also carried out at Fort William, while a new barracks was constructed at Edinburgh, which Albemarle hoped would lessen the chances of billetted men acquiring Jacobite sympathies. Wade's road-building programme was extended, Albemarle being instructed in August 1746 to use troops in order to complete the road from Dunbarton to the Western Isles as soon as possible. Lieutenant-Colonel David Watson, Deputy Quartermaster-General to the forces, assisted by William Roy, prepared between 1747 and 1755 the map known as the Duke of Cumberland's map of the mainland of Scotland, which was based on a military survey of Scotland.

Fort George was not required for the task for which it was constructed. Indeed, a striking feature of the military after-effects of the '45 is the extent to which Scotland was not occupied for long by a substantial force. Lord Glenorchy had written to his daughter on 15 April 1746, 'I have often repented taking out the iron bars from the windows and sashing them, and taking away a great iron door, and weakening the house as to resistance by adding modern wings to it. If it had remained in the old castle way as it was before, I might have slept very sound in it, for their whole army could not have taken it without cannon'. Albemarle had stressed the need to dominate Scotland by force, writing to Newcastle in February 1747, 'Upon the whole I think this kingdom can never be kept in awe but by a sufficient military force'.[39] However, Whig grandees did not need to redesign their mansions after 1746. The government decided that troops in a few strategic strong points, supported by the navy, were all that was required in the military sphere to keep the menace of a Jacobite revival at bay. The defence of the Low Countries was swiftly re-established as the military priority to be supplanted in the Seven Years War (1756–63) by North America and the defence of Hanover.

Many of the soldiers who took part in the conquest of Canada were Scots. They reflected the creation of a new working relationship between the British state and Scotland, in particular Highland society. It was difficult to guess in the aftermath of the '45 that such a relationship would be created. In August 1746 John Farquharson of Invercald wrote to Loudoun to complain about the consequences of the disarming of the clans, for he had given in the arms of:

> . . . my people . . . in what miserable state and situation this premature disarming has put my interest in, and some of my neighbours who have followed my example, beyond any others in the kingdom. The thieves have already found it to tend much to their account to attack us in our present defenceless condition there being in these eight or ten days bygone four or five different parcels of black cattle and horses taken from our doors, while others in our neighbouring countries not yet disarmed continue safe.

The same month the JPs, Deputy Lieutanants and other leading Argylshire proprietors held a meeting at Inverary and drew up a memoir complaining that they would be left vulnerable to Jacobite sympathizers if obliged to disarm.

In December 1746 Sir William Yonge, who had been Secretary-at-War

Advertisement offering a reward of £30,000 for the capture of the 'son of the Pretender'

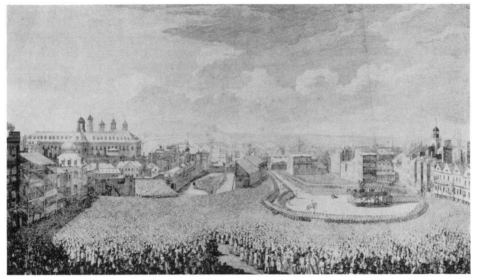

The execution of the Earl of Kilmarnock and Lord Balmerino

during the '45, a post he had since exchanged for the sinecure of joint Vice-Treasurer of Ireland, offered the Commons, then discussing the impeachment of Lord Lovat, of which he was one of the managers, 'a long invective on Jacobites and a deduction of the implacable spirit that tribe of men have been possessed with ever since the Revolution, that no ties of gratitude, benefits, pardon, emoluments could ever soften'.[40] Lovat was impeached and executed in accordance with the law in cases of high treason, which allowed defendants help from counsel only on strictly legal points. Yonge, however, then moved for a change in the law allowing counsel to such defendants.

Trials were held after the '45 and those of the leaders attracted much attention, but the government was more concerned not only to punish those it held responsible and thus alter the balance of power within Highland society, but also to prevent a recurrence of the rebellion by destroying what was seen as its social and governmental basis. On 25 May 1746 Thomas Sherlock, the influential Bishop of Salisbury, wrote to Weston, 'two things, I am sure, ought to be well considered this session; the state of Popery and the state of the Highlands. There were great laws in the last case in the year '15 – but never executed – and perhaps, the main thing to be provided for, is we secure an execution of the *king's* laws in the country; which is at present under the absolute *will* of the lairds'. He returned to this theme on 10 June 1746:

> . . . the acts made upon the rebellion in 1715 were in many respects deficient, and in others never executed; the vassals dare not take the advantage even of an act of Parliament against their superiors, nor if they dared, have they any disposition to it. And the forfeited estates having been granted away, the Crown has no more power there, than it had before . . . The forfeited country being put under a proper government, supported by a sufficient military force, will not only be kept quiet itself, and in time civilized; but it would be a barrier against

the *now* well affected clans, should they ever alter their mind; to which there wants nothing but an alteration in the affection of the chief . . . I am afraid the bill for the Highlands will be little more than articles between the ministry, and the Scotch members of parliament; if so, what reason have I to be a party to them? I shall expect nothing from them that will be of real service: the North Britains are so attached to the usages of their country, so —— [word obscure] of the superiorities, so jealous of all attempts to introduce regular government, even into these parts, where sometimes they will complain, that there is none, that I am afraid their national prejudices will not let them, and their great influence will not suffer others, to do what is right.

In August 1746 Albemarle was instructed to try to prevent cattle stealing, an important part of Highland life.[41] Legislation of 1746 and 1747 sought to weaken the independence of the Highlands. The Disarming Act of 1746 imposed fines for the carrying and concealing of arms, listed illegal arms as including broadswords, made searches for such weapons legal and ordered imprisonment for those who did not pay the fine. The wearing of Highland clothes or of plaid was prohibited to all with the exception of serving soldiers. John Campbell MP, a Lord of the Treasury, was unenthusiastic, though he wrote to his factor, 'I have thought that the poor Highlanders who are distressed by wearing breeches might be very agreeably accommodated by wearing wide trousers like seamen, made of canvas or the like. Nankeen might be for the more genteel. But I would have the cut as short as the philabeg, and then they would be almost as good and yet be lawful'. The same year an act was passed to suppress nonjuring meeting houses, which, according to Joseph Yorke in March 1746, 'are deservedly stiled the seminaries of Jacobitism'. This was a common theme. Fletcher wrote the previous month that 'the nonjuring Episcopal meeting houses are nurseries for nursing and spreading disaffection' and should not be tolerated. Fawkener claimed that April that Catholic and nonjuring meeting houses were 'nurserys and schools' of rebellion. In 1748 the Earl of Findlater, a loyal Scottish peer, wrote to the Duke of Bedford asking for mercy for a Jacobite, Sir William Dunbar of Durn. He argued that mercy:

. . . can do no hurt to the public interest, providing it be made a condition of his pardon, that his children, who are all young, shall be educated in principles of strict fidelity to his Majesty. The family was always zealous for the Protestant and Revolution interest, until the late Sir James Dunbar, father to this man, had the misfortune to marry a Jacobite wife, who introduced nonjuring ministers among them.[42]

The act stipulated that the ministers should qualify themselves by taking oaths and that they should pray for the king by name, thus making it clear that the Pretender was not intended. Those who attended services held by ministers not thus qualified were to lose their civil rights and be fined.

In 1747 the principal hereditable jurisdictions were abolished. Regalities were abolished, their jurisdictions assumed by the royal courts, while heritable sheriffdoms were similarly abrogated and their powers transferred to the Crown, so that Scottish sheriffs would be appointed annually hereafter, as in England. Not all who suffered were opponents of the Hanoverian establishment. John Campbell, who spoke against the bill, lost the hereditary sheriffdom of Nairn, though he was compensated with £2,000. Baronial courts were not, however, abolished, though their jurisdiction was limited, being removed from the sphere of criminal offences. Initially it had been proposed that these courts also should be abolished, a measure supported by Cumberland, but Hardwicke wrote to him on the first anniversary of Culloden to explain why the ministry had changed its mind. The letter is worth quoting at length for the light it throws on the factors influencing policy towards Scotland and the pragmatic nature of government policy:

> 1. The poverty of the country, where their farms are so small, and their tenants so poor, that it is universally represented as absolute ruin to them, if they shall be obliged to travel far, and employ lawyers to obtain redress in such trifling demands.
>
> 2. All the people of Scotland, even the most zealous for the Bill concurred in this viz: Lord Findlater, Lord Leven, Dundas, Craigie, etc.
>
> 3. As almost all the lands in Scotland are erected into Baronies, the English began to cry out against the prodigious sum, which the purchase of the Barons jurisdictions would have made the satisfaction to be paid amount to, which would have been a dangerous weight upon the Bill.
>
> 4. These jurisdictions, which don't exceed what our Lords of Manors in England have, are so inconsiderabie in themselves, and so spread and divided, that, when the powers of the great Lords and Chieftains are taken away, I really think they will (as now restrained and guarded) be of no ill consequence. Upon this head I will venture to throw out to your Royal Highness an argument from history, which has some weight with me, though it comes from a hand scarce to be quoted in public, nor mentioned to any prince, but one of your Royal Highness' penetration, and largeness of thought, I mean Cromwell. That usurper abolished all the great heretable jurisdictions at once, without giving any compensation for them; but at the same time preserved and established, in the Barons courts, nearly the same jurisdiction, which is reserved to them by this Bill . . . Nobody can imagine he would have done it, if it would have left an influence capable of giving disturbance to his government.[43]

From this letter it is clear that the ministry was motivated by prudential considerations rather than by a drive for 'root-and-branch' change. The measure, which became an Act on 17 June 1747 and which greatly angered Argyll and the Whig Lords in Scotland, can be presented as a fundamental move that ended the rule of overmighty subjects in Scotland, but caution is necessary in advancing such a conclusion. The social context has to be considered. There was no expropriation of all the major landlords, no attempt to create an alliance between the Crown and those who would be regarded as gentry in England. The social, economic and political influence of the nobility remained considerable.[44] More long-term political changes were as important as the legislation of 1746–7 and possibly what gave it weight. In effect Scotland, like many dependent parts of multiple kingdoms or federal states, was losing its capacity for important independent political intiatives. This affected both the Highlands and the country as a whole. In neither was it a case of English pressure on an unwilling people, for in both political changes profited, and were in part shaped by, local politicians.[45] This also affected the campaign for change after the '45 for, while altering judicial arrangements, the ministry was not proposing to extirpate Scottish management by replacing apparently reliable Scottish politicians by Englishmen sent to govern Scotland. After the '45 the Duke of Argyll, the leading Scottish 'undertaker', as the managers of government business in

Ireland were called, found his influence curtailed by that of Cumberland and was ignored in his attempt to delay the bill for the abolition of heritable jurisdictions, which would affect him and which he feared would be seen as English punishment for the rebellion. However, he remained a powerful figure whose support was necessary in the management of Scottish MPs, and his 'principle of caution and compromise above all else' ultimately prevailed.[46]

A work was published in Edinburgh in 1746 which made clear its belief that legislation would extinguish the Jacobite menace; 'Superiorities display'd: or Scotland's grievance, by reason of the slavish dependence of the people upon their great men; upon account of holdings or tenures of their lands, and of the many and the hereditary jurisdictions over them. Wherein is shown, that these have been the handles of rebellion in preceding ages, especially in the year 1715: and that, upon their removal, and putting the people of Scotland on the footing of those in England, the seeds of rebellion will be plucked for ever'. Clearly, it would be foolish to deny that the legislation did produce significant changes, though the fate of the programme to annex Jacobite estates and use them to create a new social order in the Highlands should induce caution in exaggerating specific effects. Nevertheless, it would be inaccurate to place great emphasis upon it. The defeat of the '45 was important less for the changes that followed it, than for the failure of a rebellion that might well have changed both political relationships within Scotland and those between Scotland and England. This argument should not be pushed too far. In 1745 the Scottish Jacobites feared that Charles Edward was too interested in England and his refusal in his proclamation of 10 October to promise the repeal of the Act of Union worried them. The prince was willing to say that his first parliament would revise the Act, but it was clear that Scotland was a stage on the march to London, just as for William III the invasion of England had been designed to serve anti-French objectives. However, had Charles Edward succeeded then Scotland would have been a valuable basis of support in the face of possible future English resistance, and it is likely that there would have been many changes there, including that of the established church, which would have reverted from Presbyterian to Episcopalian.

A sense of wider perspectives is provided in 'some remarks on the change of manners in my own time 1700–1790' by Elizabeth Mure. She wrote that in the early years of the century 'some part of the old feudal system still remained. Every master was revered by the family, honoured by his tenants, and awful to his domestics'. She claimed that national wealth increased considerably after the '45, whereas 'before the Union, and for many years after it, money was very scarce in Scotland. A country without trade, without cultivation, or money to carry on either of them, must improve by very slow degrees'. The change in social attitudes was related to that in religious matters:

> Whether the genius of a people forms their religious sentiments, or if religion forms in some measure the manners of a people I shall leave the wise to decide. I shall only observe, that while that reverence and awe remained in the minds of man for masters, fathers, and heads of clans, it was then that the awe and dread of Deity was most powerful. This will appear from the superstitious writing of the time. The fear of Hell and deceitful power of the Devil was at the bottom of all their religious sentiments. The established belief in witchcraft (for which

many suffered) prevailed much at this time; Ghosts too and apparitions of various kinds were credited; few old houses were without a ghost chamber that few people had courage to sleep in. Omens and dreams were much regarded even by people of the best education. These were the manners of the last century, and remained in part for thirty years in this.

The change in manners in the new generation was very remarkable. The Union with England carried many of our nobility and gentry to London. Sixty of the most considerable people being obliged to pass half of the year there would no doubt change their ideas. Besides many English came to reside at Edinburgh. The Court of Exchequer and the Boards of Customs and Excise were mostly all of that nation; at least all the under officers were . . . It likewise became the fashion for our young men of fortune to study for some years in Holland . . .

The changes Miss Mure attributed to the '45 were not those of a new English ascendancy:

From this time the country took a new form. Whether the dread of arbitrary power disposed us for more liberty, or if another cause, I shall leave the more knowing to determine, but surely it had powerful effects on the manners. It was then that the slavery of the mind began to be spoken of; freedom was in everybody's mouth. The fathers would use the sons with such freedom that they should be their first friend; and the mothers would allow of no intimacies but with themselves. For their girls the utmost care was taken that fear of no kind should enslave the mind; nurses were turned off who would tell the young of witches and ghosts. The old ministers were ridiculed who preached up hell and damnation; the mind was to be influenced by gentle and generous motives alone.[47]

With the passage of time Jacobite sympathies became less pressing and the reality of a separate Scottish political world more distant. These trends might have appeared irreversible by 1744, but in the following year the Hanoverian regime rapidly collapsed in Scotland and the surviving important centres of resistance were held by troops loyal to George II, rather than loyal Scots. The military weakness of the latter was shown by the fall of Inverness to Charles Edward in February 1746. To argue, therefore, from the fate of the '45 that Jacobitism was somehow an irrelevance, that the Stuart cause was bound to fail, is as dangerous as claiming the converse on the basis of the collapse of Hanoverian authority in Scotland and north-west England. There was no sense of inevitable victory in the response of the ministry to the invasion of England. Such a view had been advanced by ministers, such as Tweeddale, concerned to deny the truth of or minimize the importance of Charles Edward's arrival on the west coast, but they had been proved wrong by the fall of Edinburgh. Tweeddale was pushed from office on 4 January 1746, the Secretaryship of State for Scotland being left unfilled until 1885, when it was revived by Gladstone.

W.A. Speck closed his recent fine study of the '45 by claiming that 'The Forty-Five had not seriously threatened to remove George from the throne. Instead of revealing that the dynasty was essentially unstable, it demonstrated as nothing else could have done just how firmly established the Hanoverian regime was'.[48] It could instead be claimed that the '45 had presented such a threat and had revealed just such an instability, but that its failure led to the firm establishment of the Hanoverian regime. It thus closed a long period of instability and instead provided the basis for a fundamental recasting of British politics in which Toryism lost its Jacobite aspect, thus facilitating the dissolution of the Whig–Tory divide over the following seventeen years. The relationship between England and Scotland became essentially one of the willing co-option of the powerful Scots through patronage, with no alternative Jacobite or nationalist focus of loyalty and with a diminishing emphasis on coercion. Indeed the loyal Whig Sir Charles Hanbury-Williams was shocked to hear in January 1753 that six English regiments had been given to Scots, but George II, who controlled army patronage, felt it safe to thus promote Scots. Alexander Murray of Elibank played a central role in the so-called 'Elibank Plot' of 1751–3, a series of projects, that included the murder or seizure of George II as a prelude to an invasion by Charles Edward, that were betrayed by Alistair MacDonell, the British agent Pickle. His brother James, who had served in the West Indies in 1741, the defence of Ostend in 1745, the L'Orient expedition of 1746, that against Rochefort in 1757 and that to Louisbourg in 1758, played a major role, commanding the left wing, in the battle on the Plain of Abraham on 13 September 1759 which led to the fall of Quebec. The leading London opposition newspaper, the *Monitor*, asked on 27 October 1759, 'Can Britain ever forget how much she is indebted to a Murray, whose example and intrepidity taught and led on his Highland laddies to mow down the enemy with their broadswords, like grass under the scythe'? Murray subsequently defended Quebec against a French attempt to recapture the city in 1760, and was Governor of Quebec 1760–3, Canada 1763–6 and Minorca 1774–82 before becoming a full general in 1783 and Governor of Hull. Similarly Lord John Murray, half-brother of Lord George Murray and of the Marquis of Tullibardine, who was recognized by the Jacobites as the Duke of Atholl, was appointed an ensign in the Guards on Wade's recommendation in 1727, was a loyal supporter of successive ministries as MP for Perthshire 1734–61, was aide-de-camp to George II in 1743, became Colonel of the Black Watch in 1745, served at L'Orient in 1746 and Bergen-op-Zoom in 1747 and died the senior general in the army in 1787.

If Jacobitism appeared increasingly to be an irrelevance in Scotland, its international fate was no different. *The First Book of the Lamentations of Charles . . . for the loss of the battle of Culloden*, a ministerial publication of 1746, claimed that the French had used the Jacobites to help gain Flanders. The negotiation of a general peace two years later lessened the need for foreign powers to turn to the Jacobite option and led to the reaffirmation of the Hanoverian position. 'James III' published a protest against the treaty, while Fielding wrote of the impact on the British Jacobites, 'that universal dejection, which, from the first signing the Preliminaries, began so visibly to discover itself; and since the completing the definitive Treaty, hath so totally overspread the whole party'.[50] After the treaty had been signed the British government insisted on France carrying out her promise to expel Charles Edward even though it brought considerable embarrassment to Louis XV. Newcastle wrote that 'till that is done, a perfect harmony and good correspondence cannot be restored with the court of France'.[51] The principal source of foreign support for the Jacobites between the War of the Austrian Succession (1740–8) and the Seven Years War (1756–63) was Prussia, but it was easier for Frederick the Great to pursue his feud with George II by threatening to invade Hanover, though in 1753 he sought to encourage Jacobite conspiracy in Britain.

The Seven Years War brought a revival of French interest with the idea of mounting an invasion, though the French were well aware of Jacobite weakness. In April 1755, as the conflict between Britain and France in North America threatened to become a general war, Rouillé, the French foreign minister, wrote to Mirepoix, the envoy in London that the Jacobites were not capable of overthrowing the British government and that any plan seeking that end was chimerical. A memorandum of the same year stated that it would be foolish for France to invade Britain unless she had control of the sea and that that would require the destruction of the British navy.[52] In August 1755 'James III' approached the French government, claiming that while Anglo-French relations had been good he had kept his distance, but that now war appeared likely that the only way to obtain a solid peace would be to restore the Stuarts. Arguing that he enjoyed considerable support in England and Scotland, he stated that the arrival of a French force would lead the Jacobites to rally, and that if they could not invade from France, an invasion from Sweden should be attempted. James regarded an attack on Hanover as complementary, as he claimed it would indirectly increase the chance of a revolution in England. In October 1755 the Jacobites added details of their alleged support in Wales. The French reply was limited to compliments.[53] French plans for an invasion of England in the early stages of the war paid little attention to the Jacobites and in March 1756 Rouillé wrote to Bonnac, the envoy at The Hague, denying any concert with the Stuarts and asserting that history revealed that the overthrow of the British government could come only from domestic action.[54] A Jacobite proposal in January 1756 that the French invade between Rye and Winchelsea with 6,000 men, carried from Dieppe and Boulogne in small ships while the British fleet was held back by adverse winds, was regarded as underestimating the strength of the British army.[55]

French interest in attacking Britain[56] culminated in 1759 in a planned invasion that was prevented by the British naval victories at Lagos and Quibéron Bay. Newcastle complained in April 1759 that the threat was not taken seriously enough, 'I see there is a disposition almost everywhere to despise the notion of an invasion here, in Scotland, or in Ireland – notwithstanding that, nothing is more true, than that this has been, and is still the design of France'. Frederick the Great had been dismissive of the idea of an invasion in 1756. The British envoy, Andrew Mitchell MP for Elgin Burghs, who had been Tweeddale's Under Secretary when Charles Edward invaded, reported on 12 August, 'with regard to an invasion of His Majesty's kingdoms, he looks upon it, as a wild and romantic scheme, which can never succeed, unless there was a party within, to favour the invaders, that however, it will be proper to look narrowly after the known enemies to the government'. In fact the French plans were very extensive, and fears increased during the course of the summer of 1759.[57] In an interesting repetition of the situation in 1744–6 both confidence in and concern about the likelihood of the navy preventing any expedition were expressed, as was the suggestion that French preparations were principally intended to intimidate the British ministry into keeping forces at home and thus reducing their efforts against France.[58] In 1756, when an invasion had been threatened, Henry Fox, the Secretary of State for the Southern Department, had written to the Duke of Devonshire, 'if invasion or threats of invasion from France can effect the keeping of our fleets and troops at home, while they send regular troops, with their fleets to North America, the object of the war will be lost the first year of it'.[59] Robert Harrison wrote on 2 October 1759 from a warship at Plymouth, 'Sir Edward Hawke still continues off Brest, where the enemy lies in the same posture they have done all summer, and I fancy will lie, so long, as a fleet so formidable as ours appear before their harbour'. The Duke of Bedford, Lord Lieutenant of Ireland, was less confident and on 29 August 1759 informed Pitt of his opposition to sending troops from Ireland to secure Bengal:

> Though I do not think in the present situation of affairs, whilst there is so great a fleet at sea, and descents are daily making upon different parts of the French coasts, that there is any fear of an immediate invasion of Ireland, yet when the season of the year shall render it imprudent to carry on these operations under the protection of a great fleet any longer, it is very possible, under the favour of long nights, for the French to throw over in small crafts such a number of troops as may surprise Cork or other considerable seaports on the neighbouring coasts to them, or – which is still more dangerous – land such a body as may be sufficient in those popish and disaffected countries to make a place of arms.

Bedford added that the Irish population was discontented and that the British fleet could be shut up in the Channel by a westerly or a south-westerly wind.[60] However, despite Jacobite claims of discontent and support for them,[61] national discontent in Britain was less during the Seven Years War than in the previous conflict, thanks to greater success in war, a military strategy that could more readily be presented as serving national goals, and the absence, after the formation of the Newcastle–Pitt ministry in 1757 of the political uncertainty and sense of betrayal that had characterized the period 1742–4 and, though to a lesser extent, the following two years. In addition, discontent was no longer linked with or translated into Jacobitism. It was clear in 1759 that, if they invaded Britain the French would have to do so with substantial forces and conquer her. There was no real prospect of a Jacobite rising. In June 1759 Mitchell wrote to Robert Keith, one of the disproportionately large group of Scots in the eighteenth-century British diplomatic service, 'the French have begun to play off the Pretender, which will only serve to make them more hated and Jacobitism more contemptible, if possible, than it was before'.[62] In consequence, Bedford's fears were misplaced. There was no likelihood of the French entrusting a substantial force to small boats.

Jacobitism was further attenuated by the accession of George III in 1760 with his stress on being a British monarch and his conscious distancing of himself from a Hanoverian identity and consequent commitments. When, during the next Anglo-Bourbon conflict, France and Spain chose to benefit from British domestic problems, the beneficiaries were rebellious American colonies, not Scottish Highlanders. Naval power was again crucial, while America was divided between rebels and loyalists, as Scotland had been. However, whereas in 1688–9, 1715–16, and 1744–6 it had been difficult to envisage any result that did not affect all of Britain, the American rebels benefitted from their distance from Britain. Not only was it difficult to suppress a rising at such a distance, but it was possible to advance realistic goals of political separation, on the part of the rebels, while George III and his ministers could be driven to accept a partition of his dominions. There had been attempts to link Jacobitism and the cause of an independent America. In 1759 the French minister Choiseul suggested to Charles Edward that he go to America and drive the British out, a proposal supposedly based on advice from Boston. In 1775 some Bostonians apparently offered the prince the crown of America.[63]

Similar whimsical ideas had been advanced before. 'James III' had been discussed as a possible King of Poland, an elective monarchy, in 1733. Corsica for Charles Edward was suggested on a number of occasions, including 1741 and 1755. The granting of a territory to a prince with whom it had no or few connections was not unheard of. Territorial equivalents for pretensions, an idea that flourished from the 1690s until 1748, produced some surprising suggestions, exchanges and consequences, but the princes favoured in this period had more active sponsors than the Jacobites. Though there is little reason to doubt the sincerity of Louis XV's support for the Stuart cause in 1744–6, he expended more effort during the War of the Austrian Succession on his cousin Don Philip, younger son of Philip V, who also became his son-in-law. At the end of the war Don Philip became ruler of the Duchies of Parma and Piacenza, a formerly independent principality to which he had a claim through his mother, a Farnese princess. There was no chance of comparable diplomatic pressure being exerted on behalf of the Jacobites as the major peaces of the period were compromise settlements.

Charles Edward had thus been correct. It was necessary to conquer Britain to restore the Stuarts; their cause could not triumph at the conference table. The failures of 1744–6 left him without purpose, and it was not surprising that his fragile personality deteriorated under the stress of disappointment and marginality. Increasingly he became a somewhat disagreeable curiosity, travelling furtively around Europe, drinking heavily and subject to paranoid suspicions. The prince did not die until January 1788, but by then Jacobitism had been long exhausted as a cause. When James died in 1766 Charles Edward was not recognized as king by the Pope. The estates forfeited as a result of the '45 were restored to the heirs of their former owners in 1784. On 22 November 1788 *Felix Farley's Bristol Journal* reported, 'In a town in the North of England, on the Revolution day, a party met to drink health to the *old cause and family* – they were in number thirty, and we suppose comprehend *all* of that opinion in the three kingdoms'.

Charles Edward's adversary at Culloden did not die in exile, but the Duke of Cumberland, who died in 1765, also tasted the bitterness of defeat. In the aftermath of Culloden he was treated as a hero in England by the Whigs, though the extent of his popularity may be doubted, and there was a measure of revulsion at his treatment of the rebels. The thanks of parliament were voted for Culloden on 20 April and by 6 August 1746 he had collected a parliamentary Act providing him and his heirs with £25,000 annually, the Rangership of Windsor Forest and the freedom of the cities of London and York. Handel's Oratorio 'Judas Maccabaeus' was composed in his honour, just as George II had

Louise de Stolberg, Countess of Albany, married Charles Edward in 1772, artist unknown

been greeted on his return from Dettingen with the 'Dettingen Te Deum'. The anniversary of Culloden was celebrated publicly for several years. Cumberland was literally and metaphorically a man of considerable weight. Newcastle attributed to him the government's decision in November 1747 to support a certain number of troops in the United Provinces in face of the opposition of much of the ministry, and wrote in terms that indicated Cumberland's influence, 'His Royal Highness's great weight, and authority; his knowledge of the fatal consequence in Holland, which might attend the too rigorously insisting here, upon what strict justice and rules of proportion, might justify; his solid reasoning thereupon ... produced so good an effect that, if all my brethren were not convinced, they, at least, acquiesced in His Royal Highness's opinion'.[64]

However, Marshal Saxe was to be far harder prey than Charles Edward. The duke was out-generaled in the last years of the War of the Austrian Succession and must bear some of the responsibility for the failure to defeat the French.[65] Nevertheless, his military reputation was not ruined until the resumption of conflict with the Seven Years War. As commander of a German army ordered to defend Hanover against the French, Cumberland was defeated at Hastenbeck and forced to sign at Kloster-Zeven an agreement obliging him to disband his army.[66] This convention was condemned by George II, his ally Frederick the Great, the British ministry and British public opinion. The agreement was broken while the disgraced duke resigned all his military posts. George II criticized Cumberland to Newcastle, telling him 'a scoundrel in England *one day* may be thought a good man *another* In Germany, it is otherwise, I think like a German'.[67] Cumberland took an active part in the ministerial politics of the early 1760s but he never regained the promise, influence and reputation of his early years. Charles Townshend sent his mother a favourable account of the duke after his death, writing of:

> ... the strength of his understanding, the firmness of his mind and the importance of his services to the state, and I am mistaken, if succeeding ages, when his actions are read and interpreted without the prejudices of his own time, do not allot him a very high rank in the history of this country. He would have enjoyed perfect popularity even in his life, if, after having saved this kingdom, he had possessed an ambition above the endeavour to be the minister of it.[68]

Most judgements are less charitable. As a man he was popular with few, as a politician he was distrusted by many and as a general his only major success had been at the expense of an outnumbered and outgunned force of hungry men, obliged to fight on disadvantageous terrain as a result of poor generalship. There were brave men on both sides at Culloden, but it is difficult not to feel sympathy with the Jacobites. Some historians write of Jacobitism as an historical irrelevance and the '45 as bound to fail. The episode can indeed be presented in more than one light, but precisely because of this the notion of pre-ordained doom is unsatisfactory, a schematic gloss that neither does justice to the contradictory indicators of late 1745 nor to the sense of uncertainty that characterised the thinking and actions of contemporaries. For the sake of a pattern or a pat conclusion it is too easy to overlook the seriousness of what was the biggest crisis to affect the eighteenth-century British state.

NOTES

1 A Change of Dynasty

Two valuable introductions to military history are M.S. Anderson, *War and Society in Europe of the Old Regime 1618–1789* (London, 1988) and G. Parker, *The Military Revolution* (Cambridge, 1988). See also J. Black, *A Military Revolution? Military Change and European Society 1550–1800*, to be published 1991.

An important recent corrective to much work on 1688 is offered by E. Cruickshanks (ed.), *By Force or By Default? The Revolution of 1688–89* (Edinburgh, 1989). J.R. Jones, *The Revolution of 1688* (London, 1972) and W.A. Speck, *Reluctant Revolutionaries. Englishmen and the Revolution of 1688* (Oxford, 1988) can be recommended as can C. Wilson and D. Proctor (eds.), *1688. The Seaborne Alliance and Diplomatic Revolution* (1989), while J. Childs, *The Army, James II and the Glorious Revolution* (Manchester, 1980) is the best guide to the military situation.

1. B[ritish] L[ibrary] Add[itional] MS 63780 f.293.
2. New Haven, [Beinecke Library], Osborn Files, Lowther.
3. D. Davies, 'James II, William of Orange, and the Admirals', in Cruickshanks cited above.
4. Paris, A[rchives du Ministère des Affaires] E[trangères], C[orrespondance] P[olitique] Ang[leterre] 167 f.124.

2 Civil War, Plots and Risings 1689–1723

G.H. Jones, *The Main Stream of Jacobitism* (Cambridge Mass., 1954) is a valuable older work. The best works on Ireland are by J.G. Simms, *The Williamite Confiscation in Ireland, 1690–1703* (London, 1956); *Jacobite Ireland, 1685–1691* (London, 1969). W. Troost, *William III and the Treaty of Limerick* (np. 1983) is important. The major work on the '15 is J. Baynes, *The Jacobite Rising of 1715* (London, 1970). Recent studies include G.V. Bennett, *The Tory Crisis in Church and State 1688–1730: The Career of Francis Atterbury* (Oxford, 1975); P. Aubrey, *The Defeat of James II's Armada 1692* (Leicester, 1979); J. Garrett, *The Triumphs of Providence. The Assassination Plot, 1696* (Cambridge, 1980); B. Lenman, *The Jacobite Risings in Britain 1689–1746* (London, 1980); E. Cruickshanks (ed.), *Ideology and Conspiracy: Aspects of Jacobitism 1689–1759* (Edinburgh, 1982); Lenman, *The Jacobite Clans of the Great Glen 1650–1784* (London, 1984); P. Hopkins, *Glencoe and the End of the Highland War* (Edinburgh, 1986); L.B. Smith, *Spain and Britain 1715–1719. The Jacobite Issue* (London, 1987); Cruickshanks and Black (eds.), *The Jacobite Challenge* (Edinburgh, 1988); J. Gibson, *Playing the Scottish Card. The Franco-Jacobite Invasion of 1708* (Edinburgh, 1988); A.M. Scott, *Bonnie Dundee, John Graham of Claverhouse* (Edinburgh, 1989); D. Szechi, *Letters of George Lockhart of Carnwath, 1698–1732* (Edinburgh, 1989).

1. B.L. Add. MS 47028 f.62.
2. San Marino, California, H[untington] L[ibrary], Lo[udoun papers] 7885.
3. B.L. Add. MS 37361 f.31.
4. B.L. Add. MS 47028 f.6, 82–3.
5. London University Library, MS 93, f.4, 8, 7, 9.
6. B.L. Add. MS 47028 f.41.
7. B.L. MS 63093, nos. 33, 34, Add. MS 47028 f.97; New Haven, Manchester corresp. vol. 15, Manchester to Deputy Lieutenants, 26 September.
8. Hertford, CRO. D/EP F131 f.6.
9. Edinburgh, S[cottish] R[ecord] O[ffice] GD 135/141/4,2.
10. B.L. Add. MS 63093 no. 34.
11. P[ublic] R[ecord] O[ffice], S[tate] P[apers] 43/1 f.53.
12. Churchill College Cambridge, Erle-Drax MS 2/59; B.L. Add. MS 47028 f.160; Gateshead Public Library, Cotesworth MS CP/1 nos. 19, 32, 33.
13. 1700 treaty, Windsor Castle, R[oyal] A[rchives] Stuart Box 6 no. 22; PRO, S.P. 107/1B f.168, 280, 305, 315, 322.
14. PRO, S.P. 84/577 f.41, 55.
15. R. Molesworth, *Observations upon a Pamphlet called An English Merchant's Remarks* (London, 1717) p. 37; Hertford, CRO. D/EP F54 f.100; R.A. S[tuart] P[apers] 41/39.
16. Oxford, Bodleian Library, MS French e20 pp. 1, 41–7, 49, 51, 46.
17. SRO, GD 220/5/828.
18. Hertford, CRO. D/EP F54 f.104.
19. R.A. S.P. 44/5; PRO, S.P. 43/57; New York, Public Library, Hardwicke papers vol. 54.
20. R.A. S.P. 47/148.
21. R.A. S.P. 47/9, 48/63; AE. CP. Ang. 339 f.6–7.
22. R.A. S.P. 53/49.
23. R.A. S.P. 53/87.
24. PRO, S.P. 92/31 f.165.
25. R.A. S.P. 49/77, 50/62.
26. B.L. Add. MS 37389 f.8, 20.
27. Hertford, CRO, D/EP F54 f.120.
28. B.L. Add. MS 47029 f.121; Marburg, Staatsarchiv, Bestand 4, England 184, Sparre's report of 22 May; Stanhope to Carteret, 12 October 1722, New Haven, Osborn Files, Harrington.
29. R.A. S.P. 70/25, 74/60.
30. B.L. Add. MS 36772 f.219.

3 Decline and Revival 1723–43

In addition to works already cited R.C. Jarvis, *Collected Papers on the Jacobite Risings* (Manchester, 1972); E. Cruickshanks, *Political Untouchables. The Tories and the '45* (London, 1979); J. Black, (ed.), *Britain in the Age of Walpole* (London, 1984); Black, *British Foreign Policy in the Age of Walpole* (Edinburgh, 1985); F. McLynn, *The Jacobites* (London, 1985); Black, *Natural and Necessary Enemies. Anglo-French Relations in the Eighteenth Century* (London, 1986); Black, *Robert Walpole and the Nature of Politics in Early Eighteenth-Century Britain* (London, 1990).

1. R.A. S.P. 66/143, 148 (quote); George Lockhart, *Lockhart Papers* (2 vols., 1817) II, 143.

2. R.A. S.P. 66/110, 72/76; B.L. Add. MS 32686 f.330; Cambridge, C[hol-mondeley] H[oughton papers], correspondence 1041, 1087.
3. PRO, S.P. 92/31 f.255–6.
4. B.L. Add. MS 4204 f.345, 32740 f.305; C.H. corresp. 1199.
5. R.A. S.P. 84/7; B.L. Add. MS 46856 f.70–1.
6. PRO. S.P. 78/182 f.151; *Lockhart Papers* II, 150; Vienna, Haus-, Hof-, und Staatsarchiv [hereafter HHSta] Staatskanzlei, England, Noten 2, report of 1 January, memorandum of 17 May 1726.
7. B.L. Add. MS 32749 f.417, 14, 30.
8. R.A. S.P. 108/79, 107/41.
9. PRO, S.P. 35/59 f.182.
10. R.A. S.P. 114/166.
11. Chewton Mendip, Chewton Hall, papers of 1st Earl Waldegrave, 11 July.
12. PRO, S.P. 43/82.
13. Black, *The Collapse of the Anglo-French Alliance 1727–31* (Gloucester, 1987) pp. 202–4.
14. Cruickshanks, 'Lord Cornbury, Bolingbroke and a plan to Restore the Stuarts, 1731–1735' *Royal Stuart Papers* 27 (1986); J. Guite, 'The Jacobite Cause, 1730–1740: The International Dimension' (unpub. Ph.D. thesis, McMaster Univ. 1987); Black, 'Jacobitism and British Foreign Policy, 1731–5' in Cruickshanks and Black (eds.), *Jacobite Challenge*; W. Cobbett (ed.), *Parliamentary History of England from 1066 to 1803* (36 vols., London, 1806–20) IX, 536–7.
15. B.L. Add. MS 23789 f.9.
16. B.L. Add. MS 51390; Cobbett, *Parliamentary History* XI, 64, 940, 978–9; R.A. S.P. 221/109, 231/110.
17. R.A. S.P. 204/114, 205/6, 55, 208/87.
18. B.L. Add. MS 32798 f.6; R.A. S.P. 186/91, 138; B.L. Add. MS 32801 f.10; Farmington, Connecticut, Weston papers, vol. 12; B.L. Add. MS 32801 f.352.
19. Matlock, CRO, Catton collection WH 3429, p. 154; Catalogue for the sale of the collection of Sir Thomas Phillipps, 15th day, 26 June 1973 p. 150.
20. B.L. Add. MS 32820 f.59, 44; PRO, S.P. 90/44.
21. A.E. C.P. Ang. 440 f.8–11; Turin, A[rchivio di] S[tato], L[ettere] M[inistri] Spagna 69; PRO, S.P. 105/281 f.45; Chewton.
22. Cobbett, *Parliamentary History*, XI, 936–7; Edinburgh, N[ational] L[ibrary of] S[cotland MS] 7044 f.158–9.
23. PRO, S.P. 98/44 f.526.
24. J.L.A. Colin, *Louis XV et les Jacobites* (Paris, 1901), pp. 6–34; E. Cruickshanks, 'The Factions at the Court of Louis XV and the Succession to Cardinal Fleury, 1737–45' (unpublished Ph.D., London, 1956) pp. 262, 382.
25. Vincennes, A[rchives de la] G[uerre], A^1 2997 f.109–10.

4 The '44 and the Background to the '45

In addition to the books already cited J. Colin, *Louis XV et les Jacobites. Le projet de débarquement en Angleterre 1743–44* (Paris, 1901); H.W. Richmond, *The Navy in the War of 1739–48* (London, 1920); F. McLynn, *France and the Jacobite Rising of 1745* (Edinburgh, 1981).

1. H[istory of] P[arliament Transcripts].
2. *Sbornik imperatorskago Russkago istoricheskago obshchestvo* (148 vols., St Petersburg, 1867–1916) 64, 18 October.

3. PRO, S.P. 84/402 f.75–6; Ryder diary, H.P.; Bod. MS Don. c.106 f.174; Carlisle CRO. D/Lons/W2/1/105; H.P. Cruickshanks, *Political Untouchables*, p. 57 is wrong to argue that 'in the first fortnight of February, the English Government had no inkling that England was about to be invaded', though it is true that the ministry did not really act until after they had received Bussy's information.

4. PRO, S.P. 84/402 f.113–14; A. Baudrillart, *Philippe V et la Cour de France*, (5 vols., Paris, 1901) V, 185; B.L. Add. MS 23630 f.110; Durham CRO. D/Lo/F 743, 13; Sackville to Duke of Bedford, 6 Mar. 1744, Bedford papers, H.P.

5. H.P.; E. Hughes, *The Correspondence of Colonel Robert Ellison* (Gateshead, 1953) p. 12; Gateshead, Public Library, Ellison MS A.31 nos. 32, 34; Bod. MS Don. c.101 f.163, 106 f.186; Earl of Sandwich to Bedford, 5 March 1744, Bedford papers, H.P.

6. A.E. C.P. Bavière 110, f.7.

7. A.E. C.P. Bavière 109 f.185, 110 f.127; Farmington, Weston 14; PRO, S.P. 84/402 f.130; Bod. MS Don. c.107, f.1; Gateshead, Ellison MS A4, no. 11.

8. Farmington, Weston 14.

9. A.E. C.P. Bavière 110 f.102–6, 225.

10. A.E. C.P. Bavière 110 f.69–71, 89–90.

11. A.E. C.P. Bavière 110 f.106, 184–6, 270; A.E. C.P. Allemagne 526 f.108; PRO, S.P. 84/402 f.90; Gosforth, Northumberland CRO. ZAL 98 13/2; Durham CRO. D/Lo F743, 13; Bod. MS Don. c.107 f.17–18; HHSta Grosse Korrespondenz 277 f.717; L. Cust, *Records of the Cust Family* (London, 1927) III, 33.

12. PRO, S.P. 80/162; A.E. C.P. Bavière 110 f.188–9.

13. Farmington, Weston 3; H.L. Stowe collection, Box 192 (18); PRO, S.P. 84/407 f.4.

14. PRO, S.P. 43/36.

5 From the Western Isles to the Enterprise of England

In addition to works already cited W.B. Blaikie, *The Itinerary of Prince Charles Edward Stuart* (Edinburgh, 1897); K. Tomasson and F. Buist, *Battles of the Forty-Five* (London, 1962); F.J. McLynn, 'Seapower and the Jacobite Rising of 1745', *Mariner's Mirror*, 67 (1981); McLynn, 'Issues and Motives in the Jacobite Rising of 1745', *Eighteenth Century*, 23 (1982); J.M. Hill, *Celtic Warfare* (Edinburgh, 1986); McLynn, *Charles Edward Stuart* (London, 1988); W. Seymour, *Battles in Britain* (London, 1989).

1. Gosforth, Northumberland CRO. ZRI 27/4/8.

2. PRO, S.P. 43/36, 37; R.A. C[umberland] P[apers] 3/270; Earl of Ilchester (ed.), *Letters to Henry Fox* (Roxburghe Club, 1915) pp. 4–5.

3. PRO, S.P. 84/583 f.51, 43/111.

4. Farmington, Weston, 16; PRO, S.P. 43/36, 111; T.J. McCann (ed.), *The Correspondence of the Dukes of Richmond and Newcastle* (Lewes, 1984) p. 170.

5. McCann (ed.) *Correspondence*, p. 172; R.A. C.P. 4/136; Worcester CRO. 705:66 BA 4221; Farmington, Weston, 16. The Saxon envoy Hohberg noted that there was more concern about Flanders than Scotland, PRO, S.P. 107/62, 10, 13, 17 August.

6. H.L. Lo 7646, 7644; Bedford papers, H.P.

7. McCann (ed.), *Correspondence* p. 173–4; R.A. C.P. 4/203, 204, 201; PRO, S.P. 43/115; H.P., Ryder diary, 20 August.; R. Lodge (ed.), *The Private Correspondence of Sir Benjamin Keene* (Cambridge, 1933) p. 70.

8. NLS. 7071 f.3, 5; PRO, S.P. 54/26 f.1; H.L. Lo. 11460.

9. NLS. 7071 f.5; Trowbridge, Wiltshire CRO. Benett of Pythouse MS 413/22; Norwich CRO. 11319 26B5.; Carlisle CRO. D.Pen Acc 2689.

10. Matlock, Derbyshire CRO. Catton collection WH 3433; PRO, S.P. 98/50 f.238.

11. Farmington, Weston 16.

12. R.A. C.P. 5/29; Marburg, Staatsarchiv, Bestand 4, England 241; Ryder diary; McCann (ed.), *Correspondence*, p. 176.

13. PRO, S.P. 54/26 f.3, 91; Gosforth, Northumberland CRO. ZRI 27/4/2; McCann (ed.), *Correspondence*, p. 182; Cheshire RO., DCH/X/9a/2; Durham, Dean and Chapter Library, Sharp MS 150 pp. 3, 5.

14. Gosforth, Northumberland CRO. ZRI 27/4/11; PRO, S.P. 54/26 f.102; T. Keppel, *The Life of Augustus, Viscount Keppel* (2 vols., London, 1842) I, 217, 219.

15. Marburg, 241; Farmington, Weston 16; B.L. Add. MS 51417 f.141–2.

16. Farmington, Weston 16; Gateshead, Ellison MS A4, no. 24.

17. Durham, Sharp MS 150, pp. 5–6; Newcastle to Devonshire, H.P.; Carlisle CRO. D/Pen Acc 2689; Sharp MS 150, p. 13.

18. B.L. Add. MS 23821 f.107.

19. Bedford CRO. Russell Box 769.

20. H.L. Lo 7676; Farmington, Weston 16; Carlisle CRO. D.Pen Acc 2689; NLS. 7078 f.154; H.P.

21. Farmington, Weston 5; Cheshire RO. DCH/X/9a/2, 4; Bristol Library, Southwell Papers, vol. 9; Matlock CRO. Catton collection WH 3433.

22. *Old England*, 19 October, 1745; PRO, S.P. 105/283 f.19,21; Bedford CRO. HW 87/125; Gateshead, Ellison MS A7 no. 23; Farmington, Weston 16.

23. Leeds, Archives Office, Newby Hall MS 2506.

24. H.P.; Bristol, Southwell papers, 9; Sharp MS 150, pp. 14–16, 24, 26, 36, 38; C.I.A. Ritchie, 'The Durham Association Regiment, 1745', *Journal of the Society for Army Historical Research*, 34 (1956) pp. 106–19; Cheshire RO. DCH/X/9a/8, 9, 14, 49–50.

25. Bod. MS Don. c.107, f.120.

26. There is a copy in A.E. C.P. Ang. 426 f.430.

27. Farmington, +745.10.8.2.

28. Sharp MS 150, pp. 6, 34–5.

29. PRO, S.P. 54/26 f.90.

30. R.A. C.P. 8/161.

6 The Invasion of England

In addition to works already cited W.A. Speck, *The Butcher, The Duke of Cumberland and the Suppression of the '45* (Oxford, 1981); F.J. McLynn, *The Jacobite Army in England* (Edinburgh, 1983).

1. Aylesbury, CRO., Trevor MS 52; B.L. Add. MS 15955 f.36; R.A. C.P. 7/163.

2. Farmington, Weston 16.

3. R.F. Bell (ed.), *Memorial of John Murray of Broughton* (Edinburgh, 1898) p. 212.

4. Farmington, Weston 16.

5. Gosforth, Northumberland CRO. ZRI 27/4/3, 9; Aylesbury CRO. Trevor MS 52; PRO, S.P. 54/26 f.181.

6. McLynn, *Charles Edward Stuart*, p. 175.

7. Farmington, Weston 3; C. Gerretson and P. Geyl (eds.), *Briefwisseling en Aanteekeningen van Willem Bentinck* (Utrecht, 1934) p. 115; Aylesbury CRO. Trevor MS 50.

8. Hartington to Devonshire, 31 October, 5 November, H.P.; PRO, S.P. 36/67

f.242–9, 36/68 f.149–51, 36/69 f.105, 108, 36/70 f.209–10; G.C. Mounsey, *Carlisle in 1745* (1846); K. Tomasson, *The Jacobite General* (1958) pp. 74–6. I am most grateful for the assistance of Henry Summerson concerning Carlisle in the '45.

9. Gosforth, Northumberland CRO. ZRI 27/4/31; Cheshire RO. DCH/X/9a/11.
10. Durham, Dean and Chapter Library, Sharp MS 150, p. 25; H.P.; McCann (ed.), *Correspondence*, p. 185; Gosforth, Northumberland CRO. ZRI 27/4/35.
11. Gosforth, Northumberland CRO. ZRI 27/4/45; Sharp MS 150 p. 25; H.P.; C.E. Whiting, *Two Yorkshire Diaries: The Diary of Arthur Jessop and Ralph Ward's Journal* (Yorkshire Archaeological Society, Record Series 117 1952) pp. 108–10; Farmington, Weston 16 [24 November].
12. Cheshire RO. DCH/X/9a/9, 16–17, 21–2; R. Whitworth, *Field Marshal Lord Ligonier* (Oxford, 1958) p. 111.
13. R.A. C.P. 7/240; McCann (ed.), *Correspondence* p. 193; Cheshire RO. DCH/X/9a/26–27, 28, 38.
14. R.A. C.P. 7/240, 255, 261, 262, 274, 278, 281, 295, 301; P.C. Yorke, *The Life and Correspondence of Philip Yorke, Earl of Hardwicke* (3 vols., Cambridge, 1913) I, 472; Cheshire RO. DCH/X/9a/18–20; Ryder diary, 3 December; Bod., MS Don. c.7; McCann (ed.), *Correspondence* p. 194; Farmington, Weston 16; Sharp MS 150 p. 37. On reports of the Jacobites invading Yorkshire R.A. C.P. 7/264, 268.
15. B.L. Add. MS 32705 f.362. Misdated in McCann (ed.), *Correspondence* p. 188; Chatsworth, H.P.; R.A. C.P. 7/287.
16. R.A. C.P. 7/261, 263, 281, 285, 324, 325; Cheshire RO. DCH/X/9a/17, 28; Durham CRO. D/Lo/F/745/57; C.J. Terry (ed.), *The Albemarle Papers* (2 vols., Aberdeen, 1902) I, 114.
17. R.A. C.P. 7/288, 291, 279, 306; Cheshire RO. DCH/X/9a/24; B.L. Add. MS 51417 f.181; Sharp MS 150, p. 38; Chatsworth, H.P.
18. Aylesbury CRO. Trevor MS 51, 52, 53; R.A. C.P. 46/128, 8/77.
19. H.P.; Gateshead, A 19, no.45. On the combination of fatigue and high morale R.A. C.P. 7/295
20. Ellis to Hartington, 12 December, Wade to Devonshire, 8 December, 1745, Chatsworth, H.P.; R.A. C.P. 7/325, 349; R.R. Sedgwick, *The House of Commons 1715–54* (2 vols., London, 1970) II, 305–6.
21. Gosforth, Northumberland CRO. ZRI 27/4/44, 46; Carlisle, CRO. D/Pen Acc 2689; R.A. C.P. 8/38, 56.
22. R.A. C.P. 7/369; Yorke, *Hardwicke* I, 478.
23. Carlisle, CRO. D.Pen Acc 2689; Pelham to Lord Hartington, 9 November, Pelham to Duke of Devonshire, 19 November, H.P.; H.L. Lo. 7638.
24. McLynn, *France and the Jacobite Rising* p. 82.
25. 96 km, 60 miles. The accurate figure is 370 km, 231 miles.
26. Paris, A[rchives] N[ationales], A[rchives de la] M[arine], B7 345.
27. R.A. C.P. 7/264–6; L.L. Bongie, 'Voltaire's English, High Treason and a Manifesto for Bonnie Prince Charlie', *Studies on Voltaire and the Eighteenth Century* 171 (1977) pp. 7–29; A.G. A1 3152 no. 63; R.A. C.P. 7/346.
28. B.M. Ranft (ed.), *The Vernon Papers* (Naval Records Society vol. 99, 1958) pp. 539, 552.
29. Ranft (ed.), *Vernon* pp. 555, 559–60.
30. Keppel I, 308; NLS. 16630 f.2; Mount Stuart, papers of the 3rd Earl of Bute, 1761 papers no. 478; W. Hackman, 'English military expeditions to the coast of France, 1757–1761' (unpub. Ph.D. thesis, Michigan, 1968); P. Mackesy, 'Problems of an amphibious power: Britain against France, 1793–1815', *Naval War*

College Review (1978) pp. 19–20; McLynn, *France* p. 127. For valuable speculation on the situation in 1588, G. Parker, 'If the Armada had landed', *History* 60 (1976) pp. 358–68; C. Martin and Parker, *The Spanish Armada* (London, 1988) pp. 265–77.

31. Pelham to Hartington, 10 December, Pelham to Devonshire, 17 December 1745, Chatsworth, H.P.; B.L. Add. MS 35363 f.109; R.A. C.P. 8/43.
32. Bod. MS Don. c.7 f.180.
33. Chichester, West Sussex CRO. Goodwood MS 104 f.293.
34. Yorke, *Hardwicke* I, 481–2; B.L. Add. MS 51417 f.183.
35. A.G. A1 3152 no.78.
36. PRO, S.P. 84/415 f.55.
37. B.L. Add. MS 23821 f.444; *Cambridge Journal* 21 December 1745; Farmington, Weston 16.
38. R.A. C.P. 8/9.
39. Bod. MS Don. c.7 f.184.
40. Farmington, Weston 16.
41. Ryder diary, 29 August.
42. Bod. MS Don. c.7 f.182.
43. A.G. A1 3152 no. 91; Paris, B[ibliothèque] V[ictor] C[ousin], Fonds Richelieu 40 f.53–4, 59–61; NLS. 16630 f.3; A.E. C.P. Espagne 488 f.48.
44. B.L. Add. MS 23822 f.47; *Penny London Post* 20 January 1746.
45. London, Bedford Estate Office, papers of the 4th Duke of Bedford, John Wynne to Mr Becuda, 19 January 1746.
46. PRO, Admiralty papers 1 3830, pp. 930, 934. Wolter's reports can also be found extensively in PRO, S.P. 84/415; R.A. C.P. 10/17.
47. Goodwood MS no. 571; B.V.C. Fonds Richelieu 40 f.69.
48. R.A. C.P. 8/44; Yorke, *Hardwicke* I, 483; McCann (ed.), *Correspondence* p. 198.
49. R.A. C.P. 8/52, 80; Ellis to Hartington, 12 December 1745, Chatsworth, H.P.; A.N. A.M. B7 353.
50. Mounsey, *Carlisle* p. 149.
51. Yorke, *Hardwicke* I, 488.
52. Gosforth, Northumberland C.R.O. ZRI 27/4/50 b; R.A. C.P. 8/89, 109, 152, 161.
53. R.A. C.P. 8/161, 80; Farmington, Weston 16.
54. Black, 'The Catholic Threat and the British press in the 1720s and 1730s', *Journal of Religious History* 12 (1983).
55. C. Ferguson, 'The Retreat of the Highlanders through Westmorland in 1745' *Transactions of the Cumberland and Westmorland Archaeological and Antiquarian Society* 10 (1889); R.A. C.P. 8/57; Speck, *Butcher* p. 98.
56. B.L. Add. MS 35363 f.60.

7 From the Return into Scotland to Culloden

Speck, *Butcher* is especially valuable for this section.

1. H.L. Lo. 7651.
2. Bedford CRO. L 30/9/17.
3. Farmington 746.0.25.
4. Gosforth, Northumberland CRO. ZRI 27/4/48; R.A. C.P. 8/52; PRO, S.P. 54/26 f.286.

5. R.A. C.P. 8/96, 168, 138, 112, 168, 9/12, 43; Gosforth, Northumberland CRO. ZRI 27/4/51.
6. NLS. 16630 f.12; Matlock, Derbyshire CRO. Catton collection WH 3433, Potter, 14 December 1745; Chambers, *Jacobite Memoirs* (Edinburgh, 1834) pp. 83–94.
7. Speck, *Butcher* p. 109; Cheshire RO. DCH/X/9a/48; H[istorical] M[anuscripts] C[ommission], *Reports on the Manuscripts of the Earl of Eglinton* . . . (London, 1885) pp. 441, 440.
8. Gosforth, Northumberland CRO. ZRI 27/4/54.
9. Aylesbury, CRO. Trevor MS 54; R.A. C.P. 9/102, 110, 115, 141; Ilchester (ed.) *Letters to Henry Fox* pp. 5–8. See also G.H. Rose (ed.) *A Selection from the Papers of the Earls of Marchmont* (3 vols., London, 18, 31) I, 281–92.
10. Norwich CRO. 11319 Hobart MS 26 B5; Marquise Campana de Cavelli, *Les Derniers Stuarts à Saint-Germain en Laye* (2 vols., Paris, 1871) I, 154; Gateshead, Public Library, Ellison MS A7, nos. 28, 30; NLS. 16630 f.4.
11. Chambers, *Jacobite Memoirs* p. 98. On the strategic importance of Stirling, J.J. Sharp, 'Stirling Castle', *British Heritage* 8 (1987) pp. 62–8.
12. Chambers, *Jacobite Memoirs* p. 99.
13. Gosforth, Northumberland CRO. ZRI 27/4/57; R.A. C.P. 10/28; E. Charteris, *William Augustus, Duke of Cumberland. His Early Life and Times* (London, 1913) pp. 247–8.
14. Gosforth, Northumberland CRO. ZRI 27/4/60, 59.
15. R.A. C.P. 9/89; Yorke, *Hardwicke* I, 496; R.A. C.P. 10/74; NLS. 16630 f.40, 16621 f.1; Yorke, *Hardwicke* I, 496–7, 500.
16. Yorke, *Hardwicke* I, 506; NLS. 16630 f.68, 16616 f.239; R.A. C.P. 10/13–14; PRO, S.P. 54/26 f.286–7.
17. NLS. 16630 f.68; Beinecke, Osborn Shelves, Pelham Box.
18. Darmstadt, Staatsarchiv, E1 M10/6.
19. B.L. Add. MS 23821 f.456–7; NLS. 16630 f.44; B.L. Add. MS 23822 f.92, 183, 113; R.A. C.P. 7/365, 10/45.
20. Bod. MS Don. c.7 f.189.
21. PRO, 30/29/1/11 f.300.
22. H.P. Chatsworth transcripts; Bod. MS Don. c.7 f.191; Munich, Bayerisches Hauptstaatsarchiv, Bayr, Ges. London 217, 11, 21 January; PRO, S.P. 84/416 f.61; Gerretson and Geyl (eds.), *Briefwisseling . . . van Willem Bentinck* p. 167; R.A. C.P. 8/77.
23. PRO, S.P. 84/416 f.36; Gerretson and Geyl (eds.), *Briefwisseling* p. 167.
24. PRO, S.P. 84/416 f.80–1; Aylesbury CRO. Trevor MS 54, Hyndford 13 January; Manchester, John Rylands Library, Eng. MS 940, no. 53.
25. Aylesbury CRO. Trevor MS 54.
26. Aylesbury CRO. Trevor MS 55, Horatio Walpole, 14, 27 Febuary; B.L. Add. MS 51417 f.218, 57307 f.25.
27. PRO, 30/29/1/11 f.299; Bristol Library, Southwell papers, vol. 9.
28. Aylesbury CRO. Trevor MS 54, 31 December, 55, 21 February.
29. A.N. A.M. B1,83.
30. Aylesbury CRO. Trevor MS 54, Horatio Walpole, 17, 31 December.
31. Aylesbury CRO. Trevor MS 54, 55, 17 December 1745, 27 February 1746 (quote).
32. R.A. C.P. 10/131, 11/12, 11/62; NLS. 16621 f.26, 21, 29, 33; Cheshire RO. DCH/X/9a.
33. Bedford CRO. L 30/9/17.

34. Chichester CRO. Goodwood MS 103, no. 241; McCann (ed.), *Correspondence* p. 208.
35. NLS. 16630 f.62, 66, 96, 107; Bod. MS Don. c.107 f.261.
36. Gosforth CRO. ZRI 27/4/62.
37. R.A. C.P. 9/12, 43; NLS. 16621 f.3, 41; Gosforth CRO. ZRI 27/4/64.
38. Yorke, *Hardwicke* I, 510–12.
39. Aylesbury CRO. Trevor MS 56; NLS. 16621 f.34, 42, 81.
40. J. Childs, *Armies and Warfare in Europe 1648–1789* (Manchester, 1982) pp. 106–7.
41. NLS. 16616 f.240–1, 16621 f.41; PRO, S.P. 54/30 f.3–4, 152–4; Ilchester (ed.) *Letters to Henry Fox* pp. 8–9; Chambers, *Jacobite Memoirs* pp. 106–7.
42. PRO, S.P. 54/30 f.1, 12, 85.
43. B.L. Stowe MS.158 f.202; Yorke, *Hardwicke* I, 516.
44. PRO, S.P. 54/30 f.13.
45. NLS. 16621 f.94; PRO, S.P. 54/30 f.85, 143; Yorke, *Hardwicke* I, 519–20.
46. McLynn, *Charles Edward Stuart* pp. 238–9; NLS. 16621 f.103; *Albemarle Papers* I, 3.
47. PRO, S.P. 54/30 f.89, 143, 145; NLS. 16621 f.103; Ilchester (ed.) *Letters to Henry Fox* p. 10.
48. Chambers, *Jacobite Memoirs* pp. 120–1; Yorke, *Hardwicke* I, 519.
49. PRO, S.P. 54/30 f.145.
50. Chambers, *Jacobite Memoirs* p. 122.
51. *Albemarle Papers* I, 2.

8   Culloden and its Aftermath

J. Prebble, *Culloden* (London, 1961) is a powerful work. K. Tomasson and F. Buist, *Battles of the '45* (London, 1962) is useful. Excellent recent brief accounts are provided by Speck, *Butcher* and McLynn, *Charles Edward Stuart*. An important study of the consequences in Scotland is provided in A.M. Smith, *Jacobite Estates of the Forty-Five* (Edinburgh, 1982), while the correspondence of the 2nd Earl of Albemarle, Commander-in-Chief in Scotland after Cumberland's departure, was printed by C.J. Terry (Aberdeen, 1902). A valuable edition of an important work of ministerial propaganda is provided by W.B. Coley (ed.), *Henry Fielding: 'The True Patriot and Related Writings'* (Oxford, 1987). A different perspective is provided by M. Pittock, 'New Jacobite Songs of the Forty-Five', *Studies on Voltaire and the Eighteenth Century*, 267 (1989) pp. 1–75. Material on other movements can be found in O. Subtelny, *Domination of Eastern Europe. Native Nobilities and Foreign Absolutism 1500–1715* (Gloucester, 1986) and L. and M. Frey, *Societies in Upheaval. Insurrections in France, Hungary, and Spain in the Early Eighteenth Century* (London, 1987).

1. Chambers, *Jacobite Memoirs* p. 82.
2. Gosforth CRO. ZRI 27/4/66.
3. R.A. C.P. 21/261.
4. Maidstone CRO. U1590 C708/2.
5. Chambers, *Jacobite Memoirs* p. 121.
6. McLynn, *Charles Edward Stuart* p. 251.
7. Bedford CRO. L30/9/17/3.
8. They did not have to use their bayonets.
9. H.M.C. *Eglinton* p. 443; B.L. Stowe MS 158 f.211–12, 214; PRO, S.P. 54/30 f.183–7.

10. The regiment that Stanhope (cited p. 166) was with.
11. Yorke, *Hardwicke* I, 523–4; NLS. 16621 f.110.
12. Ilchester (ed.) *Letters to Henry Fox* p. 10. Aylesbury CRO. Trevor MS 58.
13. D.E. Showalter, 'Tactics and Recruitment in Eighteenth-Century Prussia', *Studies in History and Politics* 3(1983–4) pp. 19–20; B.P. Hughes, *Firepower. Weapons Effectiveness on the Battlefield, 1630–1850* (London, 1974) p. 85.
14. Taunton CRO. Trollop-Bellew papers, DD/TB 16 FT 18.
15. M. Roberts, *The Military Revolution 1560–1660* (Belfast, 1956).
16. Black, 'The Military Revolution' *Teaching History* 52(1988) pp. 34–6; Black, *A Military Revolution? Military Change and European Society 1550–1800* (London, 1991).
17. Gosforth CRO. ZRI 27/4/65.
18. Most recently by Speck, *Butcher* pp. 148–55.
19. H.M.C. *Eglinton* p. 444; NLS. 16616 f.179, 16621 f.118.
20. NLS. 16630 f.124; Whiting (ed.), *Jessop Diary* pp. 131–2; Gosforth CRO. ZAL 98 13/2; *National Journal* 26 April 1746; Bod. MS Don. c.108 f.53; *General Evening Post* 8 May 1746.
21. NLS. 16621 f.39, 16630 f.66, 16621 f.179, 181; Ilchester (ed.) *Letters to Henry Fox* pp. 9, 13–14; PRO, S.P. 54/30 f.12–13; Chichester, Goodwood MS 106, no. 480; *Albemarle Papers* I, 5. On mistreatment of loyal Highlanders ibid, I, 83.
22. McLynn, *Charles Edward Stuart* pp. 290–1.
23. 17 Geo. II cap. 39; B.V.C. Fonds Richelieu 40 f.82; R. Lodge, *Studies in Eighteenth-Century Diplomacy 1740–1748* (London, 1930) pp. 153–6.
24. B.L. Add. MS 32807 f.44; *Old England* 7 Feb. 1747; S.R.O. G.D. 248/572/8/1; Turin, A[rchivio di] S[tato], L[ettere] M[inistri] Ing[hilterra] 53, 22, 26 Sept.; R.A. C.P. 28/221, 29/87, 96, 113.
25. S.R.O. G.D. 248/572/8/2.
26. McLynn, *Charles Edward Stuart* pp. 310–25, quote p. 312.
27. PRO, S.P. 78/331 f.446, 88/68, 19 March.
28. AE. CP. Hollande 402, f.22.
29. PRO, S.P. 105/308 f.307; A.S.T. L.M. Ing. 53, 17 January; R.A. C.P. 20/241.
30. Beinecke, Osborn Shelves, Pelham Box.
31. Far less has been written on Hispano-Jacobite relations than on their Franco-Jacobite counterpart, M.J. Carpio, *España y los ultimos Estuardos* (Madrid, 1954) is the major work.
32. *Albemarle Papers* I, 214; *Penny London Post* 13 January, 10 Febuary 1746.
33. J. Basarab, *Pereiaslav 1654: An Historiographical Study* (Edmonton, 1982) p. 71; B.L. Add. MS 23810 f.368.
34. Reading CRO. Trumbull MS.133/11/1; B.L. Add. MS 57308 f.77; *Memoirs of Thomas Jones* (London, 1951) p. 44; J. Moore, *A View of Society and Manners* (London, 1779) I, 395.
35. L. and M. Frey, *Societies in Upheaval. Insurrections in France, Hungary, and Spain in the Early Eighteenth Century* (London, 1987) pp. 49–56.
36. J.C.D. Clark, *English Society 1688–1832: Ideology, Social Structure and Political Practice during the Ancien Regime* (Cambridge, 1985); J.M. Black, *Europe in the Eighteenth Century, 1700–1789* (London, 1990).
37. Clark, 'English History's Forgotten Context: Scotland, Ireland, Wales', *Historical Journal* 32 (1989); Black, *Robert Walpole and the Nature of Politics in Early Eighteenth Century Britain* (London, 1990), pp. 106–19.
38. H.M.C. Eglinton p. 444; *Albemarle Papers* I, 289–90.
39. *Albemarle Papers* I, 138, 220–1; O'Donaghue, *William Roy (1726–1790): Pioneer of*

the Ordnance Survey (London, 1977); Bedford CRO. L30/9/17/3; *Albemarle Papers* I, 357.

40. H.L. Lo, 11444; *Albemarle Papers* I, 222–4; Bod. MS Don. c.109 f.46.

41. Farmington, Weston 3. The major study of this subject is B.F. Jewell, 'The Legislation Relating to Scotland After the Forty-Five', (unpub. Ph.D. thesis, North Carolina, 1975); *Albemarle Papers* I, 138.

42. Sedgwick, *House of Commons* I, 525; B.L. Add. MS 35363 f.116; NLS. 16621 f.31, 136; Findlater to Bedford, 5 November 1748, Bedford papers, H.P.

43. R.A. C.P. 21/261.

44. L. Leneman, *Living in Atholl* (Edinburgh, 1986). There is an important review of this book by M. Pittock, *British Journal for Eighteenth-Century Studies* 11 (1988) p. 214.

45. B. Lenman, 'A Client Society: Scotland between the '15 and the '45', in Black (ed.), *Britain in the Age of Walpole* (London, 1984) pp. 69–93; D. Szechi, 'John Bull's Other Kingdoms: The Government of Scotland and Ireland' in C. Jones (ed.), *Britain in the First Age of Party, 1680–1750* (London, 1987) pp. 243–59; Lenman, 'Scotland and Ireland 1742–89', in Black (ed.), *British Politics and Society from Walpole to Pitt 1742–89* (London, 1990) pp. 81–100.

46. A. Murdoch, '"The People Above" Politics and Administration in Mid-Eighteenth-Century Scotland' (Edinburgh, 1980) pp. 33–9; M.S. Bricke, 'The Pelhams vs. Argyll: A Struggle for Mastery of Scotland, 1747–8' *Scottish Historical Review* 61 (1982).

47. *Selections From the Family Papers Preserved at Caldwell* (Glasgow, 1854) I, 260–2, 266–7, 270.

48. Speck, *Butcher* p. 203.

49. B.L. Add. MS 51393 f.132.

50. *First Book* p. 8; B.L. Add. MS 32813 f.156, 32815 f.138; *Jacobite's Journal* 5 November 1748.

51. PRO, S.P. 84/432 f.248–9.

52. AE. CP. Ang 438 f. 349, 439 f.272.

53. AE. CP. Ang. 439 f.278, 371–2, 287.

54. A.N. KK. 1402 p. 257.

55. AE. CP. Ang. 440 f.26–7.

56. AE. MD. Ang. 54, CP. Ang. 442 f.112–18.

57. B.L. Add. MS 32890 f.149; PRO, S.P. 90/66; C. Nordmann, 'Choiseul and the Last Jacobite Attempt of 1759', in Cruickshanks (ed.), *Ideology and Conspiracy* pp. 201–17; B.L. Add. MS 35418 f.181.

58. Hull, University Library, Hotham papers DD Ho 4/9.

59. History of Parliament, Chatsworth transcripts, 31 January 1756.

60. Bedford Estate Office, papers of 4th Duke.

61. AE. CP. Ang. 440 f.24–5, 29, 43, 441 f.126; N. York, Public Library, Hardwicke papers, vol. 136, secret intelligence, 26 January 1756.

62. B.L. Add. MS 35482 f.205.

63. F. McLynn, 'Unpopular Front. Jews, Radicals and Americans in the Jacobite World-View', *Royal Stuart Papers* 31 (1988) pp. 10–12.

64. *Bristol Journal* 21, Ap. 1750; B.L. Add. MS 32810 f.297.

65. Different assessments are provided by Charteris, *Cumberland* and Whitworth, *Ligonier*.

66. W. Mediger, 'Hastenbeck und Zeven', *Niedersächsisches Jahrbuch für Landesgeschichte* 56 (1984).

67. B.L. Add. MS 35417 f.92.

68. B.L. Add. MS 63079 no. 79.

INDEX

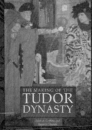

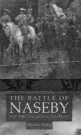

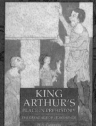